EDITH NEWMAN DEVLIN was born in 1926 and educated in Dublin at the Diocesan School, Alexandra College, and Trinity College. She was awarded an MBE for services to literature (1988) and an honorary D.Litt. from Queen's University Belfast, also for services to literature (1993). She has been a lecturer to adult students in the Extra-Mural Department of Queen's since 1968.

Speaking Volumes

A DUBLIN CHILDHOOD

EDITH NEWMAN DEVLIN

THE
BLACKSTAFF
PRESS
BELFAST

First published in March 2000 by
The Blackstaff Press Limited
Blackstaff House, Wildflower Way, Apollo Road
Belfast BT12 6TA, Northern Ireland
with the assistance of
The Arts Council of Northern Ireland

Reprinted April 2000, August 2000, 2002

Typeset by Techniset Typesetters, Newton-le-Willows, Merseyside

Printed in Ireland by ColourBooks Limited

A CIP catalogue record for this book
is available from the British Library

ISBN 0-85640-672-4

To Olive and Hugh
who also remember these things

CONTENTS

FOREWORD

The following pages are an account of my impressions as I grew up in Dublin in the 1930s and 1940s, the years which followed Ireland's independence from Great Britain (1921). They are not judgements, rather impressions of my little world at a special time in Ireland's history. I was a protestant child (Church of Ireland or Anglican) living among a scant number of poor protestants and an overwhelming number of poor catholics in a run-down but lively and resilient Dublin, where the harsh conditions of the great economic slump bore down particularly hard on the poor. At that time the catholic church was closely allied with the state and there was a strong catholic ethos not only in the laws of the land but in every street in the city. Although I was born and raised in Dublin, my parents came from the two opposite ends of Ireland, from the 'hard' North and the 'soft' South, and from two very different protestant traditions. My mother belonged to the Church of Ireland; my father was of stern Presbyterian descent but by the time I was born had become a 'militant' protestant agnostic who found himself living in the midst of a profoundly affirming catholic culture which he detested, and in this confusing atmosphere I grew up.

I tell of my strange home in the gate lodge of what was then popularly known as a madhouse or lunatic asylum and of my wandering the streets of Dublin at will. When not playing or cycling, I was reading in those television-less days. Books and I grew up together, and I was lucky that in those pinched times I was able to come by them easily, through my father who not only was a great reader himself but encouraged his children to read, through the nearby

1

lending library, through Sunday School, through the Church of Ireland Scripture exams and through school, all of whose prizes came in the form of books which we could choose ourselves from the APCK shop in Dawson Street. Books formed my imagination, my ideals, my notions of what life was about. These notions changed and enlarged over the years as I came to read more and more intelligently, and they are changing still. Music was not a strong influence in my youth though I heard and loved hymns in church, my father's favourite songs on an old gramophone with a huge horn, and the stirring music of the brass bands in the Phoenix Park.

'Reading maketh a full man...' said Francis Bacon. T.S. Eliot said that a man capable of experience is in a new world in every decade of his life. Literature is not the only way of being in a new world but it is an important one. To be in these new worlds, we must first be 'capable of experience', that is, capable of escaping from the bonds of a few confining ideas and narrow judgements, capable of keeping our minds ever open to new impressions and new ideas, capable of being in touch with our living past. The past is not 'a foreign country'; it is all around us, it has formed our present and is flowing into the future in that living stream which is our common human experience. Architecture, painting and sculpture are the most visible presence of the past, music the most invisible and most accessible to most people, and literature the most common: words are the most important carriers of our civilisation, of our values and attitudes. History is an important way of recovering the past; it interprets and reinterprets according to our changing insights, agreed facts and events of the past. Literature is another kind of history; it is the *living* history of human awareness, the very *feel* and *flavour* of what it is like to be a human being, in any time, in any place. It gives us the feel of things rather than the meaning of things. It is the opposite to abstraction and generalisation. It enables us to imagine and picture situations and feelings that are not our own and to experience our own feelings more fully. But without the supreme pleasure of shape and pattern, line and measure, expressed in living words, it would have no effect on us.

Literature, too, has had a powerful influence in the formation of our common culture, giving us ways of thinking about ourselves in which we can recognise our Englishness, our Irishness, our

Frenchness. Even if we have not read the classics of our literature, they have influenced us by filtering down through lesser books, through journalism, television and so on. We see and feel and think about things differently because Constable painted the way he did and Charles Dickens wrote; we see suffering differently because of the Bible. Without literature, the race has no memory and without memory, conscious or unconscious, we have no identity; we do not know who we are.

Autobiography is another attempt to recover the past. In this book I have tried to recover my own childhood and youth, tried to describe how my life and books were so closely interwoven that I can truly say not only that books have given me great pleasure, but that I have learned almost all I know from them, and I am still learning. In literature, I came to see my own experience better identified, better understood and better expressed.

The dominant influence in my young life was my father, whose wish to do the very best for his children was overcast by his inability to understand our feelings, an inability which led to hurt and resentment on our part, though I could not, at that time, have given a name to the part of me that was wounded. It was books which led me to understand that it was my *feelings* which were in revolt. It was books which made me see *imaginatively* that it is the way our feelings ebb and flow which really determines our lives rather than our reason. I have confined myself here, among many books, to those which first revealed this important truth to me.

Education is now a mass industry with information and training offered for every conceivable function, yet the classics of literature are read and studied less than ever before. The need to educate the imagination and the feelings is not well understood, yet it is the arts and especially literature which move us and keep us awake in this world. In *A Defence of Poetry* (1821), Shelley wrote:

> We have more moral, political, and historical wisdom, than we know how to reduce into practice; we have more scientific and economical knowledge than can be accommodated to the just distribution of the produce which it multiplies. The poetry, in these systems of thought, is concealed by the accumulation of facts and calculating processes. There is no

3

want of knowledge respecting what is wisest and best in morals, government, and political economy, or at least what is wiser and better than what men now practise and endure ... we want the creative faculty to imagine that which we know; we want the generous impulse to act that which we imagine; we want the poetry of life.

Literature is made of words, those slippery little customers which influence us every day whether we know it or not, words we use to others and to ourselves, the tone, the suggestions, the inflections which vibrate on the emotions, words used to dominate or persuade, words used to justify the self or to deceive it. What is new today is that words have become an immense industry poured over us from books, television, newspapers and marketing agencies twenty-four hours a day. Constantly battered as we are, we drown in ephemera. To whom do we listen? We are bored with this less-than-honest language; we are weary of cliché, language which has gone dead, and jargon, language which has never been alive. It is to translate our living world into a dead language. It does not touch us. Truthful and creative language is the mark of a great writer. It raises our sense of life and enriches our being. If it is great poetry it resonates in the mind and never after leaves it. We have to fight all the time to keep language honest and creative. We need to keep in touch with language used in this way, for, in an important sense, 'The limits of my language mean the limits of my world' (Wittgenstein).

This book is not a work of literary analysis directed to specialists who increasingly talk to one another in esoteric language over the head of the ordinary reader. It speaks, I hope, to those who read good books and love them and who would like to continue to do so.

DUBLIN

There were no neutered tom-cats in our part of Dublin. No one in the poor streets around us had ever heard of an operation for neutering cats. It would have made them laugh to think of it. Operations of that kind cost money, and while they might be afforded by the rich Dubliners of Rathmines or Dalkey who had little else to do with their money, the poor of Dublin in the slums of the 1930s had difficulty enough feeding their children without paying for a cat to lose its sex. The very idea! And so we children were treated at night to the terrifying music of the alley cats on the roofs and in the backyards of the little streets around Bow Lane. They put the fear of God into us. Woken abruptly by a low, rumbling sound, I listened, straining in the darkness of the bedroom to identify the noise. I was afraid to wake my sister, sound asleep beside me in the bed, for she was nearly nine years older than me and not nearly so frightened. Then it came again, louder this time and more prolonged, to be joined by another terrifying rumble, deep-throated and sinister, as if from the depths of some savage jungle. I shivered in my warm bed. Was it cats . . .? Or could it be the banshee . . .?

Annie Byrne, our maid-of-all-work, hadn't she told me that banshees sounded like the wailing of cats? And I knew that the banshee wailed when a death was about to take place. Merciful heavens! Now I remembered! Hadn't a bird flown through the window right into the kitchen that very morning, and that meant, no doubt of it, a death on that very day itself. Was it my death that the banshee was wailing? My heart turned over in my chest at the thought, and palpitations shook my whole body. I wondered, as I had often

5

wondered before, if I had a 'bad' heart and whether I would live until morning. Annie Byrne had told me that I was too suggestible for my own good, for she was the only one I could confess my fears to, the only one in our house who knew what terrors I went through in the dark of the night. I began to perspire with the fantasies in my head. I would die in the night for sure, and when my father found me dead in the bed in the morning, he would blame me for dying in such a ridiculous way. Then I was shot through by another awful thought. Perhaps the Devil himself was coming to get me! People in Bow Lane said that he sometimes came in the middle of the night to 'bold' children and carried them off in their sleep when the parents were not looking . . .

Suddenly there came a horrible, long-drawn-out scream, then another and another, the whole rising to a blood-curdling climax. Yes, now I knew it was cats; that was the way they went on when the toms were fighting. Cats, yes . . . sure it was cats all right. But didn't Annie say that the Divil (as she called him) often disguised himself as a black cat with green eyes, the kind that witches have when they fly through the sky on their broomsticks, and creep in through your window at night to grab you? Hadn't I seen a black cat just about teatime sitting near the house and staring at me in a funny way with its green eyes? Panic seized me. Just then another eruption burst in upon the night, male against male in a fury of tooth and claw, hissing and spitting and screaming ferociously. Yes, it was only cats, that was sure.

I knew very well it could have been the Devil all the same. I knew he existed and stalked about our street. My friend Martha told me that his favourite time for 'making a swoop' was at twilight when it was just turning dark and he would not be noticed. She said he disguised himself as a 'respectable man in a suit an' all', and in the dim light of the gas lamps you would have a terrible time making him out. The sure way to spot him was to look at the ankles of the man in front of you, for the one thing he could not hide was his cloven hooves. You should look between the end of the trousers and the shoes where the sock should be. We would call out breathlessly to one another as we went up Steevens's Lane on the way home for tea. 'There is the cloven hoof!'; and we would take to our heels and run until we had to stop for breath. Then how we laughed at our near escapes! The fright was, in a strange way, part of the thrill of our half-believing, half-disbelieving fantasy-filled imaginations. In the light of day all our fantasies melted away, but always revived as darkness fell. When I awoke in the morning after the nightmare caterwauling, everything looked calm and ordinary again, but clumps of fur on grass or pavement spoke of the night's battles and tom-cats limped home with bloody wounds on side and neck. They sat and licked themselves clean again, the tongue endlessly busy, restoring themselves to normal as if nothing unusual at all had happened in the night.

Then there were the she-cats who were always producing unwanted kittens. I dreaded to see their little bodies grow plump, for I knew full well what that would lead to. I made ready a bed for the new kittens in a small cardboard box which I kept hidden for such emergencies. I carefully padded it with copies of the *Evening Herald*, and placed it on the roof of the outside toilet where a ledge protected it from view. There I hoped the mother would bring her babies into the world in peace. I watched every day to see if she had gone into the box. Then I saw her in it, turning herself round and round in the newspapers and finally settling herself. I climbed the ladder regularly and waited. There they were at last, four or five tiny balls curled up between their mother's paws and stomach. I sneaked out saucer after saucer of milk, and trembled lest they be discovered. The little miaows soon gave the game away. Annie, who came from the country and had no sentimental feelings about cats, either mothers or babies, climbed up the ladder, snatched the kittens, and plunged them unceremoniously into a bucket of cold water. I pleaded and begged for them to be allowed to live. 'I will find a home for them, I promise I will!' But it fell on deaf ears. 'It is all part of life,' Annie would say. 'If you didn't do this the backstreets of Dublin would be awash with cats, and there would be no livin' in cleanliness and dacency any more, they breed that aisy.' My father went further and took the explanation onto a philosophical plane. 'The population of the world has to be controlled,' he said, 'as this planet could not support the superabundance of life which an over-generous mother nature constantly pours forth. Mother nature, to ensure the survival of the species, has created a countermechanism in the form of flood, pestilence and famine to offset her excesses. If she did not do this, there would be universal famine, and nobody would have enough to eat.'

My imagination was transfixed by this awful prospect. I wondered why mother nature was so badly organised. I knew I could have planned things better. It was all part of the great struggle for survival, my father said, complacent in the knowledge that he himself had been in that struggle and had come out of it victorious. The Dublin streets round our house abounded with this surplus of nature, poor scrawny cats and dogs whose plight made my oversensitive heart despair. I often came upon one of these strays and tried to sneak it into our backyard when my father was not looking, for although never harsh to animals, he disliked them in the house. 'They are dirty and covered in fleas; they only bring disease with them.' I must learn to accept the ways of the world or I would 'go under'. No use snivelling foolishly about it. So when I managed to smuggle an animal in, my heart was in my mouth for fear of what my father would say or do. Occasionally, I managed to hide a dog for a week or more, and there was many a crisis. One pup chewed off the heel of my father's shoe, and there was a frenzy of gluing and patching before he came back and discovered me. Another dog pulled down the curtains in the kitchen, reefed them in bits, and chewed up the curtain pole. I was again discovered, and dreadful rows ensued. The animal was thrown out and I was told in no uncertain terms that I would follow it if ever I brought in another one. My father had a great command of rhetoric, especially of the violent kind, and he terrified me when he was in a rage.

I once hid a big tom-cat for over a week in a large shed in our backyard. I called him Sergeant because he had three white stripes across his black back. Unfortunately, I had also hidden an injured pigeon called Polshee in the shed, and one morning I went in to find a few feathers and a pool of blood where Polshee had been. Sergeant had a very big appetite and no discretion at all about keeping out of my father's way. He was chased out of the house and yard over and over again. He came back in as jaunty as ever, and miaowed under the kitchen window. I sneaked out meat which I had hidden from my dinner and sat with him in the rain under a raincoat. This sight enraged my father. What a sentimental weakling of a daughter! I would catch pneumonia for sure, and where would I be then? In hospital where my father would have all the worry of looking after me. But he would not do it. I need not think he would. He would let me be taken to hospital in an ambulance, and I could die there. One night shortly after this, in a ferocious feline struggle, Sergeant fell into a barrel of tar. In the morning, an abject, black, sticky mess dragged itself slowly into our kitchen and collapsed on the floor in front of us. My father gave one look at the cat and pronounced that it would be dead before night. No one ever considered giving him a quick death at the vet's, for that alternative, like neutering, cost money and was not open to people like us. True, there was a van provided by the veterinary college in Ballsbridge which collected sick animals for free treatment, but as Sergeant's emergency happened during wartime when there was next to no petrol in Dublin, it would certainly not come out for a dying cat.

I knew the veterinary college well. I had often taken unwanted kittens and sick animals to it. Annie Byrne told me that the students needed sick animals from the poor parts of Dublin to experiment on, for if they died in the process no one would know or care. It was the same in the Dental Hospital, she said: the poor had to put up with ham-fisted students who were being trained and who had generally no idea how to do the job 'right'. I was always deeply suspicious of these institutions after Annie's words, but there was no other alternative, and to the veterinary college we had to go. It was a long way from James's Street to Ballsbridge where the 'toffs' lived. Martha and I, with our bundle of 'waste', would get on the tram at the Fountain. To avoid paying we tried to judge the time finely so that when the conductor was busy with the people getting onto the tram, we could slip off unnoticed. Sometimes it worked and sometimes it did not. From Trinity College we would then walk the mile to Ballsbridge. When we had handed in the sick animal we would start home again, crying most of the way.

But Sergeant was so black and sticky that we could not carry him into a tram. I was going to have to watch him die. Strange to say, against all common sense, he survived. Day after day he lay prone on a piece of old sacking beside the kitchen range. I tried to force spoonfuls of milk into his mouth and down his throat, but without any hope that he would be able to stagger to his feet again. A whole week went by. I noticed one morning that he was making weak

9

efforts to lick the tarry mess off his fur. Patiently and slowly he kept at the task, a little longer each day, until there was a bare patch of skin in the middle of the black mess. It was such a repulsive pink and black mottled sight that I could hardly bear to look at it. Gradually, more and more patches appeared in the black as the unrelenting work of recuperation went on. At last, a macabre object, half bald, half tar, stood up on its feet again, triumphant. Little patches of new fur had been slowly growing in the bare parts, all now of different lengths, and they made of Sergeant the most comic object you could set your eyes on.

This heroic feat, this impossible return to life, struck my father's imagination with great force. From the day and hour that he saw that the cat was determined to live, he took a new interest in it. His former dislike turned to open admiration. Instead of throwing him out of the house, to our utter amazement he bought him every day a pennyworth of lights from the butcher to increase his fighting chances. It was my task to cook that repulsive foamy, pink lung in an old pot. The cat, fat again and furry, followed my father everywhere thereafter. They walked up and down together in front of the Gate like two fellow-travellers who thought the same thought and shared the same philosophy. Sergeant returned to the tiles at night and contributed his part to the nocturnal music of our streets, fortified now as never before by his daily pennyworth of lights, which helped to make him king of the cats in our neighbourhood. For my father that cat symbolised the strength of the will, the quality of character he most admired and which he unceasingly advocated in his children. Had he not been in the business of survival himself when, at seventeen years of age, he had left a loveless home, joined the Royal Navy, and set out, unsupported, to face a hard life at sea? Now in 1931, having lost his young wife to the lingering death of cancer, he was alone and had to fend for his five children in the harsh economic climate of the Great Depression. He was in the business of survival once again. This is the tale of the youngest and weakest of those children who had to undergo all the rigours of his philosophy when not yet five years old.

MY BEGINNINGS

I should have died by rights. On the night that I was born, six weeks prematurely, in the front bedroom of the second teacher's schoolhouse in Swords, near Dublin, the local doctor, called in to attend my mother, was drunk. Having managed somehow to deliver the baby, he staggered away leaving the weakened mother and the still weaker baby to get on as best they could with living. The baby was rescued just in time from being completely smothered by blankets which had somehow got over her head when the exhausted mother was sleeping. My aunt told me later of the panic of that event and the tragedy that could have ensued. Like Sergeant the cat, the baby survived and struggled on from one crisis to another, her life all the time threatened with extinction. Everything was tried but with little effect. Finally, the doctor suggested a last remedy: 'Take her to her mother's native air', and to Bantry, County Cork, I was taken where, it seemed, I rallied. How long we stayed there I do not know. I was never able to ask my mother about it as she died before I was at the age of asking questions. I was nearly carried off several times after that by whooping cough, bronchitis and two doses of pneumonia, but I managed to scrape through until, at the age of seven, having been dosed every day with cod liver oil, malt extract and Parrish's Food, and purged every Friday night with senna tea, I suddenly took a turn for the better, and was even able to go to school. Since then I have always looked on seven as my lucky number and never get a ticket or a document without checking to see if there was a seven on it or a multiple of seven. If there were I should be in luck!

My mother's native air was the temperate, mild, moist air of west Cork. It is now a place of pilgrimage for me, for I never lived there with her as did the other children, nor was I able to hear stories of her girlhood from her own lips. Like all children, I accepted without thinking the situation as it was after my mother's death. Comparisons we learn as we grow older, and roots we look for when we are older still. It was to be many years before I visited her grave in the protestant part of the graveyard of the old Franciscan priory overlooking the sea in Bantry.

If you look at the map of Ireland, you will see that in shape she has her back to England and Wales and her head and feet stretching far out to the Atlantic towards the Americas. In one sense that is the right direction to face for she has had, over centuries, to watch thousands of her impoverished sons and daughters depart from her shores in search of work in the New World. The west of Ireland in the nineteenth century and right up to the Second World War often saw more dollars than sterling in the shops, and American newspapers were often the only ones to be found in the homes of poor farmers. To this day the size and strength of the Irish contingent in the USA speaks of those dread years of emigration.

There is scarcely any town in Ireland in so beautiful a situation as that of Bantry in west Cork. It lies at the head of one of the six long inlets of the Atlantic which dig deep into the land at this heel of Ireland and bear the names of Dingle Bay, Ballinskelligs Bay, Kenmare Bay, Bantry Bay, Dunmanus Bay and Roaring Water Bay. Their turbulent and stormy waters are held back by line after line of rugged mountains which seem to be compacted by nature to defend this last stronghold of Europe against the assaults of the ocean. The Gulf Stream washes these shores and warms the land to such a degree that semi-tropical flowers, arum lilies, fuchsias and palms grow wild in the hedgerows and around the cottages. So mild and wet is the climate that enthusiastic gardeners have come here especially to create beautiful subtropical gardens. A Scotsman, John Allen Bryce, made a world-famous Italian garden out of the wilds of Garnish Island in this soft and coaxing air.

The town of Bantry squeezes itself neatly into the small wedge of ground lying between two hills that run down to the bay, which is twenty-one miles long and four miles wide and beautiful in all its length. 'Were there such a bay lying on an English shore, it would be a world's wonder,' wrote William Thackeray, the English novelist. Wherever you stand, wherever you look, exquisite harmonies of sky, sea and land captivate the eye and entrance the soul. 'O all ye works of the Lord, praise ye the Lord, praise Him and magnify Him for ever.' Bantry was very remote when my mother was a girl, far from everywhere at the land's end of Europe, 60 miles from the city of Cork and 220 miles from Dublin. Its market square, at the sea end of the town, brought farmers in from the countryside with milk, butter, eggs and chickens for sale. As they had to rise early to make the long journey to the town, the public houses opened at 7 a.m. to supply them. Horses and carts thronged the square; there was dung everywhere, and women had to hold their skirts up to avoid walking in it. Pilchard fishing had once been a thriving industry and had a big export market to Spain, Portugal and Italy. By the end of the seventeenth century the pilchards were fished out, and the trade came to an end. It was revived from time to time over the centuries and is now, once again, flourishing.

The protestant gentry, the Earls of Bantry, lived in the beautiful Bantry House overlooking the bay. The sons of this gentry, as elsewhere in Ireland, often went to school in England, joined the fleets and armies of the Empire, came home to Ireland, and hung up their regimental flags in the local Church of Ireland. But they did not, for all that, consider themselves English. All around them were protestants who went to the same church but had a different social standing. They were small farmers like my cousins, artisans and shopkeepers like my grandfather, who were no richer than their catholic neighbours. Their forebears had lived in west Cork since the sixteenth and seventeenth centuries. With the failure of the Desmond rebellion against the English in the sixteenth century, the lands of the rebels, including the vast O'Mahony estate, were confiscated and granted to the protestant Earl of Bandon. To this day Bandon has a large concentration of protestants. After the Cromwellian wars of the seventeenth century there was another big transfer of lands from Irish to English owners. The Earl of Anglesey alone was granted 100,000 acres, and smallholdings were given to English soldiers who had fought in the Cromwellian armies. Other protestants, Huguenots, arrived directly from the Continent, where

13

they had been persecuted for their faith. Our relations, the Duke-lows of Durrus, must have descended from the French Huguenots, Duclos. My mother's family on her father's side, the Newmans, had certainly originally been small planters from England but her mother was a McCarthy of native stock and a catholic. From all accounts these descendants of planters got on well with their catholic neighbours and they helped each other on their small farms but . . . they went to different churches on Sunday.

My history begins with my grandfather, James Newman. His wife, Jane McCarthy, owned a public house in the town called the Sailors' Rest. He is described in the 1911 census as a butterbuyer and wine merchant. Butter was bought from farmers all over the country and exported in large quantities. There were four girls and a boy in the Newman family and plenty of room for them all in the six bedrooms above the pub. My maternal aunt told me how lively that household was. My grandmother was steeped in Irish country lore: she had tales of banshees, keeners, fairies and leprechauns, as well as saints and martyrs. She spoke English with an Irish idiom, saying 'Musha mo croidhe' in a lilting, caressing Cork accent. My grandfather's lore was less extensive but he was a cheerful man and extremely gregarious, just the right man for a pub for he was known as 'the man with the greatest eye for a horse in the whole county of Cork'.

While far from the heart of Europe, Bantry had nevertheless had its history on the world stage. Foreign governments at war with Britain had from time to time sent ships and soldiers to this treach-erous back door of Europe to help the Irish rebels against their com-mon foe, the English. In 1602 a Spanish force came to the help of the rebels and was besieged and defeated at Dunboy Castle at Bere. In 1796 a French fleet of forty-three ships arrived in Bantry Bay with the famous protestant Irish patriot Theobald Wolfe Tone on board. The French government had been reluctant to send this force but was persuaded to do so by the brilliant French general Hoche. He intended to land, seize Cork and possibly Dublin. Bad weather and worse communications caused the French fleet to disperse even before leaving Brest. The ship carrying General Hoche failed to ar-rive in Bantry Bay at all, and in the general confusion and terrible easterly winds, the ships which had managed to reach the bay were unable to disembark the men. This gave Richard White of Bantry time to alert the authorities and to summon up the Volunteers (for this action an earldom was conferred on him). Eventually, the French ships had, one after another, to turn about and make for home.

In 1900, when my mother was a girl, the memory of the Great Famine was still vivid and bitter. It had been particularly ferocious in west Cork; catholics and protestants had worked together to relieve the sick and dying, many of whom were brought on carts from outlying Schull and Durrus to the workhouse in Bantry. More than half the population of Bantry died in these terrible years.

The Royal Navy was not unknown in remote Bantry. The deep ports of Ireland were favoured places for naval manoeuvres, and Bantry Bay, free of rocks and sandbanks, was ideal for the purpose. The fleet came regularly to its base at Berehaven, a fine natural harbour protected from the open sea by the long island of Bere. The clear four-mile stretch of water allowed the ships to calibrate their guns and at Bere they refuelled and had repairs carried out. The fleet went out into the Atlantic on manoeuvres up the west coast of Ireland and over to Scotland. My father told me that they often put into places in Scotland for the night solely because the captain wished to dine with friends whose houses lay on shore. Sailors went to the local pubs to enjoy themselves and even further afield to Bantry town where each ships's company went to its own favourite pub. Sailors also came to Bantry from elsewhere to join their ships and might stay a night or two in a local pub while waiting to do so. My grandfather's pub, known locally as 'the Protestant Pub', was able to accommodate many of them (eleven sailors were registered as being on the premises at the time of the 1911 census). They were welcome there for they had money to spend and lively talk, singing and dancing would be on the cards for all to enjoy. Many of the girls of the area married sailors, for local practice often dictated that they might otherwise be married, if at all, to a man many years older than themselves.

In February of the year 1909, warships of His Majesty's Navy entered the bay and anchored, as usual, off Berehaven. Among them was the battleship HMS *Bulwark*, and as it came into view, a young man could be seen on the bridge beside the captain. He was twenty-nine years old, wiry, keen and intelligent-looking. He was a chief petty officer and chief yeoman of signals, and his job was to go ashore in Bantry and set up in the local post office a communications centre between the fleet and the Admiralty in London. The post office was only two doors away from the Protestant Pub where the Newmans lived. (Some years later connecting doors allowed a passage to run inside between the pub and the post office to ensure safe access in rebellious times.) This was his first visit to this corner of Ireland since he had joined the navy twelve years before, although he had been in many more remote and exotic places during that time. He was an Irishman born and bred from the oblique opposite corner of Ireland, 240 miles as the crow flies but much more by road or rail. He, too, had been brought up on the shores of a beautiful long inlet of the sea, in the town of Newtownards at the head of Strangford Lough in the county of Down. From early boyhood he had a passion for the sea and ships and he knew the names and dimensions of every ship in the navy. Large ships could not get through the narrow mouth of Strangford Lough, but he had only to walk the six miles across the neck of the narrow Ards peninsula to the open sea and the harbour of Donaghadee, then one of the busiest ports in Ireland, to see them. He often hung about the recruiting office where young boys like himself could join the Royal Navy when they were seventeen years of age. His father had forbidden him to go to sea but he was biding his time.

Any similarities between Bantry and Newtownards were purely geographical, for although Ireland was not yet partitioned, everyone knew that the north-east of the country was very different in mentality from the relaxed and sleepy south-west, and was inhabited by very different people. Ulster, too, had been 'planted' after the Flight of the Earls in 1607, not only with English but with dissenters and covenanters from south-west Scotland and the Borders. Their arrival increased the Scottish influence in this corner of Ireland where Scots had been coming to settle even before the Reformation. It was, after all, only eighteen miles between the closest points of Scotland and Ulster. Scottish houses could be seen with the naked eye on a clear day from the Antrim coast and it was quite usual, I was told, for churchgoers to row across to Scotland for morning service and return home the same day. Marriages were frequently made between the two peoples; my father's mother was a Stoupe from Ayrshire. Belfast grew to be a great industrial city, and in my father's time had more the air of a city like Glasgow or Liverpool than Dublin or Cork, with its tight working-class streets, its smoking factory chimneys, and its wealthy middle-class suburbs.

The alert-looking sailor who went ashore with his men to set up a communication's centre in Bantry post office was to be my father, and the eldest daughter of the owner of the pub was to be my mother. The two opposite corners of Ireland were to meet in that marriage and the two protestant cultures were to understand each other then as little as they do now.

The Protestant Pub (since renamed the Boston Bar by an Irishman returned from the usa) still stands four-square in William Street. It is a well-kept building with a large dwelling house above. My grandfather was Anglican in religion and was cousin to the Anglican Newmans, farmers of nearby Scart. Like their catholic neighbours, the Anglicans had big families and many of them had to migrate to find work, sometimes to Dublin and sometimes to Belfast, where their strong physique made them particularly suitable for the police force. One of my mother's cousins, Bob Newman, became a chauffeur in Dublin and another, Jim Newman, became a head constable in Belfast.

Eva, eldest of the four daughters, was twenty years old when Hugh Gaw appeared in the Protestant Pub. She and her sisters, Dot, Ella and Jenny, were not only lively and attractive, they were well educated. Eva, after finishing her education in the Church of Ireland school in Bantry, remained there for a year as an untrained teacher. She was then chosen to go for professional training to the Church of Ireland Training College in Dublin. This must have been a huge transition, for she was a close member of a large, happy and easygoing family and had never before left Cork. She was now to go to the big metropolis in a sort of boarding school bondage. Was she excited? Was she apprehensive? If, as I deeply suspect, she was like her younger daughter, she would have been both. And what a journey she had to make at the beginning and end of every term! First, trunks had to be loaded onto an 'outside' or jaunting car to take her to the station for the slow journey by train the 60 miles to Cork city, there to board a faster train for another 160-mile journey to Dublin. From Kingsbridge station in Dublin a cab conveyed herself and her trunks the two or three miles to the college, Kildare Place near Trinity College. The discipline at the college was strict. Men and women lived in separate departments and even ate separately. Students rose at 7 a.m. and attended religious service. Then came classes until noon. Marks were given for neatness and proficiency. All students were expected to join the Temperance Society and to take the pledge (of total abstinence). Candidates for admission were earnestly invited to meditate on the following:

> Cultivate an humble, teachable disposition. Come to your work as learners. Consider the importance of the charge you propose to undertake, – to sow the first seeds of Divine truth in immortal beings, and to watch over their opening characters and minds, rooting out the evil and implanting good. Who is sufficient for these things? No one in his own strength: seek therefore, earnestly, God's help in prayer; address yourself to every occupation in the spirit of prayer, and of dependence on the Divine blessing.

And:

> Avoid all negligence in your personal appearance. Let your manners be cheerful, sober, and decorous. Remember that you are to be as lights set on a hill that cannot be hid; that you are expected to exemplify in your conduct all that you teach. We would attach high importance to your office; not that you should be exalted thereby, but that you may seek strength not your own, and in that strength be careful to maintain good works.

Did the camaraderie of the students relieve Eva's certain homesickness? I can never know. The food was plain, inadequate and monotonous, and needed to be supplemented by food parcels from home. The college rhyme tells all:

> Three between four of us,
> Happy and glorious,
> It's well there's no more of us
> God save the Queen!

Her sister Ella took her place as an untrained teacher in the Bantry school. Later as a young teacher in west Cork she had to cycle sixteen miles from Bantry to her school in all weathers. She got wet, caught colds and fevers and eventually the dreaded tuberculosis. My father told me that he found her dying in Bantry and brought her to Dublin to see a specialist, but it was too late. She died aged thirty-five and lies beside her sister in the priory graveyard in Bantry. Her photograph hung in our home, young, smiling, curly-haired, a stranger to me. My mother's next sister, Dot, married a soldier and went out to India with him. She wanted to come home to have her first baby, but the birth, which happened prematurely on board ship, went tragically wrong, and both she and her baby were buried at sea. The youngest, Jenny, followed her sisters to Kildare Place and became a teacher in Dublin. She married and lived there until her death at sixty-seven years of age. She was the only one of those sisters I was to know and remember. The only son, Jack, not being interested in, or able for, a profession, remained unmarried in Bantry, doing odd jobs for a living. He died of a heart attack in middle age. Although I never met him, I have a warm place in my heart for him because he loved animals, and on the day he died and for many days afterwards they said that the howling of his animals was like the howling of twenty banshees.

James Newman's wife, Jane McCarthy, was not a co-religionist. Although catholic, she agreed to let her children be brought up in their father's religion. This was possible before the days of the Ne Temere decree promulgated by the catholic church, which obliged the non-catholic partner in a mixed marriage to agree to have all the children brought up as catholics and the catholic partner to try to influence the other's family to become catholic. This decree was to deplete severely the Anglican community in Ireland. It happened in the mixed marriages of my sister and two of my brothers, all of whose children had to be brought up as catholics. History does not relate how painful it was for Jane McCarthy so see her children brought up 'out of the Faith'; but that she never gave up her own is certain. In one of my very few early memories, I see myself walking hand in hand with a figure clad in long black garments. We turn aside from the main road and go through a gate towards a large building; there in front of me I see a big dark rock with candles blazing on it and a waxen statue of a lady in blue and white looking down on it. Terrified, I pull at my grandmother's arm and cry to go home. This was the grotto of the catholic church in Bantry.

From what I have heard, the Newman children had a carefree home and were loved and indulged by both parents. Their social life revolved around the church, with tennis, picnics, dancing, boating and cycling the order of the day. I had heard that my mother, before her marriage, was in love with her first cousin on her mother's side, one Tadg O'Sullivan. He, too, was a teacher in training, and was intelligent and generous like herself. They went out together on long bicycle rides in the country or along the shore of the bay, but belonged to different churches. The great barrier which divided them was not only religion but blood. Eva's father, alarmed by the degree of consanguinity, was against the match. When a young sailor from the North of Ireland asked for her hand, he thought him a far more suitable husband for his daughter. Eva did not agree. It is said that she was locked in her bedroom 'until she came round'. I always wanted to get at the truth of this romantic story and one day, many, many years later, I asked Tadg if it were true. He laughed in his usual pleasant way but would not be drawn. 'Your father was a fine man and one with the greatest command of the English language I ever met.' If there had been no truth in it, I thought, he would have denied it. I was confirmed in my suspicion. Tadg was to marry within a year and was to lose his own wife in childbirth. His daughter, Elmire, still lives in Cork and her distinctive Cork accent, her ready sympathy and easy cheerfulness are qualities which I imagine my mother to have had.

Hugh Gaw and Eva Newman were married in the Church of Ireland in Bantry in April 1911. She was twenty-two and he thirty-one. Her mother must have had a sore heart at the prospect of Eva leaving home in a town where she knew everybody to live with strangers in a strange land. Naval quarters were to be their destination. We do not know whether she loved her new husband well enough to bear it for his sake, but her letters home, according to my aunt, were 'coming down with homesickness'. Within a year she was expecting her first baby. She came back to Bantry for the birth of her son, James Cecil, but she returned after a few months to Devonport, where her husband was stationed in naval barracks.

She was alone with her baby for the greater part of the day. This pattern of living dramatically changed when war broke out in 1914. Her husband was posted to the battleship HMS *Erin* on 14 August and spent most of the war at sea, with occasional home leave. My mother spent those years, gratefully, I must suppose, back in Bantry with her kindly relations. A daughter, Olive, was born to her in February 1918, and the three of them settled comfortably into the Bantry life my mother loved so well. She told her eldest son, who reported it to me many years later, 'I am a west Cork woman and never will be anything else.' Had her husband tried to make her something else? While she was safe in Bantry, her husband was in the thick of the war at sea, including the Battle of Jutland in May 1916.

His homecomings to Bantry, not only during the war years but right up to 1920 when he retired from the navy, brought violently to an end the happy, carefree, indulged life his son was leading there with his doting mother and grandparents. My father was furious: there was no discipline, meals were movable feasts and bedtimes erratic. He set about changing all that and bringing a bit of good naval discipline into Cecil's life. From then on a caustic and critical presence was among them. His son was not likely, he thought, to shape up for the professional position he intended for him on such a regime. He was packed off forthwith to a boarding school – to Ranelagh School in Athlone – to be set on the right way. Cecil was miserable and his indignation was intense. My worried mother was even forbidden to send him parcels 'to make up' to him. From that experience grew a dislike of our father which was to last all his life. He always vigorously declared himself a Cork man, and would have nothing to do with the northern part of Ireland.

Another son, Hugh, was added to the family, and my mother, now with three children to care for, resumed her teaching. My father, a chief petty officer, having completed twenty-four years' service in the navy, was due for retirement. His record was so good that he was offered further training for a commission. This was unusual at the time when it was very difficult to rise from the lower deck. Not only was my father tired of being away from home and family but my mother was most reluctant to leave Ireland again. He turned down the offer, and this, I believe, he always held against her. He left his depot ship, HMS *Vivid*, on 13 April 1920 and came back to Ireland for good. He viewed this event, in retrospect, as a disaster, and from then on he saw himself as a man who had taken a wrong turning. He had landed himself, at a time of widespread unemployment, in a country where he could find no job equal to his ability, and where the narrow outlook of the catholic church nearly suffocated him. His profound feeling of being part of a large and historic empire, his free-thinking mind, his extensive self-education, were deeply scandalised by the transition.

Soon there was to be more trouble in Ireland. The rebellion of 1916 against the British had finally resulted in the Treaty of 1921 which partitioned Ireland in two, six counties in the North to be part of the United Kingdom and twenty-six counties in the South to be independent but with dominion status. De Valera declared against the Treaty together with other republicans. A bitter civil war followed in 1922–3 in which terrible atrocities were committed. (The pro-Treaty party was successful but in 1932 de Valera's party succeeded to power.) Tensions were running very high in west Cork and British ex-servicemen were not the most welcome of incomers. In 1921 he had a very bad experience which he never disclosed to me, but my brother, Cecil, got to know of it. One night during those violent times, the IRA cornered him. They stood him up against a wall and prepared to shoot. One of the men shouted, pointing to my father, 'No stop! He is Eva Newman's husband. Let him go!' (This was his second miraculous escape from death. In the autumn of 1914 he was ordered to go to the Falkland Islands on HMS *Good Hope*, one of a squadron of five ships which were to patrol the South Atlantic, but another man took his place. The ships were blown to pieces by German warships at the Battle of Coronel, and there were no survivors from the *Good Hope*.) This experience and his own last-minute reprieve took a heavy toll of his nervous system. Some time early in 1922, the Protestant Pub was burnt down, presumably by the IRA. Olive, then a little girl of three or four, remembers seeing the burnt furniture stacked in the yard and remembers crying inconsolably at seeing her little wooden dolls' pram, made by her grandfather, among the wreckage. The family then took refuge with my mother's cousins in nearby Scart.

I next find my mother doing substitute teaching in the Church of

22

Ireland school in Adare, and shortly afterwards in Roscrea. During that time a third son, Frank, was added to the family. What my father did during this time I have never been able to ascertain, but his temper could not have taken well to this purposeless existence. The education of his children was now his great passion. He determined to move to Dublin where good schools were to be found. My mother was appointed second teacher in the Old Borough School in Swords, eight miles from the city, and the whole family moved into the schoolhouse which adjoined the school proper. Still in use as a school, this is a handsome, long, low eighteenth-century building set back from the road by a large playground. Though the schoolhouse looks big from the outside, it is quite small within – a parlour downstairs, small kitchen behind, two bedrooms upstairs, and a toilet in the yard outside. My mother's life must have been hard at that time, for not only had she to do her job as a teacher, but she had four children to look after as well as an irritable and disgruntled husband to cope with. I can imagine her shock when, in these circumstances, she discovered she was expecting a fifth child. It was perhaps not surprising that I was born prematurely. At two weeks old I was taken to be baptised (unusually early for a protestant child) as my hold on life was so precarious. In the baptismal roll of St Columba's church in Swords I am recorded as having been baptised two weeks before I was born, which is stranger still!

My mother and father could not agree on a name for their new child. My father wanted to call me Edith Florence after the two famous nurses he so much admired, but my mother wanted to call me Hazel Newman after her own family. As they walked up the hill to the church carrying the baby in long christening robes, my brother remembers them still arguing. Eventually they decided to toss a coin, and my mother won, but when the moment came during the service to 'name this child' my father stepped forward and said 'Edith Florence' and the deed was unsportingly done. My father was not a man to be bested, especially by a woman. I was thus given a name which many Dubliners could not pronounce; there is no 'th' sound in the Irish language, and it is often lost in the English spoken in Ireland. It became in various mouths 'E-dit' or even 'E-dee-it' and a constant source of embarrassment to me. Everyone in the family, except my father, called me 'Bubbles' for it appeared that I very much resembled a little girl called Bubbles in an advertisement for Pears Soap.

I was only two months old when the family left Swords and moved to Dublin city. My mother was appointed to St Peter's Church of Ireland school, a town school with no accommodation for the teacher. For some months she had to finish her time in Swords and make the long journey there and back by bus. My father now had a big problem. Where were we to live? Where was an able-bodied man to get a job? It was his wife's cousin, Bob Newman from Bantry, who came up with a good suggestion. There was a vacancy for a lodge-keeper in St Patrick's Hospital, where he was a chauffeur to the chief medical superintendent. He would put in a word for him and was sure that an ex-serviceman with a good record would be favourably looked upon by the hospital authorities. My father got the job and we all moved in. A parlour, a kitchen, a scullery and three bedrooms was a decided improvement on the schoolhouse in Swords, but how my mother felt about moving from a schoolhouse in the country with a certain status to a gate lodge in a poor part of Dublin, I can only guess. My brother Hugh, then six years old, remembers his arrival at the lodge. Our mother was holding his hand in hers as they walked together up Steevens's Lane to see the new house. She told him cheerfully that there was a big brass bell on the wall which he could press to summon his father. He would love it! She was to live there for almost five years with her five children until her death in September 1931 at the age of forty-one. I was to spend the first seventeen years of my life in that house, twelve of them without a mother and under the iron rule of a worried, frustrated and sometimes violent father.

SWIFT'S HOSPITAL
FOR THE INSANE

Hardly anyone in Dublin knows the exact location of St Patrick's Hospital although many have heard of it. Hidden away in what was once a poor, run-down part of the city, it is one and a half miles from the city centre and from the better-known city hospitals. Known locally as Swift's Hospital because of its connection with the Dean of St Patrick's who left all his money to found it, it lay quiet and private behind its high walls. Everyone in Dublin knew that Dean Swift was 'mad'; few knew that he was a world-famous writer, feared by the great in England for his devastating satire, but loved in Ireland for scourging certain injustices of English rule there. In his own time he was a sort of hero to the Dubliners, who loved to see the mighty put down by wit and irony. Harsh to his political and ecclesiastical enemies, he was tender and generous to the poor. He boasted to the poet Alexander Pope, 'I walk the streets in peace without being jostled nor ever without a thousand bless-ings from my friends the vulgar. I am lord mayor of 120 houses, I am absolutely lord of the greatest cathedral in the kingdom, am at peace with the neighbouring princes, the Lord Mayor of the city and the Archbishop of Dublin.'

His political and ecclesiastical barbs make great reading, but it is *Gulliver's Travels* which has given the greatest pleasure of all his books and reached the widest public. As a child I loved the fantastical stories of big people, little people and flying islands, without the least idea that these were, in fact, a powerful allegory on the human condition. Everything he put his pen to is racy and witty. In

Holyhead in Wales, while waiting, bored, for the boat back to Dublin, he scribbled:

> Lo here I sit at Holyhead,
> With muddy ale and mouldy bread . . .
> All Christian vittals stink of fish,
> I'm where my enemies would wish.

Nobody savoured more than Swift the ironic parallel between the noble and the tawdry. He wrote:

> Then, seated on a three-legged chair,
> Takes off her artificial hair:
> Now, picking out a crystal eye,
> She wipes in clean, and lays it by.
> Her eyebrows from a mouse's hide
> Stuck on with art on either side,
> Pulls off with care, and first displays 'em,
> Then in a play-book smoothly lays 'em.
> Now dextrously her plumpers draws,
> That serve to fill her hollow jaws.
> Untwists a wire; and from her gums
> A set of teeth completely comes.
> Pulls out the rags contrived to prop
> Her flabby dugs, and down they drop.

His lifestyle in the deanery in a poor part of Dublin was by no means luxurious. He lived, he said, in a corner of a vast unfurnished house where Tom, his groom, was frequently drunk and not one of his servants was able to read or write properly. In spite of the discomfort and remoteness of his situation he conducted all his life a vast correspondence with literary friends in England. He remained the embattled dean until his death. That he had the poor of Dublin seriously at heart is clear from his decision to leave all his money to found an asylum for the weak-minded poor of the city. No such institution then existed in Ireland, and even in England the provision was inadequate. A young Frenchman, émigré from the revolution in his own country, visited Ireland in 1796 and noted in his book *A Tour of Ireland*:

There is no place of shelter for the weak-minded of Cork. It is a hideous spectacle to see them in the streets. For the most part, it is true, they are quiet but it is cruel and humiliating to see human nature so degraded, that an effort should be made to separate them from society.

Ten years before his death, on 17 July 1735, Swift wrote: 'I have now finished my will in form wherein I have settled my whole fortune in the city on trust for building and maintaining a hospital for idiots and lunatics.' This will decreed that the income from the lands which Swift ordered his trustees to purchase in any province of Ireland except Connaught

> shall be laid out in purchasing a piece of land situate near Dr Steevens Hospital, or if it cannot be there had, somewhere in or near the city of Dublin, large enough for the purchase herein after mentioned, and in building thereon an hospital large enough for the reception of as many idiots and lunatics as the annual income of the said lands and worldly substance, will be sufficient to maintain: And I desire that the said hospital may be called St Patrick's Hospital.

The governors of Dr Steevens's Hospital were willing to lease the site adjacent to their own, and St Patrick's Hospital was completed in 1757. It could accommodate fifty resident patients and ten day-patients. Swift intended that the patients should be cared for free of charge, and in fact the only charges made were sixpence a week for washing and a deposit of one pound to meet possible funeral expenses. Swift knew very well of the public humiliation of idiots such as happened in the Bethlehem Hospital (Bedlam) in London where lunatics were exhibited to the public for sport or for money. He ordered that 'no person whatsoever shall have access to the patients except in the presence of the governors or by order of the state physician or surgeon general'. Lest he be considered sentimental in his care for the Irish, he wrote in 'Verses on the Death of Dr Swift':

> He gave the little wealth he had
> To build a house for fools and mad;
> And showed, by one satiric touch,
> No nation wanted it so much.

27

Dubliners would enjoy this witty little piece even though aimed at themselves. But did Swift, too, go mad in the end? Although a very strong man physically as well as mentally, and a great walker around the streets and environs of Dublin, by 1731 when he was only sixty-four years of age, he was far from well.

Deaf, giddy, helpless, left alone,
To all my friends a burden grown,
No more I hear my church's bell,
Than if it rang out for my knell.

He felt himself increasingly helpless and depressed in the following years. In July 1740 he wrote: 'I have been very miserable all night and today extremely deaf and full of pain. I am so stupid and confounded that I cannot express the mortification I am under both in body and mind...' In 1742 a commission of lunacy was appointed to investigate Swift's condition. It decided that Swift 'hath for these nine months past been gradually failing in his memory and understanding, and of such unsound mind and memory that he is incapable of transacting any business, or managing, conducting or taking care either of his estate or his person'. He lived for another three tormented years in this dreadful darkness of mind. The following description was given of his condition:

He walked ten hours a day, would not eat or drink if he stayed in his room. His meat was served up ready cut, and sometimes it would lie an hour on the table before he would touch it, and then eat it walking. About six weeks ago, in one night's time, his left eye swelled as large as an egg... and many large boils appeared under his arms and body. The torture he was in is not be to described. Five persons could scarce hold him for a week from tearing out his own eyes.

Swift died, mad or sane, on 19 October 1745 and was buried in his own cathedral in Dublin. What a terrible irony, it was felt, that a man such as Swift who used all the formidable force of his reason to mock unreason, should at last have succumbed to unreason itself! There was even a rumour that his servants accepted money for admitting strangers to view him. 'And Swift expires, a driveller and a show,' wrote his contemporary Samuel Johnson, who was himself terrified of losing his reason at the last. (He had a paralytic stroke when he was seventy-five years old, and his first effort, when he realised what had happened to him, was to test his mental faculties by translating the Lord's Prayer from Latin. 'It was not good but I *knew* it was not good,' he said.)

During the seventeen years that I lived in the lodge of St Patrick's Hospital, I knew very little of Swift's life and his connection with St Patrick's. Pressures other than history weighed upon me during those years, and it was only long afterwards that I became interested in the great man.

Even today you would have no reason to pass St Patrick's Hospital if you did not live in one of the nearby streets, for it is on no main thoroughfare. To reach it from the city centre you would have to pass through the heart of old Dublin, past the Castle, centre of political power in the days of the Union, and into the bustling Thomas Street. Here, street hawkers still advertise their wares in raucous Dublin accents as they did in my day when, with cheerful indifference to germs and dirt, they spat on the red apples and polished them vigorously with the tail-end of a dirty shawl. Blissfully oblivious to the danger, we paid a penny when we had it for the most polished and spat-upon apple we could lay our eyes on. We had to keep a sharp eye on these women for everyone knew that they could, in a twinkling of an eye, substitute a bad apple for a good one and 'diddle' you.

James's Street, the continuation of Thomas Street, was our home territory. We knew every house, every shop, every railing, every grating in its lower length. Once fine town houses, now tenements, dirty and neglected 'relics of ould dacency', they were let out to five or six poor families; small huxters' shops sold bull's-eyes, humbugs and violently striped boiled sweets in rows of tempting glass jars; others offered thick slices of black 'gur' cake; others buttermilk in churns, tinned beef, sausages, lemonade, sweetie cigarettes and mounds of broken Kit-Kat and broken biscuits, delicious debris from nearby Rowntree's and Jacob's factories. Flood's shop, near the church, was nearly bare except for a barrel of ginger beer on the counter, its tap carefully turned inwards towards the back shop to prevent daring little boys from helping themselves. Hill's, the grocer, sold the best bacon, fruit and biscuits in James's Street but was expensive. We did not deal there, but I was drawn like a magnet to its big rectangle of pressed dates, trampled down by dirty foreign feet, my sister said, and I would have sold my soul for a pennyworth. Mr Hill would dig me out a wedge with his knife, the size depending on his mood of the moment, and wrap it up in a piece of old newspaper.

Hassell's, next door to the chemist, was our grocer. His shelves, counter and back premises were coming down with sacks of flour and sugar, chests of tea lined with gleaming silver foil, big pyramids of cool butter newly decanted from strong wooden butter boxes, and huge sides of bacon. Madeleine, his assistant, and I were great friends in spite of the difference in our ages; she supplied me with a running commentary on the state of her many romances and as she was dark-haired and pretty I believed her. 'He won't leave me alone. He hangs round the shop every evening near closing time. He's daft about me, so he is!' 'Is he nice, Madeleine?' I asked, for something to say. 'Nice? I wouldn't use that word at all. It's passionate he is, burning with love for me and dying to take me into his arms the minute he gets a chance. But I don't mind telling you, I prefer Aloysius Fogarty. He's more of a man somehow and so well spoken. If only I didn't have a dark suspicion that he is married already, the brute!'

Mr Hassell often let me help in the shop on a Saturday afternoon. These were the days before packaging and Sellotape when everything had to be weighed up and put into bags ready for the customer. This was 'to play shop' in earnest. I loved to plunge the big scoop into the sack of sugar and bring up piles of cascading grains, to fill them into a stout bag made ready on the weighing scales, to preside like an adult at the scales, and to turn down the corners of the bag expertly and seal them off. Above all, I loved to weigh up the butter. I cut a likely piece from the big creamy pyramid on the cool marble slab, I fashioned it into shape with a pair of wooden clappers, added to it here, took away there, slapped it, rounded it and turned it under my hands into a symmetrical little creation which I then placed on a piece of wet greaseproof paper, folded this up at the ends and handed it to the customer. When the shop was very busy, Mr Hassell let me work the till. I loved to press down the buttons nonchalantly as if I were an expert; I watched the numbers come up on the little window at the top, then the drawer open with the ping of a bell, to reveal the little troughs inside, crammed with notes and coins. When, at the end of the afternoon, Mr Hassell sent me home with a two-shilling bit and a bag of broken biscuits, I considered myself well paid.

Guinness's brewery dominated both sides of James's Street. A line of offices solidly took up one side while the great vats, hidden from view by a high wall, took up the other. The heavy, rich odour of hops and malt hung over the street. It was *our* smell. The catholic chapel, home to our catholic neighbours seven days a week, stood grey and bleak behind a small paved area enclosed by railings. Our church, with its spire, its diamond-paned windows and surrounding green churchyard and tombstones betraying its rural origins, was more beautiful. The Fountain, a small raised area in the middle of the street, divided the lower part of James's Street from the upper. A few trees, a plinth or monument, public toilets and a drinking trough for horses made it into a little island of its own. It was the rallying point for the neighbourhood. There old people met to chat; there little boys gathered to catch pigeons and tie pieces of string to their feet so that they could not fly; there we got on and off the tram; there in great excitement we lined up to be handed into army lorries by young soldiers during the tram strike; there we watched the crowds gather to listen to election rallies, and there we once saw the great de Valera himself! My father warned Hughie not to go near 'that arch-traitor', but Hughie defied him, went, was caught and was dragged ignominiously back and beaten hard with a walking stick. And there, too, I once saw poor women in shawls, prostrate on their knees, praying for God to rescue them from the End of the World and the Final Judgement which they believed were at hand.

To the right of the Fountain, off the main thoroughfare, a small hill descended on one side to Kingsbridge station and the Liffey and on the other to Bow Lane, Cromwell's Quarters and the old road to Kilmainham. At the apex of this hill stood the handsome, wrought-iron gates of St Patrick's Hospital between the high granite walls which enclose the piece of land Swift's executors leased from the adjoining Steevens's Hospital. Behind these walls, secret and confined as a convent on a Dublin street, lay Swift's hospital for the insane.

When, in 1926, at two months of age, I came to live in the Lodge, St Patrick's was an expensive private hospital with a first-class reputation. Patients came to be treated from all over Ireland. The alternative for the mad poor of Dublin was Grangegorman, a large institution to the north of the city. Unlike St Patrick's, it was well known and 'You must be just out of Grangegorman' was a common Dublin jibe. The Lodge stood just inside the gates at the top of the avenue that led down to the hospital, its lovely eighteenth-century façade slightly austere in the Irish fashion, discreetly hidden from view by a line of trees. The administrative offices occupied the ground floor with the private apartments of the chief medical superintendent above. Behind stretched the long shank of the hospital proper into beautifully kept, enclosed gardens. A wall with a deep drop on the hospital side separated the avenue and the Lodge from the hospital and the patients. The Lodge, a handsome little granite house in the same symmetrical style as the hospital, was adorned with a classical portico and a window on each side, a pleasing harmony to the eye which was carried over into two formal flower beds in front trimmed with box hedges (my father planted them with wallflowers in winter and snapdragons in summer). Alone among the crushed and overpopulated little streets round about, the Lodge enjoyed its own green space with a garden to one side and a big chestnut tree to the other. Into this tree I disappeared at regular intervals to live a life of adventure as rich as any of Alice's in Wonderland.

After I left the Lodge, nearly fifty years were to pass before I saw it again. Some time ago I made up my mind to revisit it. I was surprised to find myself distinctly nervous as I made my way up James's Street towards the Fountain. I hesitated before turning to look over at the Lodge: I was not prepared for the shock. The handsome gates were gone, replaced by a cheap metal-tubing construction more fit for a gate in a field than for a lovely eighteenth-century complex. To my astonishment it stood open and unattended (our gates were locked and bolted at all times). Gone, too, was the big brass plaque which my father polished first thing every morning. I knew it by heart: 'St Patrick's Hospital, founded by Jonathan Swift, D.D 1667–1745'. The dark green front door of the Lodge had been painted bright blue and, most extraordinary of all, the house had shrunk to half its former size. The back part had disappeared (from subsidence, I was told) taking with it my father's bedroom, our kitchen and our scullery. Gone, too, were the flower beds, the side garden and the crab-apple tree, all the lovely colour replaced by a grey dreariness of asphalt. I peered through the curtainless window into our parlour; it was now a featureless, bare room with a few tools and a gas jet on a dirty table. The deep window ledge was still there, the ledge onto which, come the first spring sunshine, I squeezed myself with a book and was in heaven. There, too, was the porch-step on whose cold, granite stone I was said to have caught the pneumonia that nearly killed me. I walked down what once was our garden path, past the bedroom window through which I had often passed out my sister's good clothes for some rendezvous kept secret from my father. The backyard, daily scene of our pains and pleasure, was nothing now but an ill-kempt and foreshortened space. I could hardly take in this mutilation of my childhood home. I enquired of a passer-by where I might find the main entrance. 'In Steevens's Lane,' was the reply. I walked slowly down the lane, its rough wall familiar still to my touch. At the bottom, the once inviolate wall had been breached and a large opening with a security hut allowed people to pass in and out unchallenged.

My father's business had been to monitor strictly the movements of all persons who entered and left the hospital and to render a daily account of their movements to the hospital authorities. He was conscientious in this, as he was in everything he did. When the bell rang in the Lodge, he rose, took the keys from the hook inside the parlour door, went out and enquired the business of the caller. If legitimate, he opened the small gate for pedestrians and the big double gates for cars and horse-drawn vehicles. He then wrote on a slate with a piece of chalk 'lady to see patient; entered 11.30 a.m., left 12.30 p.m.' and so on. In the afternoon, he transferred these entries into an official ledger in his best copperplate handwriting, ruled them off with a line of red ink, and took it at four o'clock precisely to the hospital office for inspection, at the same time collecting the day's letters for posting. On rare occasions I had to take this ledger to the hospital myself. I hated having to ring the bell and stand awkwardly waiting for the door to be opened. I was in awe of the officials, thinking doctors and secretaries very important people. I had often seen Mr Coe, the principal secretary of the hospital, slip in and out of the side gate like a shadow. He was so important that he had his own key and he never spoke to me.

I was particularly in awe of Dr Leeper, the chief superintendent, for he was the most important person in the whole hospital. He came and went in a black saloon car driven by a liveried chauffeur, my cousin Bob Newman. I never dared wave at Bob when Dr Leeper was in the car. It was rumoured that he suffered from gout and was often confined to his rooms, and gout, we were knowingly assured, was brought on by too much rich eating and drinking. This condition, belonging as it seemingly did to the wealthy classes, made us even more awestruck. We never knew the real reason for gout, nor that he was an excellent doctor who did much to improve the condition of the mentally sick.

The sound of the bell punctuated our every day. We all hated having to 'mind the Gate'. No matter what the weather, no matter what you were doing, when the bell rang you had to jump up at once and obey its summons. Bolting and unbolting the double gates was hard work. Frank and Hughie, being two strong boys, bore the lion's share of the work when my father was out. 'Whose turn is it?' was the signal for the endless disputes between them. Sometimes I had to take my turn; I knew it was not a young girl's job, that people would pity me when, in the full glare of the headlights, they saw me draw back the heavy bolts and pull open the Gate. I dreaded, when at a good girls' school in Dublin, having to open the Gate for my music teacher, Mrs Ferguson. She came every Saturday in her little baby Austin to play the piano for the patients during the showing of the silent film. Olive, Frank and Hughie were allowed to join the patients for this treat; I was too young to be included. They came back with such strange tales that I was glad to have missed it. Some patients came in clutching parcels under their arms, some jumped up and down and walked about during the film, some shouted out strange phrases such as 'Yes, we have no bananas!', while others, like small children, wet themselves at exciting moments.

I got my drama in another way. The back wall of our yard formed the top of the wall of the handball alley in the grounds beneath. By climbing a ladder, I could lean my arms among the broken glass on the top of the wall and see into the grounds below. From there, I could study the long, many-windowed wall of the long wards that stretched down into the gardens and hope to see something exciting on this, the men's side of the hospital. Once I saw a naked figure at a window and once I saw a mattress being pushed little by little through the aperture of a window by invisible hands. Would a body follow next? My imagination had been over-excited by too many tales of mad people in sensational books. I looked at the figures moving about in the grounds below me; some walked briskly about the paths, others huddled up, silent and morose against the cold, even in summer, while male attendants kept a casual eye on them. Most extraordinary of all were those with religious madness; they walked a short distance, fell on their knees, fervently crossed themselves and muttered prayers, then they got up and repeated the same ritual over and over again. I could not understand how religion could make anyone mad . . .

One patient came regularly to the handball alley to talk to me. He was called Mr McCoy, was about thirty years of age and had tight brown curly hair and excessively thick spectacles. When I called out 'Mr McCoy!', he turned his half-blind eyes upwards, moving his head from side to side to locate the source of the sound. His voice was gentle and cultured. I had heard that he had gone mad with too much learning of Greek and Latin at Trinity College, and could easily believe it to look at him. I could certainly understand that learning might drive a person mad. I was flattered that such a determined scholar should talk to me, a mere child, and looked forward to our conversations. Although barely able to make out my face above him, he paid me the most extravagant compliments on my appearance. 'Your head is like a beautiful rose on a slender stalk', and 'Your voice is like the voice of the Sirens.' I did not hear that kind of talk around James's Street! 'I am an impresario,' he told me. 'What is that?' I asked. 'I own opera houses all over Europe and the States and I am always on the lookout for artistic talent to sing in them. I was the one who discovered the greatest voices of our time and gave them their debut in La Scala and the Metropolitan in New York. I will do it all and more for you!' I was deeply impressed and even agitated when he asked me to sing an aria for him. I promised I would do so soon. Martha's sister, Sarah, would help me. She was always practising operatic songs, her voice mounting to the top notes with impressive ease. We were sure she was going to be a star. So was she.

She undertook to teach me 'I dreamed that I dwelt in marble halls', and although I could never sing as she sang, I managed to master it to her satisfaction. I got up on the ladder and waited for Mr McCoy. Totally uninhibited because of the distance between us and because I believed he was mad, I burst into song. He threw back his head and blinked up at me like a night owl. 'Wonderful! Wonderful! What a voice! Of course it needs to be trained. I will hire a professional to teach you. Then your name will blaze in lights above my opera houses all over Europe and America!' Although I knew he was suffering from delusions, one part of me believed him and hoped that, when he 'came out', these wonderful fairy tales would come true. I do not know what happened to Mr McCoy but I do know that even in madness he was a perfect gentleman.

As I passed through the entrance into the once forbidden grounds, I was surprised to find my heart beating violently. The habits of seventeen years were too much for me. I expected a hand to descend on my shoulder and a voice to say 'What do you think you are doing here?' I walked nervously on. I could not, at first, make out the long line of the original building because it was hidden by the many new structures which had been put up since my time. Signposts gave directions to all the secret places of the past. I put my hand on the handle of a door and to my amazement it yielded. All the doors in our time were strictly controlled by lock and key. In a state of heightened emotion, I passed along a corridor, came to another door, unmanned and unlocked, went through and with mounting fear and excitement suddenly came out into an open space. I saw a desk with a nurse behind it, and all round about it, open side-wards with patients in bed talking to their visitors as in any normal hospital. I was completely taken aback by this sight: where were the mental patients I had seen in my childhood?

I spoke to a nurse. 'I used to live in the Lodge of this hospital. It is fifty years ago now. My father was the lodge-keeper. I lived here till I was seventeen but it all looks changed . . .' 'Would you like to see the main apartments?' he offered. 'The main apartments?' I gasped inwardly. These were the apartments of the great Dr Leeper, strictly private, unvisitable, impenetrable to the inhabitants of the Lodge. 'Could I really see them?' I asked. I followed him along a gleaming waxed stairway, recognising in a flash the beautiful stained-glass window (which I had often glimpsed from the hall when on visits to the dentist), and quickly on to the holy of holies, the old secret powerhouse of the whole complex. A row of exquisitely polished doors lay before the eyes of the lodge-keeper's daughter, Dr Leeper's drawing room, his bedroom, his study. But as I gazed, I saw appended to each solemn door the names of medical consultants, of waiting rooms... The mystique had gone. I felt unbearably deceived.

The nurse left me to return to his duties. I walked on, times past and time present suspended in a strange confusion of mind, down stairs, along corridors, through doors, and then I saw it – the old madhouse I knew of padded cells and straitjackets and locked doors: there before me was the original gaunt iron staircase set in the grim vault of a stairway and caged in from top to bottom by iron rods in case a patient might throw himself over. I shivered at the sight. I walked on as if in a dream until I found myself in the long, symmetrical, vaulted corridor of the basement apartments where I had occasionally come with my father to see the matron, Miss Einthoven. The rooms off this sculpted corridor which once held great piles of vegetables, churns of milk brought in from the hospital farm at Lucan, and hindquarters of beef and pork, were now cold and impersonal offices. Agitated now by the flood of memories that assailed me, I found my way slowly back to where I had come in, walked through the open gate and back up Steevens's Lane, numbed by what I had seen.

EARLY YEARS

I was nine days off my fifth birthday when my mother died. I wonder how they celebrated my birthday that year. I have a sharp, retentive memory but, try as I may, I cannot put a face to the shadowy figure who was my mother. I continually search my memory, desperate to draw out of its depths an image, a smile, a gesture. I feel two hands gently pull a knitted green and white jacket over my shoulders . . . I see a hand, with a wooden spoon, turning strawberry jam round and round in a big preserving pan; it carefully lifts off the scum and places it in a saucer. No face, no body is visible . . . I am in bed, sick; a figure comes through the door, opens a large handbag and holds out an apple and an orange towards me . . . I see a tan, knitted cardigan hanging behind the door. I know it is my mother's . . . I am in the kitchen; I see a woman's figure leaning against the table; my father is standing beside her. I hear an angry voice. I think the woman is crying . . . I am outside the house playing in the garden; my Aunt Jenny opens the kitchen window, leans out and says, 'I will give you a penny if you keep very quiet' (my mother is dying) . . . We are all sitting around the kitchen table having our tea; suddenly my father gets up, gathers me up in his arms and carries me into the adjoining bedroom. He shuts the door on the bright kitchen scene and I am alone with him in the half-dark. The blinds are down and there is a frightening stillness in the room. My father leans over the bed with me in his arms. I look down; there is a veil over a face. My father draws it back and I see, not my mother's face, but the cold, stiff, yellow face of a strange woman, eyes closed, nose horribly pinched. I scream hysterically.

My father replaces the veil over the face and carries me out of the room, still screaming, and back into the kitchen.

The house is full of people; they are talking in whispers and although it is morning, the blinds have been pulled down. People are constantly coming in and out of the parlour door. There is a big black crêpe bow pinned to it and a white card edged with black. My father is wearing a black band on the arm of his coat. Through the open porch door I can see a strange black carriage, long and narrow with glass sides. Two black horses are attached to it, the huge black plumes on their heads sweeping up and down with the motion as they paw the ground. Men in tall black hats hold the horses' heads; my father, with some other men, appears from the bedroom carrying a long wooden box with brass handles on the sides. They go through the door and hoist the box awkwardly onto their shoulders. Horses, carriage, men, the box go through the Gate and turn down Steevens's Lane. I scream and sob, terrified. Two hands lift me up and carry me into the kitchen. My mother had started her last journey, back to her home in Bantry.

After her death, no one spoke of her again. The word 'mammy' was never again heard in our house. No relations came to speak of her. No photograph was ever displayed on wall or table to keep her face before us. It was as if she had never existed. My father lived until he was eighty-five years old. I nursed him in his final illness, and in his last few weeks he brought himself, against all his inclinations, to speak briefly of his own mother. He never mentioned his wife's name. I wanted desperately to take this last chance of asking him about her in those weeks of comparative intimacy between us, but I could not bring myself to broach the long-forbidden subject. The constraint built up over all the years was too absolute. I had to let her die a second time in my memory. Why did my father keep silent? Did he believe that tears and sentiment weakened the spirit and shook the resolve? Certainly, he was not a man for looking backwards; it was rather the future that was always ahead to be won. Or was there, deep in him, some complex psychological tangle? I can never know. Unwittingly, he had dammed up my natural feelings and by impoverishing my early memories had weakened me for the very future he was preparing me for.

What Virginia Woolf calls 'the deepest layers of our mental soil' are laid down in early childhood and it is the mother who lays them down, there to nourish the emotional roots of our being for the life that lies before us. Memory, in my case, was all but obliterated. Memory which, conscious or unconscious, is always acting upon us, making us what we are, acting both backwards and forwards, creating our sense of identity beneath the stream of time. Our identity is our inner self and our sole reality; it is that bundle of sensations, impressions and thoughts which goes through the days, months and years but which exists outside and beyond chronological time. The poet Auden writes, 'All our intimations mock/The formal logic of the clock.' Time and emotion are not fixed like the seasons; as we turn over 'memories' and meditate upon them, they surge unexpectedly and unreasonably up out of the past upon our present, and they change under our scrutiny. They may become more vivid, warmer or more painful than at the first experience; they follow the secret and irrational seasons of the soul. Memories are not necessarily weaker than first impressions. They grow and change us. They should not be spoken of too exclusively in the past tense.

I think continuously about my mother as I grow older. I look at her photograph, I search for familiar lineaments in eye and mouth. Not many years ago, I became infected with a virus and developed ME. I became so weak and disordered in my body and for so long a time that I thought I might die. This imagined proximity of death made me think more intensely of my mother. I began to search in every corner of my conscious memory for a trace of her whom I might soon meet. I could find nothing. I brought myself to ask my brother Hugh about her, knowing that he suffered under the same constraint as myself. 'Can you remember our mother?' ('Mammy' would have been too shocking.) Surprised by this unexpected question, he stumbled and was silent. 'You were eleven when she died; you must remember something.' Slowly, he began to tell me the little he could remember. 'I used to wake in the night and hear her groaning with pain in the next room. I heard her say, "I would not mind dying were it not for the children", and I prayed and cried and cried and prayed until I fell asleep. When she died, I knew God had let me down.' This brought too shockingly near an image of a suffering dying woman, the thought of whose pain was more than I could bear. And in all that pain, she was worrying about her children, worrying about their motherless future in the hands of a difficult and untender father.

Out of the depths of my subconscious memory came a new 'memory'. I saw a bedroom and on a bed a white-faced woman with eyes closed, moaning and restless, while a hired girl alternately fanned her wasted face and placed cold cloths on her forehead. That image haunted me. I had been searching for another, happier image of an active, smiling woman holding me in her arms and swinging me about. I turned to my sister for help. 'You were thirteen when our mother died. What was she like before she was sick?' She was even more embarrassed than Hugh. She shrugged me off with 'I can't remember.' I persisted. 'But you must remember! You were thirteen!' Finally, she admitted, 'I don't want to remember. I have shut out all that part of my life from my mind.' Were there painful memories I knew nothing about? I was sure of it. Better not to bring the subject up again. I had to let my mother die for the third time.

Many years later, I met, for the first time in forty years, the daughter of our schoolmaster, Mr Kelly. Casually, in conversation, she introduced the name of my mother. She could remember me very well as a baby, she said. She loved to go to the Lodge on a Saturday evening to help Mrs Gaw (who was she?) bathe the new baby in the big zinc bath in front of the kitchen range. I was deeply shocked. It seemed as if someone else had lived my life for me, had done me out of what rightly belonged to me. She had known and remembered what I could not remember and she was almost a stranger! It seemed almost indecent... I still search for her, search to re-create a mother for myself and I have not given up the search. I feel her shadowy presence in one place only, in the prayers, readings and invocations of the liturgies of the Church of Ireland which my aunt told me she loved and in which she, like me, was formed. She listened, heard and repeated the same beautiful poetry of the Book of Common Prayer as I repeat. There I have found a fragile unity. 'My soul doth magnify the Lord and my spirit hath rejoiced in God my saviour.'

After my mother's death, my father took the whole care of his children into his own hands. He took the task very seriously indeed.

He was now financially less well off than he had been, for his wife's salary had been cut off from the family revenues. He had his naval pension, and £7 10s. 0d. a week as wages from the hospital, together with a free house, free coal and electricity, eight pints of free milk a day from the hospital farm at Lucan and free medical and dental attention. He could not afford to give up the job which he felt to be beneath him. He was now obliged to pay a servant to cook and clean for us, and into our lives came that line of 'maids' with whom we were to live in close proximity for many years. My father personally supervised all that went on from the choice of our underwear to the care of our education. A strict discipline was enforced such as we might have undergone on a ship. We were in the complete charge of the captain and strict obedience to his rules was always expected and rigorously exacted. Mealtimes were fixed and no excuse whatever was taken for unpunctuality. Our hands were inspected before every meal and knees and feet before bedtime. Tables had to be scoured with Vim every day, floors scrubbed and drains disinfected. No food could be refused and every mouthful was, in theory, to be chewed thirty-two times. A narrow ledge beneath our big dining table served as a secret repository for all unwanted food, and prunes, figs, pieces of roast bullock's heart and herring bones rotted away nicely on every inch of that shelf. All our food was 'wholesome', all bread wholemeal, all jam blackcurrant because it had more vitamin C than any other. At a time when our neighbours could afford only tea, bread and margarine, we had milk, meat and vegetables every day.

I was happy with my father at first. For several years after my mother's death I clung very close to him; he was my protector, my haven, my sole anchor in a frightening world. He called me 'little dear my soul' and stroked my hair and held me on his knee. Alone together when the other children were at school, I sat on the granite step of the porch and watched him lovingly as he opened and shut the Gate to those who came and went from the hospital. I stood hand in hand with him on the pavement outside the Gate and from this commanding position we could see all that was going on in the streets around us. When I ran to him to be picked up and caressed, I saw the pleasure in his eyes and when I leaned my cheek against the rough serge of his hospital uniform, I felt warm, safe and loved. My great delight was to travel on the crossbar of his bicycle on his frequent excursions into the nearby vast acres of the Phoenix Park. When I was nine years old, he bought me a little second-hand bicycle of my own and I rode along beside him, holding on to the pocket of his jacket when I needed help to get up a hill.

He called me to him to observe this or that. He would call me out to the porch to look at a sunset or a thunderstorm. When the thunder crashed above our heads I would say, 'Do you hear, Daddy, all those hundreds of Guinness's barrels falling down on top of us!', and he would tell me not to be afraid. 'This great display has natural causes which we understand. Long ago, ignorant, superstitious people thought the Gods were angry with them and would punish them. Now we know better.' (This was in line with his lifelong debunking of mystery, religion, superstition and the occult.) All the same, when I was alone in my bed at night and heard the same roaring in the heavens, I forgot his sage counsels and leaped, terrified, out of bed to cover the mirror with a cloth as did women in Bow Lane, for 'the mirror, once cracked by lightning, you'll have nothing but bad luck for the next seven years!' I pulled the covers over my head and lay prone, terrified both of the roaring of the elements outside in the sky and the thumping of my heart inside my body.

At mealtimes my father kept me next to him, sheltering his delicate child and seeing that I ate 'healthy food to keep you strong'. Each evening he called me to his knee to say my prayers:

> Jesus, tender shepherd, hear me,
> Bless thy little lamb tonight.
> Through the darkness be Thou near me,
> Keep me safe till morning light.

But it was not God who was my tender shepherd, it was my father. I finished my prayers with 'God bless my mother and give her peace and rest for ever more. Amen.' After a short while that prayer ceased to be said and with it ceased all mention of my mother.

My health was fragile and I needed to be carefully watched. For all this inadequacy, my father blamed my mother's family. 'Hadn't three sisters died young?' His own family had all been strong and he had not known of the bad health of the Newmans until long after he was married. He blamed all his children's weaknesses on the Newman family of west Cork, for 'living in that rain-soaked place would undermine anyone's health!' Only his unflagging care of my health had pulled me through, and extreme vigilance was still needed. At the first cough my father's eyes lit upon me. I did everything I could to hide the betraying signs, nearly suffocating myself under the bedclothes to conceal the noise. My father's hand was immediately upon my forehead testing for a temperature. Some hours later, the bedroom door opened and in came the dreaded figure of Dr Thompson, summoned from the hospital below. At the first sight of his dark suit and his leather doctor's bag, I started to cry. Out came the stethoscope from his bag and its cold nose began to travel all over my chest. 'Take a deep breath now. Hold it! Turn over now.' And the instrument travelled over my back. 'Say ninety-nine!' and he gazed into my open mouth. A tablespoon was sent for and its bowl forced down my tongue so that I retched and nearly vomited. Out came the thermometer from its steel case; he shook it down slowly and deliberately and placed it under my tongue. I thought he would never take it out, that he had forgotten it, that I would presently choke on it; he had his hand on my wrist, feeling my pulse. As I watched his inscrutable face, I grew more and more frightened. Would he say it? Would he? Would he say 'soldier'? Then came the fatal words, 'Be a good soldier, now', and I knew that the sentence had been given. I was to go to hospital. I burst into frantic sobs and cried convulsively until the taxi arrived to take me to the hospital, wrapped up in a blanket and sitting on my father's knee.

Still crying uncontrollably, I was carried through the gate of Dr Steevens's Hospital and along the dark corridors smelling of soap, antiseptic and polish. A starched nurse came forward and took the sobbing bundle from my father's arms. As she carried me down the ward to a vacant bed, I cried out hysterically, 'Wait, Daddy, Wait! Wait until the screens are taken away!' He promised. The nurse settled me, the screens were pulled back and my father – was gone. My crying rose to a frantic crescendo. It was the terrible anguish of a child who has been betrayed. No other heartbreak is like it. My father would not have understood this. 'You have to be cruel to be kind' would have been his attitude. 'She is in the best hands. No use my hanging about. She will soon settle down.' Strange irony that he, so devoted to our physical health, should have been so ignorant of our emotional health. I knew that my grandmother from Bantry would have broken all the rules so prized by my father but would never have broken this rule of the heart. And I would have loved her and trusted her as I could not love or trust my father.

The betrayal of a child by an adult is hardly ever recognised as such by the adult. My father, when he came to see me after my outburst of misery in the hospital ward, thought I had got over my emotion because I did not speak of it. A child's silence is often misinterpreted by adults who are keen to conclude that all is well with the child when it does not say anything. The mistake is to believe that the child is compliant because it does not complain and that it does not complain because it does not care or has forgotten. A child is always busy absorbing new impressions and new situations; it can be intensely aware of them without understanding them or being able to talk about them. It is constantly taking in at a deep level the relations of adults to each other and to itself. In this confusing flux of impressions, the child's one secure point is its close family, through which it learns to interpret the world. What is it to take as true? What it hears? What it observes? We may be sure that it is not so much what it hears as what it overhears that influences it. Anyone watching a child as it stands in the midst of adults who have suddenly let down their guard will know this. A child's feelings are often more honest than an adult's (if not better) because the adult has, over the years, been exposed to ideas about experience, what it should think or feel, what is expected of it, from parents, teachers, books, television, which interfere with the raw experience itself. Adults put too much trust in words, with which they frequently deceive themselves and others. My father justified his conduct to himself by what he believed was common sense and reason, but did he, in fact, want to avoid an emotional scene which he could not handle? The hurt inside the six-year-old was the one certainty. Why has it stood out in my memory all these years? Because it went so deep.

Who is to record the experience of a child who is, by nature, inarticulate? Literature is the great living record of what it feels like to be a human being in all its immense variety, in all times and in all places. The child's experience often goes unrecorded, but now and again has achieved brilliant expression. Henry James, the American writer, wrote a novel which sees the world from the child's point of view. *What Maisie Knew* is full of suspense, full of profound insights into an intelligent child's mind, full of tenderness and understanding, and all given to us by the ironical juxtaposition of the child's knowledge with that of the adults. When I read it in my thirties, I knew at once that it was true. Henry James was appalled in the London high society of the 1900s, which he knew intimately, by the betrayal of the child's trust by divorced parents and by the consequent suffering of the child. 'The accidental mention had been made to me of the manner in which the situation of some luckless child of a divorced couple was affected . . . by the remarriage of one of its parents,' he wrote. In *What Maisie Knew* he undertook to trace the 'noiseless mental footsteps' of a child as she is dragged through the battles her parents wage against one another and against their new partners. In the furious rows between the sexes, Maisie is the innocent onlooker and the unwitting weapon which they use to wound and damage each other. She is betrayed again and again by people whose duty it is to love and protect her. We listen to the self-justifications and self-deceptions of their words and register them as Maisie does, but with our adult knowledge we can see, as she cannot, the terrible ironies of her situation.

James is not so much interested in external events, the separations, divorces, rows and so on, as in the inner drama of the child's consciousness as it is affected by them and this he skilfully keeps before our eyes. She is 'a mite of a half-scared infant in a great dim theatre' – his image captures the position of many children in broken families. In the egotistical pursuit of their own passions, the adults pay no attention to the hidden feelings of the sensitive and intelligent Maisie and some of them actually take her horribly into their confidence in an effort to enlist her support against the others. Hers is 'an innocence saturated with knowledge', knowledge which she tries to piece together in a childish effort to love these tarnished individuals. The dramatic power of the novel comes from the juxtaposition of Maisie's innocence with the sexual passion which drives on the adults. Maisie's overpowering need, like all children's, is to think well of her parents. Her parents are not such as to invite admiration and Maisie hears them reviled and hated but the instinct is still strong. But in a series of situations devised by James, she is made to see that her mother does not like her. ' "Mamma doesn't care for me," she said very simply. "Not really." ' James adds, 'Child as she was, her little long history was in the words.' Her shallow, sporting father finds her a nuisance as he pursues women; he, also, tries to justify to himself his treatment of the child. Maisie longs to love her two governesses who swear eternal love and devotion to her, but she learns that they are ready to ditch her when her presence interferes with their own desires. To know oneself unloved is a terrible discovery for a child (as a child I never had to know that; it was the manner of loving that confused and hurt me).

However, amidst all this horror someone comes along who loves Maisie for herself. It is her mother's new husband, Sir Claude. He gives her his time, he enjoys her company (and children always know this by sure instinct), he is charming to the little girl and treats her as his equal.

> They rode on the top of buses; they visited outlying parks; they went to cricket matches where Maisie fell asleep; they tried a hundred places for the best one to have tea... They dropped, under incontrollable impulses, into shops that they agreed were too big, to look at things that they agreed were too small...

Maisie's heart is filled with love and tenderness for him. He knows her dreadful position and he hates it for her.

> 'But I give you my word... that I'll never, never forsake you. Do you hear that, old fellow, and do you take it in? I'll stick to you through everything.'
> Maisie did take it in — took it with a long tremor of all her little being; and then as, to emphasise it, he drew her closer she buried her face on his shoulder and cried without sound and without pain. While she was so engaged, she became aware that his own breast was agitated, and gathered from it with rapture that his tears were as silently flowing.

In those sentences James expressed all the pent-up emotion of the little girl. Unfortunately, Sir Claude's charm is not felt by Maisie alone; all the women feel it and react to it but in a different way to Maisie; even the 'kind of greasy greyness' that is Mrs Wix, her governess, falls passionately in love with him physically. Mrs Beale, her former governess and her father's handsome new wife, adores him.

'I'm awfully afraid of Mrs Beale,' Maisie objected.

He raised his smooth brows. 'That charming woman?'

'Well,' she answered, 'you can't understand it because you're not in the same state.'

She had been going on with a luminous 'But' when, across the table, he laid his hand on her arm.

'I *can* understand it,' he confessed. 'I *am* in the same state.'

'Oh but she likes you so!' Maisie promptly pleaded.

Sir Claude literally coloured.

'That has something to do with it.'

Maisie wondered again.

'Being liked with being afraid?'

'Yes, when it amounts to adoration.'

'Then why aren't you afraid of *me*?'

'Because with you it amounts to that!' He had kept his hand on her arm.

'Well, what prevents it is simply that you're the gentlest spirit on earth. Besides – ' he pursued; but he came to a pause.

'Besides – ?'

'I *should* be in fear if you were older – there! See – you already make me talk nonsense.'

Maisie has to learn an awful truth, that this wonderful man has a flaw, a 'weakness' for the presence of beautiful women in his life and especially for the presence of Mrs Beale. Although Maisie becomes perfectly aware of this weakness, she does not know what lies behind it and she tries, in her child's way, to disentangle him from it. She sees that for him to be what she knows and loves, good and true and loyal, he must be 'free' from having to twist and turn and dodge in his connection with Mrs Beale. And although Sir Claude knows that no one in his life has been able to bring out his finer feelings as Maisie has done, he is, at the end of a series of dramatic situations, unable to give up his 'weakness'. His passion for women is stronger than his love for Maisie. Maisie brings him to see that he could not stand up to the demands of truth and loyalty which she would make on him, were he to stay with her. It is often so: a weaker person feels continually reproached in the constant presence of a stronger one. Reluctantly, so very reluctantly and tenderly, he gives her up. Maisie has been betrayed by everyone. She is left alone at the end of the story, more loyal and brave and loving than all those around her, but abandoned, alone, bereft.

What does Maisie know? In spite of all the elements that are there to corrupt her, Maisie does not know of the sexual passion which impels these people. But what she does know is even more important. Hers is the instinctive knowledge, unique in the book, of the feelings of love, reverence, loyalty and wonder although she could not give any of them a name. James is not a determinist: he does not believe in conditioning. Maisie's is the triumph of the human spirit (at least in a child) over all that tends to corrupt it, and to have that affirmed by as great an artist as Henry James fortifies us. I, who remember my childhood well, recognise my experiences in this book – Maisie's terror when she hears the tone of hatred between adults (why do I remember the raised and angry voices of my father and mother when I can remember little else?); her self-protective instinct to 'play stupid', to avoid answering awkward questions ('she had never been safe had she not been stupid'); her horror at finding out in a lie someone she loves; her appalled fright when she hears a hitherto unknown and horrible passion in the voice of an adult ('But he was too angry to heed her – too angry with his wife; as she [Maisie] turned away she heard his anger break out. "You damned old b——!" – she couldn't quite hear all. It was enough, it was too much: she fled before it, rushing even to a stranger for the shock of such a change of tone').

I remember vividly the long weeks in hospital. The nurses came and rubbed my chest with warm oil and wrapped me in a strange cotton wool jacket. I did not know that I had pneumonia and that they were waiting for the 'crisis' when the body would either defeat the infection or be defeated by it. Then began the long, slow recovery from the ravages of that struggle. I was kept in bed for weeks, wearied and restless with the endlessness of inactive days. At six years of age, I was taken to Baggot Street Hospital with the measles and kept there for four weeks, 'two to cure the disease and two in case something might brew up'. I was alone in a room except for a small baby in a cot which never moved or cried. The nurses came to feed and change it and then went away. I listened eagerly for my father's footsteps in the long afternoons, knowing that he was sure to come and that if he were not able to get away from the Gate, he would send Hughie or Frank instead. In he came briskly in his sports coat and flannels carrying the soft hat which he always wore when outside the Lodge. I liked him much better dressed like that than in his hospital uniform. After a few weeks, I was allowed to get up and as soon as my feet touched the floor I fell down in a heap, my muscles having grown flaccid during my long stay in bed. I laughed with the nurses when, like a baby, I learned to walk again, holding on tight to the bed as I tottered around it.

Soon I was to go home. The importance of going home was marked by a ride in a taxi; only on important occasions could families like ours afford a taxi. How strange and unfamiliar the city looked! How strange and unfamiliar the Lodge! Even the furniture looked different. The maid took one look at me and exclaimed, 'Jesus, Mary and Joseph, but ye'v got very thin and white!' I looked at myself in the mirror. It was true. I was long and skinny and white-faced and my hair, which had been very curly, was lank and straight. My heart fell; I was clearly plain and unlovable. It was not the first time that an indiscreet remark dimmed my spirits and made me dislike myself. I had to spend a good part of every day lying down so that I would get strong again. I pleaded from my bed, 'Please leave the door open! Please leave it open!' for I longed for a comforting sound from the outside world. The long, lonely day came to an end when the children came in from school and played with me and my fire was lit. At night, I watched the shadows dancing across my ceiling in living patterns and fell asleep comforted.

I could read long before I went to school. I begged everyone in the family to 'hear me the headlines in the newspaper, hear me the words on the hoarding in the street, Guin – ness – is – good – for – you', and they all burst out laughing. I soon cracked the great code which men and women have devised for talking in print to each other over space and time; I had made the huge intellectual leap which is called 'reading'. I could form pictures in my head from looking at black marks on a page, and would never be quite alone again. From then on, I was always the best reader in the class.

My father approved of books. They were the gateway to knowledge, he said, and without knowledge you could not be 'free', free from ignorance and superstition and narrow, bigoted ideas. He, himself, read every day; he read the plays of Shakespeare over and over again, the Bible as 'a fine collection of great stories', Gibbon's *Decline and Fall of the Roman Empire*, Josephus's *History of the Jews*, Cervantes' *Don Quixote*, a large volume entitled *Symbolism in Relation to Religion*, the poems of Burns, Shelley, Keats, Thomas Hood, Tennyson, some of the writings of Voltaire and Carlyle, and all the novels of Dickens, whom he loved. Most popular of all was the *Dictionary of the English Language*. He savoured the sound of words and turned them over and over on his tongue. His vocabulary was unusually large and he used it in everyday conversation with ease and mastery. From our earliest childhood we were used to hearing English well used. Mealtimes were a torment: we were quizzed on the meaning and spelling of difficult words, especially those whose sound did not resemble the spelling like 'pneumonia', 'psychic' and 'mnemonic'. We hated these inquisitions for they usually ended in resentment and argument. He browsed in the second-hand bookshops on the Dublin quays and would spend sixpence or a shilling on a book of poetry or a biography. All other books he found in the library.

One day when I was seven or eight years of age, he brought home ten volumes of Arthur Mee's *Children's Encyclopedia* and placed it before me. The uniformity of appearance of the covers and gold lettering had the look of required reading so I turned my eyes away from them. One afternoon, however, sick in bed and bored, I opened a volume at random and read 'Why do we not fall off the world?' and 'Why do we have two eyes?' and 'Can a fly hear?' and 'Can an animal think?' My curiosity instantly aroused, I read the answers with rapt attention, answers which were expressed in simple language a child could understand. I went on to read all the Wonder section and followed it by Great Men and Women and the Story of the Boundless Universe and All Its Wondrous Worlds. It was the most pleasurable way of both inviting curiosity and satisfying it. As there is no real education without curiosity, I was, quite unknown to myself, being educated at the same time as

I was enjoying myself. From those marvellous volumes I taught myself the rudiments of piano playing as well as a smattering of French and I spent many hours making objects from the section Things to Make and Do.

If I said I was going to the library, my father made no objection to my going out. I loved the library, which was snug and warm in the cold winters of my youth when houses were not centrally heated and our fire was lit only at six o'clock in the evening. My method for choosing a book was simple. I searched along the shelves until I came to a promising title. I opened the book and scanned the pages rapidly; if there was plenty of conversation and very little narrative I took it. I loved the smell of a new book (most of the books were dog-eared from overuse), the feel of an un-touched page, the smell of glue on a new spine. I took the book home and read the first few pages. If they were intriguing, I read on but I rarely persisted after a dull opening. When the spell of a story was cast, I lost myself in the magic world where everybody lived more vividly than anyone I knew, where rich or poor, learned or ignorant, interesting or boring, were equally alive, where all that was said was momentous and where what happened to the charac-ters mattered to me more than anything else during the time I was reading it. I wanted the good to triumph and for everything to be beautiful and true. If the book created this magic, I could not bear to leave it down and if I were obliged to do so, I lived in the prospect of picking it up again, of returning to those fascinating characters and to finding out what was happening to them. My father forbade us to read in bed. 'Sleep is necessary for health and, besides, reading wastes electricity.' For years I read in bed without his ever finding out. I took my book to bed, hid a handful of raisins under my pil-low, pulled the clothes over my head, turned on my bicycle lamp and read to my heart's content. If I heard a heavy tread outside my door, I turned the lamp off rapidly, kicked it and my book to the end of the bed and lay like a stone 'asleep'. In the morning, I mana-ged another few pages before leaving for school and on the way to school, propped the book open in front of me in my bicycle basket and snatched a few more pages between rapid glances at the traffic. If the narrative was very exciting I got off the bicycle altogether and read a few pages. I could not bear, at the end of the story, to have to part from the characters; they continued to live in my head for days afterwards and there are some who live there still.

From the age of five I longed to go to school like other children who went to the Church of Ireland national school nearby, but I was too delicate and might catch infections, so I had to wait until I was seven. 'When am I going to school?' was my continual cry. When the day came I burst into tears and refused to go through the school door. My brother Frank, leading me by the hand, at first coaxed then threatened me, but when there were no results, he opened the door, gave me a shove, and I was in. He dragged me, still weeping and sobbing, upstairs to the infants' class and as soon as I saw all the strange heads raised to look at me, I cried hysterically. A gentle pair of hands was laid on me, I was lifted up, carried along and put down in front of the biggest doll's house I had ever seen. A beautiful voice said, 'You can play with it all morning if you like', and turning, I saw Miss Barnett, the teacher of the upstairs classes. 'Put your hand into this big glass jar and choose two sweets.' I had joined the class. I loved Miss Barnett; she taught four classes at once in that room and I do not remember her ever being angry. She was very different to the people I knew in James's Street; she wore beautiful clothes, spoke in an educated accent and came from 'somewhere posh'. She kept borzoi dogs, an exotic breed we had never heard of, entered them for dog shows and showed us their pictures when they won.

One day Miss Barnett did not turn up for school and a big boy from the Master's room downstairs was sent up to keep us quiet. Two days later, Miss Barnett reappeared. Her eyes were red with weeping, her niece had died. 'It was very sad, children, she was only fourteen years old; she lay sick in bed for a long time but was always cheerful and patient because she loved the Lord Jesus. On the day she died, she lifted up her arms to heaven and cried, "Take me, Lord Jesus!" ' We were deeply impressed by this 'holy' death. It sounded just like one of the stories from the Bible which Miss Barnett told us so simply and so dramatically. We could never forget how John the Baptist had his head cut off because the wicked Salome asked Herod to do it, nor how the little baby Moses was hidden in a basket in the bulrushes by his slave mother and how he surely would have died had not an Egyptian princess found him and had him brought up as her own son. And we were all on David's side when he went out to fight the giant, Goliath, with only a sling in his hand. We made slings ourselves out of a forked branch and a piece of elastic.

At that time, there were no visual aids for children, no projects, no nature excursions. There was much learning by rote of tables, spelling, poetry and the Bible. Have I ever put so much concentration as I did then into writing 'up to the line and down to the line'? With tongue hanging out, we wrote with our 'Waverley' nibs 'The pen is mightier than the sword' and 'All that glisters is not gold'. I loved it all. I loved the games Miss Barnett invented. For mental arithmetic competitions we all stood up on our benches; if you answered correctly, you remained standing, if you did not you sat down and whoever was left standing at the end received a halfpence from Miss Barnett's glass jar. We stood in a line for spelling competitions; if you answered correctly you moved up one, if you did not, you moved down and whoever was at the top of the line at the end got another halfpenny from the glass jar.

These protestant children were poor and some were very poor indeed. The poorest of all lived in one room or sometimes two in Lamb's Court and Nash's Court, off James's Street. We were afraid to go into these courts because of the rough boys who played there. Some of the children had no shoes to their feet and very thin clothes to their bodies. They were often blue with cold. If they had no buttons on their trousers to hold up their braces, they used rusty nails instead. Their hair was shaved close to avoid both lice and barbers' fees. For a long time I thought that the pink spots on their necks were signs of measles until I learned that they were flea bites. We in the Lodge were always well clothed and were one of the few families who could pay for their books. My father was meticulous in never taking anything for which he could not pay.

At nine years of age, the time came to move downstairs to the Master's room. This was a dreaded transition, for we knew he had a cane and that he used it. The school rhyme ran:

> Mr Kelly is a very good man,
> He goes to church on Sunday,
> And prays to God to give him strength
> To wallop the boys on Monday.

He caned me once, a 'whish' on the hand that scorched my skin; I had been found with children who were smoking outside the toilets although I was not smoking myself. Mr Kelly taught me so well that when, at the age of eleven, I went on to secondary school, I was better at Irish, reading and arithmetic than anyone else in the class. He was a good and just man who wore himself out trying to do well for his pupils. He lived next door to the school in a small, private, tightly curtained, red-brick house. Every day, his lunch was carried into the school on a silver tray and every day, every child craned his or her neck to see what was under the silver plate-cover. We had never seen a dinner served like that. Mrs Kelly, a mild and gentle woman, supplied clothes and shoes out of her own pocket to the poorer pupils. She must have been sorry for the motherless little girl in the Lodge for she made me a beautiful cream crêpe de Chine dress, with a smocked bodice and puff sleeves with pale blue French dots. I loved myself in that dress; it was so unlike the serviceable clothes which my father bought for me.

My father oversaw the buying of all our clothes. He did not trust anyone else to make sure of the quality and durability of our garments. I hated our expeditions to the shops. It was humiliating enough to have a man instead of a woman ask for 'two pairs of warm knickers for this child' but when he contradicted the assistant with 'Don't tell me this is made of wool! Anyone can see it is half-cotton!' I could have died of shame. Every pair of shoes had to be a size too big so that 'you can grow into them' and every dress and coat had to have a large unsightly hem for the same reason. My father once had the idea of buying me a pair of boys' boots 'for they are tougher and will last longer'. They had a boy's tape loop at the back of the heel and I hated those boots with a hatred I have never felt for any other article of clothing. In spite of all my tears and protestations I was forced to wear them to school. Humiliated to the depth of my being, I took a kitchen knife and scored the leather all over. To the repeated question 'Why did you do it?' I hung my head and said nothing. 'Why, why?' is meaningless to a child. I could hardly give a name to my deeply felt mortification. He flew into a rage at 'this useless waste' but I did not care. Nothing could persuade me to wear those boots again.

To keep me from catching cold, I was encased for years in liberty bodices, combinations, woollen vests and, for a time, gaiters with innumerable buttons to be hooked up on the sides. I had a poor impression of myself, nothing fitted or was 'right'. This impression lasted all through my student days. To improve my appearance, I was always at work with my needle and my mother's old sewing machine, adding on, taking off, dyeing, bleaching, turning back to front and whatever else my keen eye could invent. Nothing could equal the joy of buying my first silk stockings after years of wearing thick lisle ones. I must have been about fourteen years of age at the time. I paid six and a half pence for the pair in Frawley's of Thomas Street and I looked down admiringly at my legs and at the perfectly straight seam carefully arranged at the back. My legs looked very grown-up enveloped in that sheer substance but I was strangely embarrassed at myself; these stockings seemed to be inviting people to look at me and I was not quite sure whether I wanted that or not.

The highlights of our school year in James's Street were the Christmas party and the Sunday School excursion. For days before the Christmas party I could think of nothing else. We arrived at the school dressed in our very best, the boys' hair plastered down with water and the girls' burgeoning in curls and ringlets which their mothers had put in the night before. We gathered in the school yard to be led up the stairs to Miss Barnett's room. In the middle of the room was a glorious sight, a tall Christmas tree blazing with real candles and festooned with coloured balls, trails of silver tinsel, balloons and toys. We sat cross-legged in a circle around it, the lights were extinguished, the candles blazed and every eye was raised to that magic tree. Miss Barnett struck the piano and we all sang:

> While shepherds watched their flocks by night
> All seated on the ground,
> The Angel of the Lord came down
> And glory shone around.

We were entranced; if the Angel of the Lord had descended among us at that moment in all his glory, no one would have been surprised. The piano fell silent and so did we, stilled every one by the magic of those solemn moments. Miss Barnett struck up 'Jingle Bells' and the mood changed to shouting, laughter and tears as musical chairs, oranges-and-lemons and here-we-come-gathering-nuts-in-May followed one another in happy succession.

Then came the food, laid out for all of us in the Master's room, sandwiches, sausages, biscuits and lemonade; paper hats were tried on, crackers pulled and, in the excitement, some children cried and had to be comforted. Back again we went upstairs for the magic lantern show with Mickey Mouse or Sinbad the Sailor whose antics sent us all into peals of happy laughter. Finally came the big moment, the arrival of Santa Claus with his sack of presents. I never once guessed that the scarlet figure with the long white beard was the Master himself. Each child had to shake his hand and receive a parcel from him, pink for girls and blue for boys, some of which pleased and some of which did not. Then came the time to go home, tired out with excitement and clutching our present and balloon. The Christmas party was the only glory that many of these poor children knew at Christmastide.

I loved the Sunday School excursion to Killiney strand. As there were no private cars in our neighbourhood, an excursion to the seaside was a very big occasion. We were up bright and early to make sure of an 'outside' seat on the tram which was to take us to Westland Row station. As it lurched down James's Street, swaying from side to side on its tracks, coloured streamers hung from every window and not a voice was silent. At Westland Row we poured out of the tram and up the steps to the train that was to take us to Killiney. Everyone scrambled for a window seat. Piercing blasts on the whistle, snorts of steam from the engine, and we were off. At Killiney station we were formed into lines, the wicker food hampers were lowered to the ground and we set off over the railway bridge and down to the beach below to paddle and bathe. At one o'clock the whistle blew; it was time to line up in front of the hampers and receive our individual lunch-bag and bottle of lemonade. After lunch came the games – tug-of-war, leapfrog, three-legged races, long jumps and obstacle races on the sand, with the shape of Bray Head cut out against the sky beside us. Once something very special happened: each child was presented with an individual box of chocolates with a picture of the Dublin Mansion House on the front. It was from Alfie Byrne, the Lord Mayor of Dublin. This generous offering ensured that Alfie Byrne was the only Lord Mayor we ever remembered in later life. When all was packed up, the hampers closed, the litter collected, weary, happy children piled back into the train that was to take us back along Dublin Bay to Westland Row and we left the mountains, the sea and the strand, like a dream, behind us.

THE MAIDS

When my mother was dying, we had a maid. They could be had for next to nothing. Sacred race of women – unsung slaves of penury! Ten shillings a week 'all found', the worst bedroom in the house, the worst furniture, 'servants of all work', 'good plain cooks', washing, ironing, cleaning, cooking, a half-day off a week if lucky, no holidays, no trade union to protect them from the unscrupulous, thrown out at the whim of an employer, what else could a poor uneducated girl in the Ireland of the 1930s slump expect? Then the war came. Suddenly there were jobs to be had in England, in munitions factories, in the ATS, and on the land. They left Ireland in their thousands to work there, and many of them never came back.

Some of our maids lived in, others came by the day. 'Servants of all work' in our house meant down on their knees every day scrubbing the floors, cooking, baking, washing and very little thanks for it all. Maids who came by the day were the most undependable because sometimes they did not turn up for work. 'Where is that damned woman? Too damned lazy to get out of bed. Well, she needn't expect to be paid for her idleness!' My father knew he would be tied to the Gate until 4 p.m. when we got home from school, for the maid also occasionally had to mind the Gate, and we knew that we would have to do the housework ourselves and contend with his irritated nerves into the bargain. My father never kept us home from school in these emergencies for he valued education too much to forfeit a day of it. On one occasion, when two or three days passed and no maid appeared, Hughie was sent to ferret her out and deliver her an ultimatum. He searched the streets, not being sure where she lived. She was out. No answer to the door. 'Right,' said my father, 'that trollop of a woman is finished. She is a useless good-for-nothing and we are better off without her. Take this advertisement down to the *Evening Mail* office!' In came the answers, big handwriting on cheap ruled paper. 'I am a farmer's daughter, a good plain cook, honest and reliable. In my last place for five years. References enclosed.' He picked out one or two likely candidates and interviewed them in the front parlour. I always kept well out of the way for I knew what direct, embarrassing questions my father would put to them. 'Can you clean thoroughly, not just give a quick rub over the surface? I hope you are strictly honest, for we do not want anything stolen here.' (He regularly inspected suspect maids on their way out, looking in their bags and pockets for stolen goods, which he sometimes found.) 'Have you any hangers-on? I don't want young men lounging about here.'

He seldom followed up references, preferring to rely on his own judgement of which he was inordinately proud. 'I have had men under me. I know the good from the bad.' What about women? He felt well able either to charm or to confront them. He had no intention of handing over the reins of domestic government to any woman, let alone a maid, so exacting were his standards and so absolute his control of household finance. Responsibility without power is not attractive, and they did not like the situation. But Dublin was full of poor women, and as there were too few jobs, even badly paid ones, they had to accept. There were continual arguments and fiery clashes. Some of the women could give as good as they got, and ripostes, peppered with rich Dublin expletives, flew through the heated air. My father never blasphemed in front of us children, which is curious in a naval man, but he could devastate the opposition without invoking the Deity, His Mother or the Saints, preferring to call upon the Devil instead.

Nearly all our maids were poor catholics from the surrounding streets. Annie Byrne looked middle-aged, but she was probably quite young. She lived with her sister and her sister's husband in a tiny house on Arbour Hill. She was small and wiry and had a fierce temper. Every Sunday she prepared the week's washing for six people. All the whites were put to soak overnight in the big zinc bath which had served the night before to wash us all. On Monday morning she arrived early to deal with it. She stoked up the kitchen range with coal (supervised carefully by my father, who was always afraid that the seven tons of free coal allowed him by the hospital would not last the winter). She put all the whites into an enormous black oval cauldron and brought them to the boil. Then, her head swathed in clouds of steam, she plunged and turned and poked and lifted the clothes with a wooden spoon until the perspiration poured off her face and bare arms. 'A good twenty minutes you have to give them,' she said. Then came the hauling of the steaming, sodden articles out of the cauldron and into the bucket which she carried to the scullery sink. With a big bar of yellow Sunlight soap in her hand she lent over the washing board and attacked the clothes, rubbing, scrubbing, pulling, stretching, dipping and lifting each article out of the swirling suds. There being no mangle in the house, she had to wring them by hand, deftly twisting each article to the right and into a corkscrew shape before flinging it up on the deal table behind her. After that came the rinsing, the plunging down and hauling up until the water ran clear. Even that was not the end of this intensive ritual: the sheets, pillowcases and tablecloths had to be starched and wrung out.

When all was done, Annie looked, triumphant, at her handiwork, piled up high in the zinc bath and ready to be pegged up on the line. It was a plain stout wire attached at each end to a hook in the yard wall. It happened, now and again, that when Annie had everything pegged up, shirts, sheets, underwear, socks and towels, the overloaded line suddenly snapped and her lovely washing fell down on the dirty yard. Poor Annie would go mad. 'What in God's name kind of hopeless aul' line have ye got? Can ye not buy a decent wan, ye dirty old skinflint? I'll get me sister up to ye!' And my father, who never allowed himself to be put in the wrong, shouted contemptuously back at her, 'Have you no sense in your thick head, you useless article? Could you not see that you were overloading the line? I'll take the price of it out of your wages!' Furious exchanges followed. Annie implored God and His Holy Angels to bear witness for a fool to work for such an auld divil. She was going this very minute to get her sister to come up and 'settle' him.

She would stump off down Steevens's Lane in a rage.

We gathered up the clothes and piled them up again in the zinc bath. Up would come Annie in the afternoon with her reinforcements. Her sister went first into the attack. 'How dare ye, ye old skinflint, rob a woman of her wages and kill her with the likes of the work ye'er givin' her to do, and not even a strong line to do it on. I'll get the police on ye so I will.' My father was well able for them; he loved these confrontations and would have taken on a regiment of women. I used to run off, mortified by these exchanges. The following day, all passion spent, Annie would return to work, grumbling and grousing and still invoking God and His Holy Mother to witness how she had been treated, and do the washing all over again.

Next day I helped her prepare the clothes for the iron. I loved the bustle involved. I held one end of the sheet while Annie held the other. We pulled and hauled, turned over, turned back, gathered together, let out, folded longways, folded sideways, engaged in a straightening tug-of-war, until every fold was symmetrical and ready for the iron. She had to bake bread for the family every day, 'good wholemeal bread for health'. I loved to watch her curve the dough into a 'cake' as she called it, rounding it with the side of her hand until it formed a perfect whole. A quick cut of the knife and she made a deep cross on the surface, sign and symbol that the bread was blessed. She could make a succulent Irish stew and a baked milk pudding done to a delicious crust. Annie got little thanks for her work, and only a couple of puffs at a cheap Woodbine cigarette and a cup of strong tea as a respite. She had not one minute to call her own. In one of the rows with my father, she left and never came back. Although rough and fiery she was kind to me, and kindness I needed even more than stew and milk pudding.

Bridget was with us for several years. She came by the day. Not as strong or as good a worker as Annie, she was soft and indulgent to us children when my father's back was turned. The first time she failed to show up for work, Hughie, as usual, was sent to find her. He located her in a room off the Coombe with no husband and two illegitimate children. We concluded that she must be one of those 'fallen women' we had heard about. We were amazed, and she looked so nice! It was incomprehensible. My father did not turn a hair on hearing this piece of news, for he was, he said, a man of the world. Her morals did not concern him but her failure to turn up for work certainly did. Bridget was herself in no way burdened by a sense of sin, in spite of being a good catholic. She was a born optimist, always sure that her fortune was going to take a turn for the better. Betting on horses was her main activity for bringing that change about. When my father's back was turned she whipped out the newspaper and studied form. Very ambitious, she went for a treble and kept running in and out to the nearby bookie's to see how her horses were doing. Sometimes she won a few shillings on a 'place', and once she pulled off a treble. She bought us all sweets, warned us on pain of death not to tell the boss (he strictly forbade eating between meals), and lost all her winnings the following day. Bridget brought a strong nationalist culture to us children. She taught us republican songs like 'Soldiers are we who fought and died for Ireland', and recited the stirring epic of 'How Sarsfield kept the bridge at Limerick'. She spoke of Celtic prophecies which, she darkly said, were certain to come true. 'The North will run red with blood, brother turn against brother, and all will be consumed.' I little thought that I would one day be a witness of this very thing.

Mary was a strong, buxom and fresh-complexioned girl from the country. I can scarcely remember her for she did not last long. My brothers remember her very well. They were two good-looking boys in their teens. And Mary, I heard later, took it upon herself to initiate them into the mysteries of sex.

Ann stayed with us for eight years and during all that time she was my best friend. She was a poor protestant from the country, unmarried and therefore obliged to earn her bread. About twenty-eight when she came to us, she was neat, presentable, alert and well organised, a girl who, in different times, would have acquired the education to get a job worthy of her ability. She was paid twelve and six a week, all found. I could tell her all my troubles, sure of a sympathetic ear. She worked hard to make my life as smooth as possible and to save me from rows with my father. If I brought a schoolfriend home for tea I could rely on Ann to produce something good out of her slender resources and to decorate the table with little refinements of her own devising. Though she seldom went home to visit her family in County Meath (she could not spare the money for the fares), she spoke at length about its doings, the travels of Viola, her sister, who was in the ATS in Germany, and the festivities in the big house nearby to which her brother, the farmer, was invited in scenes worthy of Thomas Hardy. She told us how her friend had come to Dublin to work and had got 'into trouble'. She returned home to have the baby, explaining that 'Dublin is a terrible place, you know; I picked this up in the bus.' Ann had a boyfriend much older than herself who worked as a restorer in a well-known Dublin antique shop. They spent all their evenings together. I liked him very much. She never spoke of marriage all those eight years so we assumed that he must be married already. His constant appearance in our house so irritated my father that he said some very unpleasant things to Ann about him. She was deeply offended and she left. I was desolate. My father, as usual, had cut off his nose to spite his face. It was not the first time he had to pay with his own comfort for his uncontrollable fits of irritability.

Mrs Quinn was an enigma. She was a thin woman with a pinched face, a pinched nose, a pinched mouth, pinched rimless spectacles, and a very pinched mind. Where my father got her from I do not know. She absolutely refused to reveal anything about herself, where she came from, where her family was, or where she was going on her day off. She turned every friendly enquiry aside. 'Have you any children, Mrs Quinn?' I asked. 'One,' she said, discouragingly. 'A boy or a girl?' I asked. 'Maybe it's a boy and maybe it's not,' she answered. 'What's his name?' I said, determined to be pleasant. 'Michael,' she said, reluctantly. 'A fine name,' I said, conciliatingly. 'And why wouldn't it be,' said she defiantly, 'and it the name of the Archangel himself!' At the end of her first week she was given her wages. She disappeared and came back hours later the worse for drink. I hurried her into bed before my father saw this new development. She thanked me next morning for helping her into bed 'when I was so tired', declared I was an angel, and that she would do anything for me. The next pay day she disappeared again and came back more drunk than before. This time it was my father who opened the door. Seeing her in this state he propelled her into her room and told her in no uncertain manner that she could take a week's notice. She never reached the end of the week; she disappeared the next day taking with her half my clothes and a great deal of household linen. My father was furious at this trick, called the police, and even walked the town streets trying to find the culprit himself. No trace of her was ever found. She disappeared into the same thin air out of which she had come.

Mrs Furey was the most exotic maid we ever had. She arrived at our house in a taxi, matter enough for astonishment. When the taxi driver deposited two beautiful leather suitcases on the pavement we were even more impressed. When the lady herself emerged we were dumbfounded. She looked like nothing more than a prize prostitute, hair dyed too harsh a red, cheeks smeared with too bright a rouge, and lips a crimson scar across her face. How could such a woman be coming to work for us for twelve and six a week? 'She won't last long' was the verdict, but in fact she lasted over a year. 'I have just arrived from California' was her opening remark. 'From California?' we gasped. 'Yes, you see I have been living in the States for the past sixteen years, but I could not stay there any longer. It was too dangerous. I had to flee. For the moment I am travelling incognito.' Incognito? I had to ask Hughie what the word meant. 'She must have escaped from Grangegorman,' said Frank. 'I had to get away from my husband, you know. He is insanely jealous and believes I am having affairs with the postman, the milkman and every man who passes by. He was going to kill me. It's true. He was so very passionate, so very possessive that he had to go into a psychiatric clinic for a time.' We wondered if she was just out of such a clinic herself. 'I have to cover my tracks. At this very moment he may be landing at Dublin airport in hot pursuit.' We did not believe a word of it. She pulled a photograph out of her bag and showed it to us. There she was in a gorgeous bridal outfit, hand in hand with a handsome man. 'Watch out,' she said, 'and if you hear any man with an American accent around here tell me at once. Meantime I shall try to recover from the fray.'

Decidedly Mrs Furey had a past. Although a poor housekeeper, her emotions having tired her out, she was pleasant and obliging. Her vocabulary was extensive and her manners (belying her appearance) courteous and refined. She spent all her spare time in her room 'writing novels'. She covered sheet after sheet of paper. As each one was completed she flung it down on the floor on top of the pile. It was a very frenzy of writing. 'Will you let me read what you have written?' I asked. 'Not until the day of publication,' she answered. That day never came. She got on very well with my father after he discovered that, although she was born and bred a catholic, she never went to mass and disliked priests as a race. 'That woman has a mind of her own; easy to see she has been out of Ireland.' For that independence of mind he was prepared to forgive her other little lapses. They got on famously together. One night poor Mrs Furey had an attack of asthma so bad that my father had to call an ambulance. She was taken to hospital and never came back to us.

OUR FAMILY

For many years after my mother's death, I was a botheration to the other children. Told continually to 'come and mind the child' or to 'take the child for a walk and be sure you take good care of her', they had other things in mind. Besides, I was on the side of the enemy, for if thwarted in anything, I had learned to cry 'I'll tell Daddy on you!', knowing that he would immediately rush to the defence of 'a helpless little child'. My eldest brother, having always hated the name Cecil, took the opportunity, when starting his first job, to call himself James. He was a stranger to me. Thirteen years older than me, he had already left home when I was five for 'a good job in the bank with a pension' (very few people then had the right to a pension). From the mysterious and faraway North where, ironically, he had been posted, he descended now and again on a big, shiny, black motorbike, disguised in helmet, goggles, leather trousers and huge gauntlet gloves. This apparition so overawed me that I was scarcely able to get a word out when he spoke to me. I knew he was different from the rest of us children for he was earning money and was independent. I could see it in the way my father treated him. Unlike us, he sat down to a half-grapefruit for breakfast and very meticulously ate it with a spoon. He preceded it with a raw egg which he swallowed down before my fascinated eyes in one awful, slithery gulp.

Acutely aware of his superior status, he bustled about playing Big Brother before us. Very tidy in his habits, he placed notices in all his drawers saying 'Keep out! This means you!' for he rightly suspected that when his back was turned, we went through all his drawers, curious to see what he possessed. Hughie and Frank were green with envy of his motorbike; they could not keep their hands off it in spite of severe warnings from James. One day, they managed to get it started in the backyard. 'Rip-rip-roar' went the engine, and highly delighted with themselves, they ran round and round the yard holding on to the handlebars. Unfortunately, they could not find how to bring it to a halt so they were obliged to keep running until, worn out and very worried, they were discovered when James came home. We hung about our big brother hoping for crumbs from the rich man's table but were usually disappointed. At Christmas and at birthdays, however, he was generosity itself. He gave each of us five shillings, newly minted from the bank. We knew that we could recoup our fortunes twice in the year. His holidays over, he donned his helmet, goggles and gauntlet gloves and with a great roar from the engine, he tore off back to the North out of which he had come.

My sister Olive (she tried 'Olave' for a time as I tried 'Edythe') was lively and attractive and very popular with the boys. My father exercised an iron control over her comings and goings and frequent rows broke out between them. She braved his anger blithely. At eleven o'clock, he locked and bolted the front door for the night. This was the time for Olive to be home. Lying in bed, too apprehensive to sleep, I listened to my father pacing up and down the parlour. The doorbell rang, the bolts were drawn and voices were raised in anger. As the shouting grew louder, I began to sob to myself in bed. Shortly afterwards, Olive came into the room, got into our bed beside me, put her cold feet on my warm ones and said nothing. She was tearless. She was often obliged to take me out and if, as it often happened, she had a rendezvous of which my father knew nothing, she knew she had a little spy in the camp. I listened hard to every confidence and took in every movement. She had to bribe me with a penny to keep my mouth shut.

Soon she was working in Guinness's brewery and earning money like James. This put her at once into the economically independent category so respected by my father. But she was a girl. He had no intention of letting her get into trouble or marry a catholic, and she had no intention of being treated like a child. Rows were so common between them that at one stage she moved out of the

Lodge altogether and into a flat on the South Circular Road but after a while she was so lonely that she moved back in again and the turbulent relationship resumed as before. It was easier to cajole a penny out of Olive than out of James. She adored Scot's Clan toffee and sent me on regular errands to Kelly's shop to buy a quarter-pound for threepence. On the way home, I always stole one, was always accused and always denied it. She was expected to look after me, to cut my hair and to make my clothes. She was good at neither. She took the scissors, began to cut at one ear and continued straight until she got to the other ear, thus giving my head the distinct appearance of a golliwog's. The dresses she made were always too short, too long, too narrow or too wide. At fourteen, I learned to dressmake myself and did a far better job.

Frank and Hughie were next in age to me. Strong, athletic and daring, they were always in mischief, always in rows and always in fear of our father. He used to haul them out of bed at night to examine their knees for dirt. If in a bad mood, he examined the soles of their shoes as well and if there were holes in them – as there often were – he rounded on them. They used their shoes as bicycle brakes! They had kicked stones with them! They had worn out the seat of their trousers! They had done every kind of badness! No use protesting their innocence; they were guilty! We were all afraid to declare the holes in the soles of our shoes. We stuffed them with cardboard to keep out the rain and it was only when the leather became white with dried-out moisture that we could hide them no longer. Frank fell into the canal when he was nine years old and was wheeled home, squeezed up in a stranger's pram, dripping wet and humiliated. Instead of being glad to see him, my father told him off severely for getting into trouble. During one of his many escapades, Hughie was impaled on an iron railing and taken to hospital but there was no tender reunion with my father for him. He was accused of being grossly careless. My father frequently beat the two of them until one day Frank, then an adolescent, hit him back. From that day, my father had a new respect for him and even gave him two shillings a week pocket money while the rest of us got nothing. With only eighteen months between them, the boys were very good at every kind of sport and were always in competition. Hughie was the stronger of the two and often taunted Frank with that fact. Many a battle I witnessed between them, fists flying and noses bleeding. These fights terrified me and I ran backwards and forwards pleading with them to stop, more often than not getting a fist in my own face for my pains.

Frank had a very different temperament from the controlled Hughie. He was a born gambler and loved the thrill of risk and chance. He would ask you to bet a sweet on two flies going up a wall and any idle moment saw him playing games of shove-penny, pitch-and-toss or poker. He was always being caught but he did not care. Original Sin, which my father denied as a theological concept, was acutely real to him in this tendency of his son. He was always warning him of the fate that lay in store for him. He himself never gambled and regarded it as a strict moral law to pay cash for everything. On the same principle, he never insured his house or his own life, for insurance to him was but another form of gambling. We seldom had any money and spent much time daydreaming about how to acquire it. We were always on the watch for a halfpenny or even a farthing (for you could buy three sweets with a farthing) which had fallen through the iron grating of a street cellar. Frank was expert at retrieving them. He tied a magnet to a piece of wire and spent hours fishing among the debris until he hooked it and drew it up. I was always pleading with my brothers to let me accompany them on their excursions and was usually spurned. Occasionally, they let me go fishing with them for pinkeens (tiddlers) in the canal at Inchicore. When they had filled their jamjars with myriad little pink fish, they got tired of it, handed me the cane and net and dived into the water. I looked at them admiringly. I knew I would never have the courage to go far under the water as they did. Lying flat on my stomach on the bank of the canal, listening to the shouts of my brothers and dipping my net into the water, I was happy and content.

But I was lonely for a special friend of my own. Forced to go to bed at seven o'clock, I listened to the shouting of the children in Bow Lane as they swung giddily around the lamp-posts on pieces of old rope or careered dangerously down the lane on home-made go-carts. Why did I have to go to bed so early? Why could I not play on the lamp-posts like them? One day, when I was about eight years old, I noticed a girl of my own age pass up and down Bow

Lane. She was slightly taller than me and blonde. I could always tell when she was coming by the sound of a hacking cough which preceded her. About a week later, as she reached the top of the lane opposite the Lodge, I looked at her and she looked at me and a flash of recognition passed from eye to eye. I plucked up courage.

'Would you ever come in and play with me?'

'What will you give me if I do?'

'This brown bead purse in my hand.'

She came in and I gave it to her. Thus began a long friendship which lasted all through my childhood, through her years in England during the war and through her married years in California until she died at the age of fifty-two. After that first encounter, I was on the watch for Martha every day. If she did not come, my spirits drooped and the day turned dreary and empty. When she did come, we set to work seriously to play. We invented games and challenges of all kinds to test our powers, both physical and mental. We played Sevens against the back of the yard wall, setting ourselves more and more complicated patterns to master. We played Piggy Beds, marking out the beds with a piece of soft stone and making a pig out of an old boot polish tin filled with wet earth. We climbed the big chestnut tree, daring each other to swing off the highest branches or to drop to the ground from greater and greater heights. We devised games and concerts in which we were film or opera stars, ballet dancers or chorus girls like the Royalettes in the Royal Theatre in Dublin. I fancied myself as Judy Garland while Martha saw herself as Jeanette MacDonald.

Martha lived in Bow Lane. I knew everybody in that lane from the tiny little private houses at the top to the bigger tenement houses at the end. All faced the wall of the hospital except for a huxter's shop at the bottom. It was a magnet for all the children in the lane because there was a grey parrot on a perch just inside the door and when anyone entered it screamed out 'Shop! Shop!' to alert the owners in the back room. In a small house at the top of the lane lived Mrs Riordan. Her husband worked on the railways in Inchicore. She was neat and pretty and even as a child, quite unconsciously, I liked looking at her. She would be leaning over her half-door as I passed, the range fire glowing in the room behind her. She had one fascinating feature: one eye was blue and the other brown. I always hoped that I would see her as I passed so that I could look into those curious eyes. She had no children because, Martha said, she had had one miscarriage after another (we thought for a long time that she had fallen out of a railway carriage) and was eating her heart out for a baby. Mrs Fox lived in a tiny house next door. She was fat and jolly in her dark overall overprinted with red flowers, as she stood at her half-door, chatting with her neighbours. She knew everybody and was always in demand for helping women in trouble or for laying out the dead of the neighbourhood.

Further down in number twenty-eight lived the Atticks, parents of my friend Martha. Mr Attick had been a corporal in the British Army during the Troubles of 1921 and 1922 and had fallen in love with a lively Dublin girl, Grace Murphy. She had had her hair cut off at the time for 'going with' a British soldier but she had persisted and had married him. They lived with their two daughters and Mrs Attick's mother in two rooms upstairs. The grandmother was a permanent feature in one corner of the living room. She was bedridden and held court underneath a red and white diamond-patterned patchwork quilt. She enjoyed a great social status in spite of her infirmity for she had been a lady's maid to an important person in Blackrock near Dublin who knew the film star Maureen O'Hara. She knew how things should be done and was always consulted on points of etiquette. You were always expected to exchange a few words with her on entering the room and whatever else she lacked, it certainly was not company for the whole life of the family was carried on around her in that room. She had two passions in life, the taking of snuff and the sucking of peppermint 'lozengers'. Martha and I were frequently sent out to buy them. I loved to watch the shopman take the snuff out of a tin with a delicate brass scoop and weigh out half an ounce of the pungent powder on a tiny brass scales with miniature brass weights, then roll it up in a 'scuff' of paper and fasten it off like a cornet. The grandmother took a dainty pinch of the powder between two fingers, lifted it to one nostril then the other and inhaled deeply.

The room was scantily furnished, a deal table in the middle covered with a piece of oilcloth, a black gas cooker with a slot meter beside it, a small table with a basin and ewer and a bucket under it for slops. An enamel bucket complete with lid stood beside the grandmother's bed for purposes I could dimly guess. There was a picture of the Sacred Heart of Jesus on a small shelf on the wall and a little red oil lamp burned constantly before it. In that poor household they were never without oil for the holy lamp. Everyone made the sign of the cross before it except Mr Attick. He was a protestant. An Infant of Prague, a squat little figure in a robe and crown, stood on the mantelpiece. Mrs Attick presided at the table, pouring out mugs of strong tea from a half-blackened teapot and adding a few drops of condensed milk for fresh milk was too dear. She held a white loaf firmly to her large bosom, spread it thinly with margarine and with a vigorous slap of her knife she deftly cut off a slice and offered it around. Occasionally, she would offer a spoon of sugar to spread on the bread and, on state occasions, a piece of processed cheese. Mr Attick came and went silently; he seldom spoke or laughed, unlike his wife, who had a great fund of salty Dublin phrases. He was always looking for work and would rise at six o'clock to walk the two miles to the docks in the hope of getting it; but he had only to open his mouth to reveal his English origins and in the depressed Dublin of the time he had little chance of being taken on. He was generally silently at work either in the living room or in the yard mending the girls' shoes or fixing up an old bicycle. I do not think I ever exchanged two words with this silent Yorkshireman. He had been gassed in the First World War and although not in the best of health thereafter, he was accepted in the Second World War for duty on barrage balloons. Many years later, he was to die, as quietly as he had lived, of cancer of the throat. Mrs Attick managed somehow on the tiniest of fluctuating incomes and I never saw her less than buoyant.

The living conditions were insanitary in the extreme, with no running water, one standpipe in the yard for four families and one outside toilet. The landlord, Mr McCarthy, lived in the house next door and shared a yard with the tenants. He kept pigs in two broken-down old sheds in the yard and fed them on the offal he collected from the hospital kitchens. He entered each day by our front gate and went out by the back gate with his cartload of swill. I often heard pigs grunting and snuffling in the sheds there but never saw them. One day, Mrs Attick went out as usual to bring up a bucket of water from the tap in the yard. I was in the room above when I heard a hysterical screaming followed by a loud clatter of feet and Mrs Attick came flying up the stairs. 'Jesus, Mary and Joseph, the heart is after goin' crossways in me! Just as I was fillin' me bucket, didn't I put me eye to the crack in the shed wall behind it and what am I after seein' starin' out at me but two twinklin' eyes of a bloody big rat! It was the size of me ar–um and it could have eaten the face of ye! I nearly fell out of me standin' with the shock I'm after gettin'!' She took a swig out of the Baby Power (whiskey) which she kept for emergencies to soothe her shattered nerves. The shortage of work and money came to an end for the Atticks when the war broke out. They left one by one for Birmingham to work in munitions factories and never came back to live in Dublin.

Downstairs in number twenty–eight lived Miss Clark in one tiny room. She was bedridden and helpless. The neighbours looked after her as best they could. As I passed her open door, I caught a glimpse of a darkened room and the end of a bed. She had no visible relations and was in a terrible fear lest she be taken by force to the Workhouse. For years, she paid a penny a week to Mr Brannigan, the insurance man, to ensure a decent burial. Mr Brannigan was the friend of the whole neighbourhood and knew everyone's business. He came once a week to collect from Miss Clark, to hear her confidences and to do little errands for her. Martha told me that he even cut her toenails. One day, when I was in the lane, a large black horse-drawn carriage drew up outside the house and a gaunt, emaciated figure was carried out on a stretcher. It was Miss Clark being taken to the Workhouse, the place which she had so dreaded. Martha told me that Mrs McCarthy, when she came to clean out her room for the new tenant, found a bundle of pound notes under her mattress, chewed to pieces by rats. Her gangrenous toes, too, had been partially chewed away.

At the end of the lane were the tenements, where conditions were even more insanitary. In the evening, women sat outside their doors on stools or butter-boxes to take the air and to chat to one another. Knowing I was from the Lodge, they would call out to me as I passed, 'Young wan, would ye ere get me a red ger-an-i-um for me winda from the hospital? Ah, sure, I'm very fond of a big rosy-red ger-an-i-um!' Alas, I could do nothing for them.

A protestant family lived in a small, narrow house beyond the

Atticks. There were nine boys in the family and the mother was always hanging out huge lines of washing. The boys went to our school and to our church and were in the Boys' Brigade with my brothers. At the very bottom of the lane, below Cromwell's Quarters, lived the roughest and toughest crowd of all. I did not know any family there but went, from time to time, with Martha when she was told by her mother to pay her respects to the dead. This was a very important exercise of solidarity in poor catholic Dublin. We knocked at the door; it was opened and I repeated after Martha, 'I'm sorry for your trouble, missus', and we passed inside into a small, stuffy room filled with people where the corpse was laid out. Terrified and fascinated at the same time, I had to steel myself to look into the coffin at the waxen face and waxen arms folded piously on breast, with a rosary between the fingers. Martha said a prayer and I pretended to do the same, hiding the fact that I was a protestant. I never told my father where I had been; I kept the two worlds quite separate in my mind but moved easily between them.

James's Street was bigger and noisier than Bow Lane. I could see the back of some of the tenements from the Lodge, the wooden triangles sticking out from the windows hanging with washing and the women calling to one another as they leaned out. One of the girls in my class lived in number one; her family was an enigma, not mixing with the neighbours as did everyone else. Her father was jewish and had married a protestant and, as a result, it was said, no jew would help him as they helped each other when in need. I used to see him pass down the street, buttoned up in an old coat, his face sallow, his expression dead. Although I often came to their rooms to call for his daughter, I was never once asked to cross the threshold.

The pawnshop, economic powerhouse of the neighbourhood, was next to the chemist. The windows were crammed with watches, jewellery, cameras and clothes, all the objects which had never been reclaimed by their owners and which were now on sale. On Monday morning early, a queue formed outside its doors and women waited, battered prams piled high with the furniture and clothes they had taken out of pawn the Friday before. I looked at them curiously. We in the Lodge were different; we never had to pawn or borrow anything. My father saw to that. Credit of all kinds was anathema to him. 'Never buy anything you cannot pay for' was his stern command; 'If you do not have the money to pay for it, do without!' But he had never been reduced to the bare level of subsistence as had these poor people.

Though drunken brawls were regular occurrences, I was always frightened to see grown-up men and women act in this violent way. A bottle might come flying through the fanlight of a Georgian tenement, accompanied by shouts and curses, or a couple of women the worse for drink would be punching and kicking each other, tearing at each other's hair and falling to the ground struggling while stockings and knickers showed and a crowd of men stood around and egged them on, shouting 'Give it to her right on the arse!' and 'Tear her fucking hair out!' The shame of it was terrible. I used to beg my father to go in and put an end to it, but he wisely did not interfere with the mood of the crowd. Boys regularly fought one another in the street, throwing off their jackets and swinging their arms into menacing boxing positions at a real or imagined insult. Everyone seemed to carry on with their lives, aggressively, on the street.

The Dublin Union or Workhouse was nearly opposite our school. The gate stood open and Martha and I often walked through the grounds on our way to Dolphin's Barn. For us it was the fascination of the horrible. In those grey and bleak buildings was concentrated all the hopelessness of the Dublin poor. The philosophy on which the British workhouse was built – 'Do not pamper the poor' – was rigidly put into practice here. Husbands were separated from wives, children from parents, so that it would be as uncomfortable and shaming as possible. We watched the inmates standing about, beaten down and despairing. They seemed a different race from the ordinary Dublin poor by the utter lack of life in their demeanour. We dared each other to enter the morgue. Martha led the way and I followed. She pushed open the door very gingerly and we stood together inside ready to take to our heels at the slightest sound. A large brown crucifix hung on the dim wall, suitable symbol of suffering. We gazed in enthralled horror at the corpses laid out on narrow marble slabs, each wrapped in a rough brown shroud, the face waxen and yellow, the hands piously crossed over crucifix and rosary beads. The absolute silence terrified us. All the stories we had heard in Bow Lane came vividly back to us. The story of the corpse which sat up and laughed so that the poor nun who was praying over it ran screaming out of the morgue, shouting 'Lord ha' mercy on us! Lord ha' mercy on us!' The story of Mrs Attick's cousin who had gone to the morgue to pay her last respects to her poor, dead husband. As she was kneeling beside the bier, the corpse suddenly gave a loud whistle. She screamed like a madwoman and fell down in a dead faint. 'She had to be taken to Grangegorman with the shock of it and hasn't got over it yet nor never will, neither.'

Martha coughed her way through months of every winter, and each winter her mother dreaded yet again the wasting disease, the consumption, the TB which had claimed so many lives in the streets around her. So every winter, she took her to the Outpatients' Department of the hospital to have her lungs examined. She was kept waiting a whole long weary afternoon to be seen by the doctor who, as usual, prescribed medicine and a tonic. Her mother went to the free dispensary at the end of Steevens's Lane to obtain them. I often saw poor thinly clad women go in and out of that sombre red-brick building opposite Kingsbridge station. I watched them almost incidentally and without pity as a child registers without reflection what is going on around it.

We in the Lodge never had to undergo the humiliation of asking for free medical treatment as St Patrick's looked after the health of the lodge-keeper's family. Once, however, I knew what it felt like to be without money and in need of treatment. When I was about sixteen years old, a small, pink rash made its appearance on my chest. It itched and itched and I scratched and scratched. It spread and refused to go away. My sure instinct was to say nothing of the matter to my father as I knew that one trouble confessed could lead to another one invented. I consulted Ann, our maid, my best friend. 'Why not attend the Outpatients of Hume Street Skin Hospital?' she said. 'Your father will never know.' On the appointed day we cycled in to Hume Street, chained our bicycles to the railings and went inside. The familiar smell of antiseptic and wax polish brought a flutter of anxiety to my stomach, reminding me of weeks spent in Steevens's Hospital. I gave my name and address and was told to sit and wait.

Wait we did, for several hours passed as a crowd of people were called one by one into the doctor's room. Suddenly came a shock as my name was called. I jumped up with an anxious heart and followed the nurse through the door of the consulting room. A middle-aged man in a white coat was sitting behind a desk writing busily. He showed no sign of registering my presence; I felt very awkward and uncomfortable. Should I say 'Good afternoon, doctor'? At last he looked up and enquired my name. 'What is the matter with you?' he asked in a cold, remote voice. I opened my blouse and stepped forward to show him the rash on my chest. 'I have had this for some time,' I said. In a commanding voice he said, 'Step back!', and stung by his tone, by the humiliation of the order, I stepped back a few paces. Was he loath to be in too close contact with the dirty poor? 'You have scabies,' he said. 'Here is a prescription for ointment. Rub it on twice a day. Take it to the dispensary on your way out.' I was back outside the door, hurt and humiliated by the distance, both physical and mental, he had put between us and ready for the warm human sympathy of the waiting Ann. I had that day learned what it felt like to be poor and at the mercy of an arrogant and ill-mannered doctor.

Such fears and fantasies were the vivid counterpart of hours of fun and laughter. These fears multiplied by night. By day, I belonged to the normal, ordinary, reassuring world of Bow Lane and James's Street but by night I was engulfed in a fantastical-imaginary world. I woke; I heard a faint rustling in the leaves outside my window; I listened, sharp to every implication of the sound. My mind at once leapt to the terrible truth: an escaped lunatic was at that very minute standing on my window sill, one leg already over the frame, poised to leap in and strangle me. My heart nearly burst my ribs with its terrified thumping. I closed my eyes tight and waited for the fingers to close around my throat . . . This happened many a night and on each occasion, my fears were as real as on previous occasions although they had proved groundless every time.

Terror-filled, too, was the visit to the hospital dentist. We did not then have regular dental inspections and it was only when a toothache became so agonising that it could be borne no longer that we had to resort to the dentist. No aspirins or other painkillers were kept in our house as taking such things was regarded as a decided moral weakness. When I was worn out with the pain, I was obliged to confess it to my father who arranged for me to see the dentist on his next regular visit to the hospital. A terrible ordeal then began. Handed over to a nurse in the hall of the hospital, I had to face my torture alone. I followed the nurse through corridor after corridor where handless doors were unlocked and locked again behind us. The terrifying feeling of being trapped in a madhouse grew stronger and stronger until it reached a climax when we came out into the female ward, the door was locked behind us and I was face to face with the patients. The dentist's room lay between this ward and the male ward on the other side. The ward was long and beautifully furnished with flowers, pictures and comfortable chairs but I took in little of this: my eyes were on one thing only, the lunatics and the closed doors of the cells which led off the ward, out of which a patient might rush at any moment and attack me.

The patients sat about or stared out of the window. I knew I was secure as long as the nurse was with me, but when she left, telling me to wait until I was called, panic seized me. Better stand still, I said to myself, and not catch anyone's eye. Loud screams suddenly came from the far end of the long ward, turning my blood to ice – that must be the padded cell, or a patient in a straitjacket! I wanted to turn and run, but how could I get through all those locked doors? I was trapped! Out of the corner of my eye, I saw a patient slowly advance towards me . . . she came nearer and nearer until her eyes fixed on mine. I had to stifle a terrible urge to scream hysterically. Mesmerised, I stood still as I felt her hands travel over my head, down my forehead, over my eyes, my nose, my lips . . . The next would be my throat! I yelled, 'Nurse! Nurse!' The nurse came quickly and gently led her away. Just then my name was called and I ran into the terror of the dreaded surgery, glad for once to escape the worse terror outside. In the chair, my tooth was extracted with such awful torture that I thought every bone in my head was breaking. Exhausted by emotion, by fear and pain, I was escorted by the nurse back through the locked doors and out into freedom.

My father loved the cheap shopping streets near Nelson's Pillar. He journeyed there regularly on his black upright bicycle. He had a commanding presence, even on a bike, and when he wanted to make a turn, he simply put out his arm with such an air of authority that the traffic immediately slowed down and gave him place. He loved the geniality of Moore Street, Dublin's vivacious open-air market where battered prams, the universal transport of the poor, overflowed with chickens, fruit and cabbages. Women in long black skirts and shawls, which often held a baby tight in their criss-cross folds, vigorously called out their wares: 'Ten a shillin' now, ten a shillin'! Live Dublin herrins!' You had to be mentally strong to withstand the battery of words they let loose at you. My father loved these verbal tussles, loved to extract a tribute from the enemy in the form of an extra herring or a couple of apples which he bore home, triumphant, on the back carrier of his bike.

Horse-drawn cabs and carts packed the streets of Dublin. Cabs stood outside the main railway stations, their owners lazily convers-ing as they waited for fares while the horses, heads deep in nosebags, jangled their bits as they chewed. I hated to see miserable, scrawny animals, ribs showing, toil along the streets, their drivers often lash-ing them with their whips and shouting, 'Get up there! Get up there!' Steevens's Lane, short and very steep, was a terrible trial for these poor beasts. The back entrance to Guinness's brewery opened on to the end of the lane and horses issued forth all day long pulling carts heavily laden with barrels and laboured up the hill to James's Street. They were the finest horses in Dublin, beautiful Clydesdales, manes brushed, feathers white above their hooves and brasses gleaming on nose and harness. The drivers were splendid, too, in top hat and uniform, poised above the reins. An extra horse was al-ways attached for the steep climb, and once at the top, it was unhar-nessed and led back down again. Private carriers often had to make one horse do the work of two. I used to watch as the beast strained and stumbled under its load, desperate to get a grip on the over-smooth cobblestones, its owner alternately exhorting and cursing it and applying his whip to its perspiring flanks. Every nerve in my body would be lacerated at the sight. Sometimes the heroic effort was beyond its powers. I remember seeing one horse give a last frantic tug, then its eyes bulged hideously, blood poured from its nostrils, dung fell steaming from its hindquarters and its legs gave way under it. Gasping convulsively, it sank down quivering horri-bly between the shafts. Men rushed to hold its head and to detach its body from the crushing shafts. It lay there, sweating and trembling violently, its great eyes standing forth in terror. Then, as I watched appalled, it gave a last huge shudder and lay still. Keefe the knacker was sent for. His horse and cart came rattling along James's Street, steel chains clanging. Down jumped the driver and fastened the chains around the body of the still steaming animal, then with a gee-up to the living beast the huge lump of dead flesh was slowly hauled up the ramp and into the knacker's bloodstained cart. The sides and back were briskly bolted down and off it went at a rattling speed to the knacker's yard for the carcass to be turned into glue. When the wind was in a certain direction, the heavy sickly smell of burning flesh almost choked me.

I was nine years old when I saw my first film. It was *The 39 Steps*. Martha and I paid fourpence each for a seat in the front stalls of the Fountain cinema, right under the screen. I had to crane my head to see what was happening. The bench was hard and had no back, the room was stuffy and the children around me kept up a noisy, boisterous personal commentary on the action, warning the 'goodies' when they were in danger by shouting out, 'He's behind you! Look out!' As the story unfolded in the magic space above me, I forgot all my discomforts and it was only when I emerged from the cinema that I felt the thud of a bad headache on my forehead. The 'pictures' were a great treat. Some people went to the cinema three or four times a week and courting couples found a warm place to embrace in the double seats in the back row. I always avoided looking at them. Going to the posh cinemas in O'Connell Street was special; the seats were comfortable and the cinema ventilated so that you did not come home with a headache. The big cinema organ played for ten minutes before the film began. Splendid in incandescent pink and white, it rose majestically out of the darkness and its sonorous notes filled the whole auditorium. As it came to a halt, the organist in dress suit and bow tie, his whole person suffused with a magic light, swung round on his stool, bowed to the audience then turned back to thunder forth a well-known tune. The screen lit up to reveal the words of a popular song and the whole audience joined in the singing. We were happy even before the film began.

There was always something interesting to be seen on the streets of Dublin. People walked out for the sole purpose of enjoying themselves, hoping for 'a bit of gas'. You might see a drunken brawl with policemen trying to separate the parties and a black Maria arriving to take them off to gaol. You were sure to see beggars and queer people behaving in odd ways, shouting or jerking their limbs or calling out, 'Your salvation is nigh!' 'Forty-coats' was certain to curse you and chase you if you looked sideways at him, and old 'Hit-me-Hard' would foam at the mouth as he swore at you. They frightened us and made us laugh at the same time. You might spot anything in the River Liffey. I often saw a dead cat or dog, its head protruding from an old sack in which it had been tied, and once I saw a dead body and gazed, horrified, as the police dragged it out of the water and into a boat while half Dublin hung over the parapet and watched the spectacle.

Now and again a dramatic event sent us scurrying to the Phoenix Park. The huge Wellington monument had been struck by lightning and great lumps of granite were lying about the grass at its base. The statue of General Gough which stood in the middle of the main road in the Phoenix Park had lost its head, cut off by terrorists, it was said. Nelson at that time was still standing upright on top of his long slender pillar in O'Connell Street in the heart of Dublin. For sixpence we could toil up the staircase inside and come out at the top beside the one-eyed admiral where we got a dizzy view over the whole of Dublin. Hawkers displayed their fruit and flowers at the base of Nelson's Pillar and visitors up from the country made rendezvous at this familiar meeting place. But the Pillar was used for a more sinister purpose: despairing people bent on self-destruction sometimes climbed up in order to throw themselves off, so the top was caged in to prevent such follies. In the 1960s Nelson would be blown off his Pillar by a terrorist bomb and it was sadly and unnecessarily demolished. None but the ideologically conscious could have associated that beloved Dublin landmark with the humiliations of Ireland's colonial past. Blowing up statues seemed an acceptable part of our lives for no one got excited about it. I had not been, therefore, surprised to see, when walking through Stephen's Green on my way to school, another military-looking statue in pieces among the flower beds: it was the equestrian statue of George II.

One day, a powerful smell of burning cocoa descended on Bow

Lane. Rowntree's chocolate factory was on fire! The rumour ran round that sacks of chocolate were lying about for the taking and we all rushed up to Kilmainham to help ourselves. Great flames filled the sky as we approached and the heat was so intense that we could not get near the chocolate. When the fire died down the following day, we returned for the plunder only to find that the chocolate was nothing but lumps of natural cocoa too black and too strong to be enjoyed!

The nurses who came and went to the hospital were obliged to hang up their keys in a long, flat cupboard in the porch of the Lodge. Footsteps advancing or retreating and the rattle of keys were the background noises of our daily existence. We knew all the nurses by name. Some came from Dublin while others had Cork or Kerry accents. We all had our favourites. I liked Kitty Devereux best: she had red hair and a pretty laughing face. Every Christmas she gave me a box of chocolates for myself but my father always took it from me saying that it would do nicely for the pantomime, a treat which he gave us every year on New Year's Eve. Each time the box passed from knee to knee in the darkness of the theatre I surreptitiously took out two chocolates instead of one and felt completely justified.

A tomboy, I was always about in the avenue climbing trees, and the nurses would call out to me as they passed. One or two of the male nurses had what I now know to be an unhealthy interest in me. 'Will you take down your knickers and let me see how nice you are?' and a hand would hold out a sweet. An instinct told me to run off. I never told my father about these incidents for fear of the scenes that would follow. It was from Martha that I heard of 'dirty old men' (they were nearly always young). Dirty men would try to entice you away and do dirty things to you, so you must always run away. The two of us, being very athletic, loved to practise our skills on the grass of the Phoenix Park. We were always at work perfecting our handstands and Catherine wheels. As often as not, a man's head would be raised from the grass nearby and a voice would say, 'Will the two of you do handstands for me? If you are good and can stay up for a long time I will take you up behind the polo field and give you sweets.' We ran off.

We rarely went to the cinema without being accosted. We

would be sitting absorbed by what was happening on the screen when one of us would feel a groping hand on a leg. We would both jump up and move to another seat. Once, the man followed. We called the usherette and she ordered him out; he moved to another seat and we sat on secure under her watchful eye. One day, after school, my father took me to see Nelson Eddy and Jeanette Mac-Donald in *Maytime*. As we sat watching, I suddenly became aware of a man's thigh pressed against my own. I looked round. A respect-able-looking man was sitting bolt upright beside me staring fixedly at the screen. He had a raincoat folded over his knee. I put my schoolbag between his leg and mine and moved nearer my father. The hand came steadily groping from under the raincoat. I moved even closer to my father, who wanted to know why I could not keep still. I dared not tell him the truth for I knew he would im-mediately rise up and tackle the man, that there would be a stand-up fight, the lights would go up and I would be the centre of atten-tion. I stood up, pushed my way past my father and away from my tormentor, forcing a long row of irritated people to let me pass just in the middle of a romantic sequence. I waited anxiously at the back of the cinema until I saw the man move away and then returned to my seat.

When I was fifteen I saw a man walking towards me reading a newspaper. All at once I saw that beneath the newspaper he had ex-posed himself. Nothing could express the horror of that sight, in that context, to a child who knew very little about sex and who had never seen her brothers naked. For days and weeks afterwards I was in a state of confused revulsion. What was this frightening thing that menaced me on all sides? I could tell no one about my fears so I devised ridiculous ways of escaping should I ever be cor-nered. As I lay in bed at night, I thought of what I would do and say in such situations. I would say that my father was a policeman; I would offer to pay him £100 to leave me alone – but what if he tried to poison me with a handshake of crushed ivy berries? I kept these fears and fantasies to myself as do all children even in sympa-thetic families, but they never left me.

When I was about nine or ten years of age, I began to like walks with my father less well. I wanted to be free from what I now thought of as 'teaching' walks; and besides, I much preferred to play with Martha. Sunday afternoon was sacrosanct to our long walk in the park together. My father had long given up asking his older children to accompany him, being one of those who get on best with young children, animals and other unargumentative beings. I began to hide from him. My favourite hiding place was the crab-apple tree in our side garden. When he rose from his siesta, he went to claim me. 'Edith, my child! Edith, my child!' No reply. 'Edith, where are you?' He passed directly under the apple tree where I was crouching. Would my brothers tell on me as they sometimes did when they wanted an afternoon free of their father's presence? My nerve generally snapped when his back was turned to me. I slipped down and declared myself. Off I went beside him, reluctant and sulky, down Steevens's Lane, over Kingsbridge and up to the Park. If he bought me an apple from the fruit shop in Parkgate Street I cheered up a bit; if he did not I sulked the more. We passed the cricket ground where the white-flannelled players were going through their rituals of bat on ball. I was determined to be miserable. My father persisted in talk, but I remained mute and unresponsive. He did not know how to deal with me or how to bring me round. So we walked on, a brisk middle-aged man and a sullen child. He, in his turn, became irritable and angry, some slight misdemeanour would raise a storm and we would return home, distanced from each other, hurt and offended.

So began the long years of non-communication. Little by little I drew away from him and we were never able to get back to the same natural loving relationship we had enjoyed when his little girl travelled blissfully along on the crossbar of his bicycle wanting no other happiness in the world but that. The habit of communication once lost is almost impossible to recover. Each side desires it, neither can achieve it. I withdrew into myself. To love your fellow man is not the same as to know how to do it. He did not know how to show his love for me because with all his intelligence, his devotion to our good (he could have taken to drink or brought in a stepmother), he lacked the most important quality of all, the imagination to understand our feelings.

Gradually, I became aware that, in some strange way, he frowned on my association with Martha Attick, that he did not like to see me enjoying myself in her company. 'You will be learning bad habits in Bow Lane,' he warned. 'The people who live there are ignorant, superstitious and thriftless. They have no ambition; they do not even want to improve their situation. Keep away from them!' Nothing could have appalled me more: not to play with Martha! It was a death sentence. So I began to deceive him. I slipped out when he was not there but on my way back up the lane I began to grow apprehensive. What if he had come back? I peered cautiously through the Gate to see if the coast was clear; already my heart was pounding with fear. Dimly, in my child's mind, I began to perceive that he did not want me to play with Martha because he did not want to see me enjoying myself without him, that he even seemed to resent laughter in which he was not included. I did not know that he was becoming more and more isolated in the midst of his children and that he did not know how to reverse this painful and frustrating situation. He sought relief for his wounded feelings in impatience and truculence. He usually calmed this nervous irritability by walking or cycling many miles, but if he was in one of his black moods we were 'for it'. It did not matter whether we were guilty or not of some supposed crime. His swings of mood were so erratic that we never knew when the blow was going to fall, and the only strategy we could develop against an unjust attack was to know at every moment of the day where we were, physically, in relation to him. No mouse was ever more wary of the cat than we were of our father.

Sometimes as we were sitting reading in the parlour or playing a game at the kitchen table, the door would open and the 'presence' would be among us. Our bodies would stiffen automatically. One child would receive the full weight of his tongue. 'Where is all the gratitude after all I have done for you? How are you going to get on in the world idling about like this? You will certainly end up in a factory!' And the litany of our sins erupted from his irritated nerves. The ranks closed: it was him versus us. A vicious circle was created in which we were all trapped. He went on justifying his lonely anger by criticising us. His moral arithmetic was simple: we owed him everything, we returned him nothing. Instead of the natural language of love and affection, he could find only the chill language of duty and obligation, which has a profoundly withering effect on the emotions.

Being met with rebellious silence, he grew more and more angry and unfair as if driven on by some terrible inner need to make himself felt. We, being children, did not understand his state but, like all children, we knew what we felt. We knew that in his more tempestuous moments, we hated him with a hatred all the more violent because it was helpless. He was a stranger to us, a stranger whom we feared. Had he been able to take us into his confidence, admit his bad temper (could a Victorian father ever do this?), talk to us as a friend rather than as an enemy, how different all our lives would have been. But that was to ask for the impossible. Like all of us, he was imprisoned inside the limits of his own nature. We were victims of a victim.

When I was born, my father was forty-seven years of age. He had lost his mother when he was seven and she forty-two. He was to lose his own wife when she was also forty-two (I early developed an obsessive fear that I, too, would die at this age). His father was a deeply religious reformed presbyterian, a brand of religion brought to Ulster from Scotland by the covenanters, passionate men who in the seventeenth century refused to accept the Anglican Prayer Book forced on them by Charles I. They made a covenant to resist to the death all forms of ecclesiastical authority and many of them died for the cause. My father told me of the glumness of his home. The Lord's Day began at six o'clock on Saturday evening and lasted until midnight on Sunday. During that time no washing was allowed, no cooking or cleaning, no shaving, no work or play of any sort. Because the wife was considered subservient to the husband in all things, his mother was sometimes punished for breaking the rules. Hell and Judgement were awful realities to his father, who was obsessed by the question of Election and Grace. Would he be one of the 144,000 Elect promised in the Old Testament? My father told me that, as a boy, he was terrified lest the ground should open up in front of him and swallow him up in Hell for ever. (Both Charlotte Brontë and Lord Byron were early exposed to this Calvinist religion, Charlotte by her aunt Branwell and Byron by his Scottish nurse; in low moments of their lives, their imaginations were overwhelmed by this terror of Hell and Judgement.)

My father was the youngest of four children of a second family (his father's first wife had died young). He loved his delicate mother and was, he said, her favourite child. The tenderness lacking in the household she lavished on him. She was often ill and he hung about her sickroom just to be with her. One day, being unusually fretful, she called him to her and told him to run to his father and ask him for a penny to buy 'a pennyworth of sweet milk for his mother'. Although afraid of his father, he summoned up his courage. To his surprise, his father gave him the penny without a word, and he brought the milk quickly back to his mother, who sat up in bed and drank it down greedily. As he came home from school the following day, he saw a crowd of people gathered around his front door. A neighbour stepped out, pulled him into her house and said, 'Your mother is very sick today and cannot have a small boy making a noise.' An awful fear seized him. Next day he ran into the street and saw a line of men moving along the road. Too small to see over the men's heads, he bent low and peered through their legs. He saw his father with several other men carrying a long box on their shoulders. His heart broke. He knew he would never see his mother again. 'That was the most terrible thing that ever happened to me in the whole of my life,' he told me on his deathbed, 'and I have never been the same since.' Was he offering me an explanation of his character? Strangely, history repeated itself. The night before he died in my house he asked me for a glass of milk. I brought it to him and held it to his lips. Although extremely weak and emaciated, he sat up vigorously and drank it down greedily. The next morning he died.

My father left school at fourteen and was put to work on a farm. Quick and intelligent, he was soon helping with the farm accounts. His father was well pleased with him. But he had not forgotten his burning ambition to join the Royal Navy. His father forbade it. The minister of religion was brought in to dissuade him, but it was useless. At sixteen, with his father's reluctant consent, he crossed the narrow peninsula between Newtownards and Donaghadee and joined the Royal Navy as a second-class boy at sixpence a week. He was posted to Rosyth, near Edinburgh, to be trained on a sailing ship and there he underwent a discipline so harsh and strict as to be unthinkable now. At sea when bad weather impended, sailors had to go aloft and, standing on ropes under the yards, had to lean over in gale force winds and gather up the whipping sails, a painful operation as their nails were often broken off by the strong canvas. On a few occasions he saw his companions fall to their deaths on the deck below. He described how the ship's company was forced to stand to attention while strokes of the lash were administered for minor offences: 'I saw bits of skin and hair flying through the air as the lash fell.' Food was very poor: 'We turned the bread over and knocked the insects out of it.' Conditions were uncomfortable and unhygienic: 'We lay in our hammocks and knocked the rats off the ropes.' And so it was until Churchill was made First Lord of the Admiralty and everything changed for the better for the ordinary sailor: 'A great man, Churchill!' My father was so affected by the cruel discipline and so impressed by Churchill's reforms that he covenanted a small portion of his naval pension to Churchill's estate.

He talked very little about his life at sea when we were children and we never wanted to ask him about it. All that remained of his naval past was kept shut up in his bedroom as if he alone inhabited the world of memories from which his children were excluded. The white ensign from his last ship lay carefully folded in a drawer of his naval chest together with his telescope, his medals (brought out every Armistice Day), his picture, young and handsome in naval uniform, a sketch showing him laughing and cavorting with a big scissors and a roll of bunting, and his naval record on a large piece of folded vellum with the name of each ship on which he served, length of service, remarks on ability ('superb') and conduct ('very good'), each signed by the captain. It might all have been a fairy story, so little reality had it for us in the Dublin of an independent Ireland where the British Navy did not exist.

He had nothing but himself to rely on in the navy, his health, his wits, his will. He was haunted by the thought of losing them in old age and thus losing his precious independence. He did not believe that tenderness in his children would rescue him when he was helpless in old age or ill-health, and sadly it took until the last few months of his life for him to know he was wrong. He had a great sense of achievement in his life at sea. He had enjoyed it to the full when Britannia ruled the waves and sailors were paid in golden guineas. He had been in danger many times. Swept off the bridge of his ship into the Baltic Sea by a huge wave, he nearly lost his life in the freezing water. The ship searched for him in the darkness and found him after an hour. He was wrapped in warm blankets and lay in his bunk for a fortnight unable to speak, his vocal cords paralysed. He had been in the thick of the Battle of Jutland in 1916 when his warship, the *Erin*, stood fourth in the line of battleships. Amidst the day-long pounding of the guns from both sides, the clamour, the cries of the wounded, the dense smoke, he had had an almost impossible task keeping up communications with Admiral Jellicoe's flagship. He told me how, at the end of that terrible day, darkness fell and all was quiet. The German ships, it was thought, were hemmed in. 'When dawn broke the next day, we looked out and behold, there was not one German ship in sight. We had let them get away!'

Fourteen years later, he was in need again of his wits, his health and his strength of will. Overseeing his five children while at the same time doing a job he disliked stretched his nervous system to the limit. The lack of trust, the willingness to blame, the injustice of his accusations hurt us most. Any attempt to defend ourselves only made matters worse, but as spirited children we did defend ourselves, outraged by these accusations. The heated exchanges which followed, the turbulence of mind, put me in particular into a state of nervous agitation which troubled me for hours and days afterwards and kept me from sleep at night. I determined to run away, to escape, somewhere, anywhere, only to fall back, helpless. I had no relations to run to, I was in the complete power of my father. This helplessness outraged me: it was unjust, it was wrong.

JANE EYRE
AND THE LIFE OF THE FEELINGS

When I was fourteen years old I read a book which strangely mirrored much of my own situation: it was *Jane Eyre* by Charlotte Brontë. I was overwhelmed by the power and intensity of the writing. In this passion-filled book I read of the helplessness and burning sense of injustice of a young girl at the hands of adults. I read the early chapters with total recognition. They gave a name to those feelings which boiled up in me when my father attacked me without cause. Jane Eyre, orphan of a poor clergyman, had come to live with her dead uncle's wife, Mrs Reed, and her three children. She was not beautiful like the conventional heroine but plain, small and penniless. I could sympathise with that. She tells her own story in the book as I am telling mine.

The opening paragraphs convey her bleak unhappiness.

There was no possibility of taking a walk that day. We had been wandering indeed in the leafless shrubbery an hour in the morning; but since dinner (Mrs Reed, when there was no company, dined early) the cold winter wind had brought with it clouds so sombre, and a rain so penetrating, that further out-door exercise was now out of the question.

I was glad of it: I never liked long walks, especially on chilly afternoons: dreadful to me was the coming home in the raw twilight, with nipped fingers and toes, and a heart saddened by the chidings of Bessie, the nurse, and humbled by the consciousness of my physical inferiority to Eliza, John and

Georgiana Reed.

The said Eliza, John, and Georgiana were now clustered round their mama in the drawing-room: she lay reclined on a sofa by the fireside, and with her darlings about her (for the time neither quarrelling nor crying) looked perfectly happy. Me, she had dispensed from joining the group; saying, 'She regretted to be under the necessity of keeping me at a distance; but that until she heard from Bessie, and could discover by her own observation that I was endeavouring in good earnest to acquire a more sociable and childlike disposition, a more attractive and sprightly manner, – something lighter, franker, more natural as it were – she really must exclude me from privileges intended only for contented, happy, little children.'

'What does Bessie say I have done?' I asked.

'Jane, I don't like cavillers or questioners: besides, there is something truly forbidding in a child taking up her elders in that manner. Be seated somewhere; and until you can speak pleasantly, remain silent.'

There is a chill in the little girl's heart. The words poetically suggest her desolation. The 'leafless shrubbery', the 'cold winter wind', 'clouds so sombre, and a rain so penetrating', a 'heart saddened by the chidings of Bessie, the nurse'. She takes refuge in a book – just as I did – to escape present misery. All at once a hand descends upon her – I recognised the shock to the nerves of the suddenness of the attack – that of her fourteen-year-old cousin, John Reed.

'What were you doing behind the curtain?' he asked.

'I was reading.'

'Shew the book.'

I returned to the window and fetched it thence.

'You have no business to take our books; you are only a dependant, mama says; you have no money; your father left you none; you ought to beg, and not to live here with gentlemen's children like us . . .'

He lifts his hand and strikes Jane. In a fury of rage she rushes at him.

'Dear! dear! What a fury to fly at Master John!'

'Did ever anybody see such a picture of passion!'

> Then Mrs Reed subjoined:– 'Take her away to the red-room, and lock her in there!' Four hands were immediately laid upon me, and I was borne upstairs.

She is thrown into the very room where her uncle had only recently been laid out in death, and faints with terror.

I thrilled to Jane's spirit. The passive verbs 'were laid' and 'I was borne' suggest the unavoidable force of the adult world which carried her along against her will, and 'the picture of passion' suggests the inner, unquenchable spirit which resisted. The combination of helplessness and rebellion I knew well.

> 'You ought to be aware, Miss, that you are under obligations to Mrs Reed: she keeps you: if she were to turn you off you would have to go to the poorhouse.'

My father threatened me with the factory floor, and idle as his threat undoubtedly was, I believed him. It seemed that I was to be grateful, like Jane, for being born and kept in existence.

> No severe or prolonged bodily illness followed this incident of the red-room: it only gave my nerves a shock, of which I feel the reverberation to this day. Yes, Mrs Reed, to you I owe some fearful pangs of mental suffering. But I ought to forgive you, for you knew not what you did: while rending my heart-strings, you thought you were only up-rooting my bad propensities.

I knew about 'bad propensities'. We learned about them in our catechism at Sunday School. We repeated that we had 'renounced the Devil and all his works and all the sinful lusts of the flesh'. I liked the sound of 'renounce the Devil and all his works'. The phrase tripped nicely off the tongue, and its balanced rhythm made it easy to remember. As for 'sinful lusts of the flesh', I did not know what they were and was not even curious to find out. Our business was to learn the phrases by heart and to repeat them. It was received wisdom and we were happy to receive it. We were, we were told, 'born into sin', but by some magical transmogrification we had been 'born again into righteousness through Jesus Christ our Lord'. The trouble was that parents and teachers did not seem to believe that we were born again. It seemed that in many cases baptism had not worked and that 'bad propensities' were still lurking inside us, bold and eager to assert themselves. Children had to be carefully watched, severely controlled and punished when necessary for the good of their immortal souls. This view was widely held. My father was always alert to the possibility of criminal propensities in his children. If Frank was caught playing cards for pennies, he was certainly on the downward path to perdition, and if Hughie was caught out in a small lie, he would certainly end up in gaol. We hated this lack of faith in us.

Dickens knew how prevalent was this attitude to children. He was appalled by it, seeing it as an insult to human dignity. He knew that unprotected children in Victorian England, orphaned by maternal death, illegitimacy, crime, disease and poverty, were particularly suspected of every kind of evil leaning. His novels are crowded with such children for England was crowded with them too: orphans of the poor, of mothers who died in childbirth or of disease. Oliver Twist is discovered in the workhouse; the illegitimate Esther in *Bleak House* is adopted by an odious and hard aunt; David Copperfield is a victim of a cruel stepfather at seven years of age; and the orphan, Pip, in *Great Expectations* is 'brought up by hand' by Mrs Gargery, his sister.

She gives dramatic expression to this attitude:

'Where have you been, you young monkey?' . . .

'I have only been to the churchyard,' said I from my stool, crying and rubbing myself [she has beaten him].

'Churchyard!' repeated my sister. 'If it warn't for me you'd have been to the churchyard long ago, and stayed there. Who brought you up by hand?'

'You did,' said I.

'And why did I do it, I should like to know?' exclaimed my sister.

I whimpered, 'I don't know.'

'I don't!' said my sister. 'I'd never do it again! I know that. I may truly say that I've never had this apron off since born you were.'

Pip is made to feel guilty for having been born, not only by his sister but by society as a whole. 'As for me I was always treated as if I had insisted on being born against the dictates of reason, religion and morality and against the dissuading arguments of my best friends.' The criminal, Magwitch, of whom Pip is terrified, turns out to have been a poor abandoned child who had to steal to live. Dickens had seen, when he worked as a reporter at the Old Bailey, the many children like Magwitch who were brought to the dock to be judged. Into the mouth of the lawyer, Jaggers, he puts the following guarded but deeply compassionate statement in their defence.

'Put the case that he [the lawyer] lived in an atmosphere of evil, and that all he saw of children, was, their being generated in great numbers for certain destruction. Put the case that he often saw children solemnly tried at a criminal bar, where they were held up to be seen; put the case that he habitually knew of their being imprisoned, whipped, transported, neglected, cast out, qualified in all ways for the hangman, and growing up to be hanged.'

Such horrible vistas were held up as possible fates for children in my day.

Jane Eyre suffered as I did from the attitude of profound suspicion and distrust of children. Mrs Reed determines to rid herself of this child so full of 'bad propensities'. She sends for the Reverend Mr Brocklehurst, manager of a charity school for orphaned girls, and tells him, in front of Jane, that she is a liar. The injustice of the accusation rouses Jane to fever pitch.

Speak I must: I had been trodden on severely, and *must* turn: but how? What strength had I to dart retaliation at my antagonist? I gathered my energies and launched them in this blunt sentence —

'I am not deceitful: if I were, I should say I loved *you*; but I declare I do not love you: I dislike you the worst of anybody in the world except John Reed; and this book about the Liar, you may give to your girl, Georgiana, for it is she who tells lies, and not I.'

Mrs Reed's hands lay still on her work inactive: her eye of ice continued to dwell freezingly on mine.

'What more have you to say?' she asked, rather in the tone in which a person might address an opponent of adult age than such as is ordinarily used to a child.

That eye of hers, that voice stirred every antipathy I had. Shaking from head to foot, thrilled with ungovernable excitement, I continued –

'I am glad you are no relation of mine: I will never call you aunt again as long as I live. I will never come to see you when I am grown up; and if any one asks me how I liked you, and how you treated me, I will say the very thought of you makes me sick, and that you treated me with miserable cruelty.'

'How dare you affirm that, Jane Eyre?'

'How dare I, Mrs Reed? How dare I? Because it is the *truth*. You think I have no feelings, and that I can do without one bit of love or kindness; but I cannot live so: and you have no pity. I shall remember how you thrust me back – roughly and violently thrust me back – into the red-room, and locked me up there, to my dying day; though I was in agony, though I cried out, while suffocating with distress, "Have mercy! Have mercy, aunt Reed!" And that punishment you made me suffer because your wicked boy struck me – knocked me down for nothing. I will tell anybody who asks me questions this exact tale. People think you a good woman, but you are bad, hard-hearted. *You* are deceitful!'

Ere I had finished this reply, my soul began to expand, to exult, with the strangest sense of freedom, of triumph, I ever felt. It seemed as if an invisible bond had burst, and that I had struggled out into unhoped-for liberty. Not without cause was this sentiment: Mrs Reed looked frightened; her work had slipped from her knee; she was lifting up her hands, rocking herself to and fro, and even twisting her face as if she would cry.

'Jane, you are under a mistake: what is the matter with you? Why do you tremble so violently? Would you like to drink some water?'

'No, Mrs Reed.'

'Is there anything else you wish for, Jane? I assure you, I desire to be your friend.'

'Not you. You told Mr Brocklehurst I had a bad character, a deceitful disposition; and I'll let everybody at Lowood know what you are, and what you have done.'

'Jane, you don't understand these things: children must be corrected for their faults.'

'Deceit is not my fault!' I cried out in a savage, high voice.

'But you are passionate, Jane, that you must allow; and now return to the nursery – there's a dear – and lie down a little.'

'I am not your dear; I cannot lie down: send me to school soon, Mrs Reed, for I hate to live here.'

'I will indeed send her to school, soon,' murmured Mrs Reed, *sotto voce*; and gathering up her work, she abruptly quitted the apartment.

I was left there alone – winner of the field. It was the hardest battle I had fought, and the first victory I had gained . . .

Quarrels, battles, victories – here was fighting talk I could thrill to! I was with Jane against the whole world! Once or twice I had stood up to my father when taunted with my dependence, as Jane had stood up to Mrs Reed. I had cried out in a high, frenzied voice, 'I didn't ask to be born!' And after that supreme effort my father had grown calmer, less aggressive, as if startled by my unexpected outburst. Jane describes the effect of these turbulent emotions on mind and body:

> But this fierce pleasure subsided in me as fast as did the acceler-ated throb of my pulses. A child cannot quarrel with its elders, as I had done – cannot give its furious feelings uncontrolled play, as I had given mine – without experiencing afterwards the pang of remorse and the chill of reaction.

Just so had my own beating heart subsided, giving place to dread feelings of guilt and remorse, self-accusation and shame, an inevi-table drop in the emotional temperature after such a violent erup-tion. Then how prostrate I was, how flattened, all my energies drained away, sick at heart, my emotions all in a turmoil! Then I knew, like Jane, 'the dreariness of my hated and hating position'. Against all my inclinations, I was being forced to utter hateful words, to feel hateful emotions, to seethe with hate when what I wanted more than anything in the world was to love and be loved. These mental battles drained me of all confidence in myself and to this day, I always blame myself for disagreements.

This sapping succession of emotions which overpower and confuse us is as well known to adults as to children, then as now. It is Charlotte Brontë who brings them into consciousness, clarifies and identifies them. It is much harder to understand our feelings than our thoughts and much harder to be honest about them. Brontë does not analyse these feelings or talk about them as would a psychologist; she brings them living before us on the page so that we can imagine them ourselves. In this way she not only enables us to imagine experiences which may be other than our own but helps us more fully to register our own experience and therefore to understand it. We have not all the same eye and ear and heart, and we have not all the same ability to imagine our own experience fully. We may be limited by lack of attention, lack of imagination, over-absorption in justifying ourselves, or by passion, anger, revenge, jealousy. We see what we are able to see, feel what we are able to feel, what is in our nature to see and feel. We make sense of ourselves in the ways possible to us with the equipment we have. It is the great creative writer who has this attention and this imagination in the highest degree. And it is the creative writer who can find the means of expressing it and can find the most perfect representation to delight and satisfy us.

I was caught up in Jane's story. What would happen to her? What would happen to me? My story, like Jane's, was yet to unfold and I was secretly writing several versions of it in my head. We all love stories, meaningful, connected, self-contained sequences of events, and we like to see our own life as meaningful in this way. If we are under an illusion in doing this, as some writers would have us believe, it is a universal one. Like a character in a novel, we come on stage in our life with a set of given characteristics, man/woman, beautiful/plain, healthy/fragile, rich/poor, intelligent/dull, and with our individual 'cultural baggage'. Our part is set in motion and the story unfolds. If our life is like a novel so does the novel copy life. The plot, that sequence of connected actions or events into which the novelist puts her characters, is like the circumstances of our life. Do we ourselves cause these circumstances to happen (free will) or do they cause us to be the way we are (fate)? Are we 'captains of our soul and masters of our fate'? Or are we culturally and genetically determined? Are we a mixture of both?

Charlotte Brontë has a purpose in this plot; it is to choose situations which will bring Jane into direct confrontation with powerful male figures so that she can challenge them and reveal a truth about human relations (free will). After John Reed comes Mr Brocklehurst. Contemporary opinion would have admired him as a charitable, Christian man dedicated to the good of orphaned girls, but Brontë, through Jane, exposes him ruthlessly as a bully, a hypocrite and a fraud. To expose a priest or a clergyman like this in my time, let alone one hundred years earlier, was well-nigh unthinkable. Charlotte Brontë's father was an Anglican priest and she herself a fervent Christian, but she knew how 'to discriminate the clergy from the man' (*Jane Eyre*). No wonder the book shocked.

The experience which Jane undergoes at the hands of Mr Brocklehurst is substantially what Charlotte and her three sisters underwent at Cowan Bridge School at the hands of the Reverend Carus Wilson. Patrick Brontë decided, after the early death of his wife, to send his girls to this subsidised church school. No one better than he to understand the value of education: he, a poor boy, one of ten children on a small Ulster farm, had, by his own initiative, got the education necessary to take him to Cambridge and a university degree. He took pains to make all his children, his five daughters and one son, acquainted at an early age with literature, painting, music and political thought. But he did not know until it was too late that the regime at Cowan Bridge was so dreadful that his two eldest daughters, Maria and Elizabeth, eleven and ten respectively, had developed typhoid and tuberculosis. Maria died in the school and Elizabeth died shortly after being brought home. Charlotte and Emily were withdrawn just in time to save them from a similar fate. We can imagine with what satisfaction Charlotte describes the school in *Jane Eyre*.

The starving girls had been served porridge for breakfast, so burned as to be inedible. The headmistress, Miss Temple (the holy association of her name is not accidental), had allowed them bread and cheese instead. The Reverend Mr Brocklehurst, on his daily visit, hears of this incident and bursts into sanctimonious rage.

'Madam, allow me an instant. You are aware that my plan in bringing up these girls is, not to accustom them to habits of luxury and indulgence, but to render them hardy, patient, self-denying. Should any little accidental disappointment of the appetite occur, such as the spoiling of a meal, the under or the over-dressing of a dish, the incident ought not to be neutralised by replacing with something more delicate the comfort lost, thus pampering the body and obviating the aim of this institution; it ought to be improved to the spiritual edification of the pupils, by encouraging them to evince fortitude under the temporary privation. A brief address on those occasions would not be mistimed, wherein a judicious instructor would take the opportunity of referring to the sufferings of the primitive Christians; to the torments of martyrs; to the exhortations of our Blessed Lord himself, calling upon His disciples to take up their cross and follow Him; to His warnings that man shall not live by bread alone, but by every word that proceedeth out of the mouth of God; to His divine consolations, "if ye suffer hunger or thirst for My sake, happy are ye." Oh, madam, when you put bread and cheese, instead of burnt porridge, into these children's mouths, you may indeed feed their vile bodies, but you little think how you starve their immortal souls!'

Poverty and self-suppression are good for the souls of others while he, his wife and children are well clad and fed. Miss Temple attempts a mild justification of her act. This brings on a near-hysterical outburst from the reverend gentleman:

'Miss Temple, Miss Temple, what – *what* is that girl with curled hair? Red hair, ma'am, curled – curled all over?' And extending his cane he pointed to the awful object, his hand shaking as he did so.

'It is Julia Severn,' replied Miss Temple very quietly.

'Julia Severn, ma'am! And why has she, or any other, curled hair? Why, in defiance of every precept and principle of this house, does she conform to the world so openly – here in an evangelical, charitable establishment – as to wear her hair one mass of curls?'

'Julia's hair curls naturally,' returned Miss Temple, still more quietly.

'Naturally! Yes, but we are not to conform to nature. I wish these girls to be the children of Grace: and why that abundance? I have again and again intimated that I desire the hair to be arranged closely, modestly, plainly. Miss Temple, that girl's hair must be cut off entirely; I will send a barber tomorrow: and I see others who have far too much of the excrescence – that tall girl, tell her to turn round. Tell all the first form to rise up and direct their faces to the wall.'

Miss Temple passed her handkerchief over her lips, as if to smooth away the involuntary smile that curled them; she gave the order, however, and when the first class could take in what was required of them, they obeyed. Leaning a little back on my bench, I could see the looks and grimaces with which they commented on this manoeuvre: it was a pity Mr Brocklehurst could not see them too; he would perhaps have felt that, whatever he might do with the outside of the cup and platter, the inside was further beyond his interference than he imagined.

He scrutinised the reverse of these living medals some five minutes, then pronounced sentence. These words fell like the knell of doom:–

'All these top-knots must be cut off.'

Miss Temple seemed to remonstrate.

'Madam,' he pursued, 'I have a Master to serve whose kingdom is not of this world: my mission is to mortify in these girls the lusts of the flesh; to teach them to clothe themselves with shame-facedness and sobriety, not with braided hair and costly apparel; and each of the young persons before us has a string of hair twisted in plaits which vanity itself might have woven: these, I repeat, must be cut off...'

He must have total power over them; he becomes enraged by even the slightest opposition to his will, and the hypocrite justifies his domination of these helpless women and girls by invoking the sanction of religion, just as my father invoked the notions of 'duty' and 'obligation'. Charlotte Brontë is very daring here: she implies that men put women under severe restrictions so as to avoid being tempted by their feminine charms. It is women who have to pay the price for men's weakness in loss of liberty and self-expression. At this time (1847) and for a hundred years afterwards, the ideal for women was submissiveness, docility and self-sacrifice. Here is a woman challenging this ideal as a self-interested male fiction.

The Brontë sisters inherited this role model for women in their lives if not in their writing. Marriage was the most honourable goal for women. It was their only hope of security. Security if not independence was, perhaps, in Jane Austen's phrase, 'the pleasantest preservative from want'. If a woman was well connected, beautiful and rich she could bargain for a husband; but the Brontës were none of these. Their high level of education was a disadvantage in a society where women were expected to be submissive and clinging. The only course open to them was governessing and it was what their father realistically hoped for them. For Branwell, the son, it was different. He was a man and could hope to enter the professions. He could do something in the world, unlike the girls. As a talented artist, he was the hope of the family, a hope that turned into bitter disappointment when he ruined himself with drink and drugs. Charlotte and Anne became governesses, and the mortifications, servitude, stultifying loneliness and penury of that position were exposed by Anne in her novel *Agnes Grey* and by Charlotte in *Villette*. Charlotte wrote: 'I see more clearly than ever that a private governess has no existence, is not considered as a living, rational human being.' They knew every patronising tone, every nuance of contempt of that position.

Charlotte longed for colour, variety, hope and meaning in her life. Her imagination pictured her life so and her sense of natural justice demanded it. Jane Eyre declares roundly 'to be alive is to know passion', but Charlotte found only self-suppression and rejection. She had to bow her passionate heart to the domestic yoke at Haworth Rectory, had to learn to subdue her fiery temper, had to endure the death of her mother, four sisters and brother, and to fall passionately in love – she a devout protestant – with a married man, a foreigner and a catholic, who did not return her passion. Finally, at thirty-nine years of age, she married (without love) her father's curate and died nine months later in sickness and pregnancy. Her friend, Mary Taylor, called her life 'a living nightmare of poverty and self-suppression'. What Charlotte could not say publicly, what she could not make happen in her life, she put into *Jane Eyre*.

It was her own powerlessness as a woman that gave her an acute instinct for discerning the will to power in others. In *Jane Eyre* the heroine does exactly this and resists it. Later in my life, I was to recognise something of it in my father. Jane, shamed and humiliated by Mr Brocklehurst and before the assembled school, longs to die. It is the women who believe in her and support her. (Thomas Hardy, in his novel *Tess of the D'Urbervilles*, gives the same integrity of feeling to the women; it is they who rally round the seduced Tess while it is the men who use her and blame her.)

Eight years later we find Jane installed as a governess in a happy home with a lovable pupil. That is as much as she could have hoped for in her position. But Jane is not satisfied. From the pages comes a great *cri de cœur* for equality of women with men, equality both of feeling and of action. This helped to make the book the most revolutionary in nineteenth-century England and caused it to be censored and abridged right up to the Second World War. It made me into a secret revolutionary from that time on.

Anybody may blame me who likes, when I add further, that, now and then, when I took a walk by myself in the grounds; when I went down to the gates and looked through them along the road; or when, while Adèle played with her nurse, and Mrs Fairfax made jellies in the store-room, I climbed the three staircases, raised the trap-door of the attic, and having reached the leads, looked out afar over sequestered field and hill, and along dim skyline – that then I longed for a power of vision which might overpass that limit; which might reach the busy world, towns, regions full of life I had heard of but never seen; that then I desired more of practical experience than I possessed; more of intercourse with my kind, of acquaintance with variety of character, than was here within my reach. I valued what was good in Mrs Fairfax, and what was good in Adèle; but I believed in the existence of other and more vivid kinds of goodness, and what I believed in I wished to behold.

Who blames me? Many, no doubt; and I shall be called discontented. I could not help it: the restlessness was in my nature; it agitated me to pain sometimes. Then my sole relief was to walk along the corridor of the third story, backwards and forwards, safe in the silence and solitude of the spot, and allow my mind's eye to dwell on whatever bright visions rose before it – and, certainly, they were many and glowing; to let my heart be heaved by the exultant movement, which, while it swelled it in trouble, expanded it with life; and, best of all, to open my inward ear to a tale that was never ended – a tale my imagination created, and narrated continuously; quickened with all of incident, life, fire, feeling, that I desired and had not in my actual existence.

It is in vain to say human beings ought to be satisfied with tranquillity: they must have action; and they will make it if they cannot find it. Millions are condemned to a stiller doom than mine, and millions are in silent revolt against their lot. Nobody knows how many rebellions besides political rebellions ferment in the masses of life which people earth. Women are supposed to be very calm generally: but women feel just as men feel; they need exercise for their faculties, and a field for their efforts as much as their brothers do; they suffer from too rigid a constraint, too absolute a stagnation, precisely as men would suffer; and it is narrow-minded in their more privileged fellow-creatures to say that they ought to confine themselves to making puddings and knitting stockings, to playing on the piano and embroidering bags. It is thoughtless to condemn them or laugh at them, if they seek to do more or learn more than custom has pronounced necessary for their sex.

The reviewers were shocked.

I followed the love story in *Jane Eyre* with passionate interest. I fell in love with Rochester, the hero (I now think him the weakest part of the book, a Byronic dream-fiction of the emotion-starved Charlotte). A wealthy, powerful man of the world, he employs Jane as a governess to his ward. Jane must again face an unequal match. She has to make him recognise her for what she is, recognise her moral courage, her independent spirit, her unshakable belief in herself. In conversation after conversation, they test each other, exploring each other's personalities and feelings. She rejects every touch of patronage; she will not be treated as an inferior. He comes to love this 'indomitable spirit'; and she, who suspects all display of spurious authority in the male, comes paradoxically to have a sumptuous delight in his 'native pith and power' – his natural authority. By a melodramatic turn of the plot (calculated to test Jane), she discovers that he is married already, that his wife is mad and locked away. She goes through a delirium of horror and confusion before forcing herself to turn down what she most longs for:

> '*I* care for myself ... I will respect myself. I will keep the law given by God; sanctioned by man ... Laws and principles are not for the times when there is no temptation: they are for such moments as this, when body and soul rise in mutiny against their rigour.'

For the modern reader, of course, this can seem priggish. Jane flies across the moors, gets lost in their wilderness, and, when almost at death's door, is rescued by two sisters and their brother, the Reverend St John Rivers. She is again confronted with a strong male personality and the quiet but inexorable will to power and domination. Erudite and handsome, St John Rivers has so much authority in himself that the independent Jane quickly falls under his spell. 'When he said go, I went, come, I came, do this, I did it.' This is the same magnetic force which compels hundreds of intelligent people willingly to give up their liberty of mind to another. Jane says:

> I was tempted to cease struggling with him, to rush down the torrent of his will into the gulf of his existence and there to lose my own.

The spell freezes her, 'My iron shroud contracted round me ...' She tries to understand the nature of this power which takes away her independence of mind.

He offers her marriage and a life of shared self-sacrifice in the mission field. Is he a heroic Christian man? Is this the love, the action, her nature craved for? She searches deep in his personality and slowly, very slowly, is able to surprise his real nature. Far from being a noble idealist, he burns with a fierce ambition to quit his monotonous life as a parish priest and to find the power his nature craves in the mission field. Under the mask of self-control, he is a ruthless egoist who believes himself a Christian hero. Who better for him to dominate, to make feel his power, than this independent, intelligent woman? She offers to go with him as his sister but he will have none of this. Jane is surprisingly frank:

'... the very name of love is an apple of discord between us. If the reality were required, what should we do? How should we feel?'

Thousands of women have had to deal silently with this situation. Rivers insists on marriage. 'I want a wife: the sole helpmeet I can influence efficiently in life, and retain absolutely till death.' This gives a new meaning to the marriage bond.

Like Mr Brocklehurst, he invokes Scripture to blackmail her. But she sees that he wants to prevent her feeling pleasure or tenderness because he cannot feel them himself. This is a sad but common reaction. Was there a shade of my father here? She finally sees that what he really wants is to subdue her nature, to change it, to violate her personality, subtly, by stealth, unknown to her. This for Charlotte Brontë is total moral corruption. Once Jane sees through this luster after power, she can resist him. She returns to Rochester whom she finds blinded by a fire which has conveniently killed his wife. By the grace of Charlotte Brontë, Jane has inherited money and found a family (the Rivers turn out to be cousins) and now, when there is no way in which Rochester can be more equal than herself, she marries him.

The tonic administered by Jane Eyre worked upon me. There and then I determined to work hard at school and to earn money, never to be dependent on fathers, brothers, husbands. No matter that the book was written one hundred years before, she spoke to me more powerfully than anyone I knew around me. For years I wanted to be like her. Was I intelligent? I doubted it. Was I independent? I was sure I was. I wanted to be like Jane in everything, even wishing myself *very* plain so that my spirit might shine through the more. When I was older and studied the book, I became more aware of the subtleties in the play of power in human relationships, the will to dominate which parades as something else and which Charlotte Brontë diagnoses so well. But that is another story.

THE CATHOLIC
AND PROTESTANT DIVIDE

M y whole childhood and youth, up to twenty-five years of age, was passed in the catholic–protestant divide and I was deeply marked by it. When I married and went to live in England, I knew, like most young Irish people of my time, that, as like as not, I would be unable to return permanently to live in Ireland because there were so few jobs to come back to. It was an assumption that everybody lived with and accepted more or less philosophically. It was the way things were. 'She's over the water working' was commonly on the lips of Irish parents. I little thought that fate would bring me back to Ireland after eight years 'over the water' and to a corner of it where the fires of the religious feud were still smoulder-ing and were to burst into a conflagration nine years later in 1969. This conflagration has blazed for thirty years and over 3,000 people have been consumed by it. We have now arrived at a provisional peace settlement; there may be no more physical violence but it will be a long time before the submerged mental violence of both sides is extinguished.

My three children have been brought up in Northern Ireland, gone to school, made friends and lived out the first eighteen years of their lives well aware of the Troubles around them. My two boys went to a city centre school where the daily music coming through the classroom windows was the scream of ambulance sirens and the heavy thud of exploding bombs. Often, they had to walk the two miles home from school because the buses had been suspended or burned out or a nearby building had been blown up and the streets were strewn with broken glass and pieces of brick. All this was such a regular occurrence that it hardly caused comment. I naturally worried about my children's safety but thought it best not to make them anxious about it so that they could lead as normal a life as possible. They told me later that they were not harmed; their real preoccupations lay elsewhere.

When I came to live in 'the Black North', as it was called in the South of Ireland, I came with all the prejudices about the place which exist in the southern mind. No one actually told you how the North was 'black' but you knew it just as you knew that the Chinese were yellow. The North was black with shipyards, black with smoking factory chimneys, black with smoke from the myriad working-class homes packed close together in rows. Dublin, by contrast, was a fine, handsome city and even the poor lived in big rooms, carved out of what had once been fine Georgian mansions. The North was black, too, with dour presbyterians, black with their cheerlessness and lack of laughter and that absence of *joie de vivre* which was the southerner's speciality. And think of the northern Sunday! The swings were tied up on the Sabbath in case the children might enjoy themselves, cinemas were closed, sport was frowned on and people remained indoors all day long, reading their Bibles! 'Sure, Sunday "up there" must be a terrible day altogether.' And as for scenery, everybody knew that the best in Ireland was to be seen in Galway and Kerry and Cork, and you would have no cause to go north to see the like of it. In all this time I was never made aware that there were catholics in the North who were not happy with their lot under the protestant and unionist dispensation, cut off from their co-religionists in the South by the 1921 border and swept, willy-nilly, into the new state of Northern Ireland, to be penned up there with their unionist foes. Perhaps I was not made aware of it because southern catholics had forgotten their existence...

In Belfast, I found the reality to be very different. True, the religious divide I had known in Dublin existed there, too, but it wore another, more intense face. In 1889, the year of my mother's birth, the protestants of what was later to be the Republic of Ireland made up 25 per cent of the population; by 1926, the year of my own birth, this had fallen to 10 per cent, and by 1968 to 2.5 per cent. By contrast, the northern protestants had remained a steady, obdurate and unyielding 60 per cent of the population of Northern Ireland, living beside the 40 per cent of their catholic neighbours and suspicious of them as a fifth column, ready and willing, they believed, to sell them into a theocratic state where the political and religious liberties they loved so well would be forever extinguished. To Great Britain they would cling, protestant Great Britain, assurer of their liberties. 'Go into a papist state? Better to eat grass!'

I discovered, to my surprise, that there was little sympathy between northern and southern protestants, not even between members of the Church of Ireland north and south of the border. I never met a single presbyterian in Dublin and that culture was completely strange to me. I learned that the nonconformist majority in the North had, in centuries past, nursed a grievance against the established Church of Ireland, which had denied them, as it had catholics, their political rights. The Established Church was seen as smug and snobbish: it smacked of popery; it called itself the 'catholic' church and was ruled by bishops just like the Roman catholics. There were to be 'no bishops in the kirk' for presbyterians; they would rule themselves as they had always done, democratically. That part of the Church of Ireland which existed in the North and to which I belonged seemed less relaxed, more defensive, more anti-Roman than the church I had known in the South.

In 1931, when my mother died, leaving us to the sole formative influence of a passionately free-thinking and humanist father, only fifteen years had passed since the Easter Rising against the British and ten since the Civil War when Ireland was dangerously divided over the conditions of the Treaty with the British. People still talked of those terrible times, of the cruel hangings of the Irish patriots in Kilmainham Gaol, and of the brutal behaviour of the infamous 'Black-and-Tan' British soldiers. The Treaty was still an issue and the question would be asked of someone whether he had been for or against it. This Treaty of 1921 which had given Ireland dominion status within the Commonwealth divided Irish people down the middle. In 1922 Michael Collins's party, which had accepted it, won the general election; the anti-Treaty party of de Valera was not prepared to accept the result and a brutal war broke out between them with atrocities committed by both sides. De Valera's party claimed to represent the legitimate authority of the Irish Republic, but he was forced to end his resistance in 1923. The Northern Ireland question created by the unionists was not solved. In 1932 de Valera won the election and he continued in office until 1948. To everyone's surprise, it was the Prime Minister from the opposing party, John A. Costello, who in 1949 declared Ireland to be a republic. My father, enraged and betrayed, rushed to the British embassy in Dublin to make sure that he was still a British national. As for de Valera, my father could hardly bear the mention of his name and we knew better than to bring it up.

The British occupier had been protestant, the Irish were catholic and so the new nation had indelibly stamped on its face the words 'catholic' Ireland. In 1937 de Valera devised a new constitution for the state: freedom of religion was guaranteed to all (there was no persecution of protestants and, indeed, they lived much as they had lived before, many of them successful professional and business people) but the special position of the catholic church was assured (the 1937 constitution was drawn up in close consultation with Rome: it was granted a special position as 'the guardian of the faith professed by the great majority of its citizens') and claims of sovereignty over the whole island were enshrined in the famous Articles 2 and 3.

With Ireland now a self-governing dominion, a great tide of nationalist and triumphalist sentiment swept through every institution in the land. Pádraig Pearse and de Valera, both deeply conservative catholics, believed in the central control of Rome over the education system: school managers should be members of religious orders; the catholic atmosphere should be cultivated in every subject in the curriculum; it was to be 'a catholic state for a catholic people' (protestant schools were exempt). A drive took place to keep Ireland 'morally pure' and censorship of books was established. This infuriated my father who believed passionately in books as a means of knowledge. 'A crass interference with freedom of choice,' he raged. He set out to smuggle as many banned books as he could from his forays to the North. As it was assumed by everyone that sexual descriptions were the reason for banning books, I was very embarrassed to see Boccaccio's *Decameron* and Joyce's *Ulysses* on my father's bookshelves.

Children and most adults were unaffected by censorship; it was a case of 'what the eye does not see the heart will not grieve for' and we could get what books we knew of on the shelves of the local library. It was later, as a student in Trinity College Dublin, that I came up against it. For us students of French literature, the books of Proust were required reading. We were astonished when we learned that they were 'on the Index' and that we would have to be taken to a special room in the college library to read them. We might be morally contaminated, it seemed, by contact with this great author. Alas, Proust's style was so convoluted and our French so poor that our excitement was short-lived; they need not have bothered censoring him. Trinity College itself, alma mater of Burke, Goldsmith and Beckett, was banned to catholics on pain of excommunication as being too 'liberal' and the few catholics who did go there, usually children of mixed marriages, often found it hard to get a job afterwards. In all my five years as a student and post-graduate student in Trinity, I never met anyone from the catholic National University of Ireland; we might as well have been on different planets for all the encouragement we were given to meet one another. In these interdictions lie many of Ireland's problems, both north and south. Such extreme measures, such obstinate philistinism had already driven Joyce and Beckett out of Ireland to the more liberal catholic Europe. After completing my degree at Trinity, I went to Paris, there to breathe quite a different air.

Language, too, became a political weapon. As English was the language of the imperial occupier, the Irish language must be brought back into its own as the language of the Irish people. In 1926 all primary schools were obliged by law to teach Irish as a compulsory subject and my mother and my Aunt Jenny had to master that difficult language to keep their jobs. My father fulminated against all these measures in what he saw as an oppressive and illiberal state. When, in 1951, a great scandal burst upon the nation, he saw himself thoroughly vindicated in his strictures. A Mother and Child scheme providing free pre- and post-natal services was about to be put through the Dáil by the Minister for Health, Dr Noel Browne (himself catholic-born but married to a protestant). The proposed legislation foundered because of strong clerical opposition to government intervention in this area.

Many people were outraged. So Irish mothers were to get no help? Not if protestant doctors were attending them!

This turn of events in Ireland may be understandable historically but we children were no historians. We did not care about the past; we lived exclusively in the present and we knew that, as protestants, we felt different. Catholic blood seemed to flow in every vein but ours. This confused and unsettled us at a deeply unconscious level for like all children, we wanted to be like everyone else, unnoticed and accepted. This unease was intensified by my father continually fulminating against the church of the land in which we lived. He forbade us to put down roots in this alien soil. We were constantly being asked to be disloyal to the place we lived in. So there we were, a small group of protestants living in the midst of an overwhelmingly conservative, catholic people with a vehemently anti-catholic father from a democratic, presbyterian culture in the North, a free-thinking, agnostic, widely read 'citizen of the world' as he proudly called himself, who found himself in the last place he would have chosen for himself, the Dublin of the 1930s, 1940s and 1950s, where what most irritated him was most concentrated. My mother, mild, affectionate, untravelled, churchgoing, might have sheltered us from his extreme, scorching statements and given us a feeling of rootedness in her own familiar culture. Had they conflicting views on Ireland? Were these the angry voices I heard raised in the kitchen as a young child? Where were we to put down roots? In what soil were we to find nourishment? 'Not here, not here!' said my father. And the grandparents and uncles and aunts, that given order of the family, whose traditions are handed down from one generation to another, from the parent to the child who takes his natural place among them, where were they? The homelands of both sets of parents were *terra incognita* to me, names only in my head. I knew only that Bantry and Belfast were somewhere on the top and bottom of the map of Ireland. Of his own parents in Newtownards, my father never spoke: it was as if he never had a home or habitation there. We were never brought to visit them nor did anyone descend to visit us in Dublin. We dared not ask about a past which my father concealed so absolutely.

Now and then he would vanish for a day or two without telling us where he was going or why. He would reappear, say nothing, and resume his routine as before. His personal life, he was making clear, had nothing to do with his children. We lost all curiosity on the subject and came to the conclusion that 'the North', to which we suspected he had gone, must be a terrible place if he never wanted to talk about it. One day, when he was out, I dared to look into the wardrobe in his room. There, at the bottom, lay a black bowler hat. What could he be doing with that? Hughie told us that he must have taken it to 'the North' to wear in the big Twelfth of July parade. We were amazed: he scarcely ever mentioned the North and never the Orange parade.

At the Diocesan School for Girls, a grammar school run by the Church of Ireland, we spent many hours in the week studying the Irish language. It was full of imagery and poetry and I loved it and was good at it. I loved the old Gaelic script and worked on it for hours, forming the letters with various personal flourishes of my own. Irish culture was also both honoured and practised. We learned Irish dancing and took part in ceilidh competitions in Dublin's Mansion House. We were taught to say the 'Our Father' in Irish and were taken, occasionally, to church services in Irish in Adelaide Road near our school. The great de Valera himself once sent his wife, Síle Bean de Valera, an Irish scholar, to give out the prizes at our prize distribution ceremony. I remember her well, a small, neat, self-effacing woman, sitting beside the protestant archbishop, Dr Gregg. We learned Irish language and history for the state examinations, a subject which could have helped us understand our own Irishness had it been better taught, but the reasons for the Penal Laws were as dry, inflexible and uninspiring as the reasons for the French Revolution; we wrote them in our notebooks, learned them, repeated them and forgot them.

In spite of being good at Irish, I knew in a vague sort of way that I was not the genuine article. Real Irish-lovers wore a *fáinne* (a circle of gold) in their coat lapels to show their true dedication. I knew that they would almost certainly be catholics and that they would not take our Irishness as seriously as their own. No word was said on the subject but we were made to feel that we were only playing at being Irish and were not the real thing. After all, we were protestants. The real lover of Irish learned all school subjects through the Irish language, and 'Are you doing it through the Medium?' was the question sometimes asked by a despairing pupil and sometimes by a triumphalist one. My protestant cousin from west Cork, Nancy Dukelow, was at a protestant school, Coláiste Mobhi, where all subjects were learned through Irish. It was strange to see a protestant girl dedicated to what then seemed a catholic ideal. At sixteen years of age, I moved from the Diocesan School to the prestigious Alexandra College, there to study for the state Leaving Certificate examination. To be successful in that examination, you had to pass in Irish. Fifteen of us entered and only five passed in Irish. I was one of them. I often wondered if the professional prospects of those who failed were blighted. I do not think so; employers were more realistic than the ideologues.

We lived on an island at the Lodge. We were separated from the people outside by locked gates and high walls. We were separated from the people in the hospital below by the fact that they were mad and we were sane; and we were separated from the administrative and medical staff by our inferior social position. We were separated from our poor neighbours by having a better house to live in, better food to eat, better clothes to wear and better schools to go to. Above all, we were separated from them by religion: we were protestants in an overwhelmingly catholic district. Had we lived in one of the wealthier suburbs of Dublin such as Rathgar, Killiney or Dalkey, going to school with our own and coming back to our own, we might well not have noticed the difference.

When I left Mount Brown primary school for the grammar school at the age of eleven, I mixed with protestant girls, most of them of the middle or lower class but living in better parts of Dublin than I did. I had to give my address as 'Street' whereas they lived in 'Parks' and 'Avenues'. If they came among the first in exams their parents gave them watches as presents. They went on family holidays to the seaside at Gorey or Connemara. I was invited to birthday parties in Blackrock and Rathmines but I was ashamed to ask them back to the Lodge. I was in some way ashamed of my own shame but I could not help it in the class-conscious society in which I lived. It was not acceptable as it is now to come from a working-class district. I tried various ruses: 'the Lodge' might pass for a big house standing in its own grounds, or 'St Patrick's' sounded as if it were surrounded by high trees in a wealthy road, not requiring a number. My sister was in a quandary when her boy-friend, who had a car, asked to come and pick her up at home. She walked boldly up the avenue from the hospital as if she were coming from a large house with a lodge at the gate. Her boyfriend, who was to become her husband, told us later that he saw exactly what was going on and laughed heartily at it.

My father had strong socialist convictions and was outraged by any infringement of the brotherhood of man by the power structures of church or state. He was no snob and we were never made to feel superior to the poor around us. He mixed easily with his catholic neighbours and took a pint of Guinness with them daily in Reilly's pub. It was not for social reasons that he forbade me to go down Bow Lane to play; his reasons were religious. He wished to protect his children from being influenced by the mental and moral attitudes of the catholic church, whose ideas and practices he detested. We were young and impressionable; he was safe, we were not. We must be carefully watched in case we slid into undesirable attitudes, laziness, inertia and passivity which dulled all initiative and inhibited progress. He wanted passionately to give us the right start in life, that rigorous discipline, wholesome food and high level of secular education which he believed to be the only means of rescuing us from the deep ignorance into which the ultra-conservative catholicism of his day had plunged its people.

His argument went like this. Catholics had been taught to accept authority in all matters, moral and spiritual, and to question nothing. They were not even trusted to read the Bible for themselves. Their priests encouraged them to remain in deep ignorance so as to increase awe and respect for themselves and their institutions. They were not, as we were, 'free' men and women able to think about problems and come to decisions ourselves. We were responsible for ourselves and to ourselves. No ecclesiastical authority had the right to tell us what to do or think. We were never to forget that our free will was our birthright. My father knew; he was a citizen of the world and had had his mental horizons enlarged by seeing what life was like outside Ireland. Moreover, he had read widely and could judge. Deep in his mind was the conviction that the Reformation was one of the great liberations of human history and that this liberation had not yet been won in Ireland. He would go further: the world would be a better place without any religion at all for its history was very bloody. Catholics had been made supine; they were encouraged to put all adversity down to 'the will of God' whereas it was the will of men that brought about most suffering.

You could see the results of these attitudes in the streets around us. Catholics accepted everything that came to them and made no effort to better themselves. They had no ambition because it had been crushed out of them. All around us you could see decent people who had been reduced to unconscious mental slavery. We might all be poor but the difference between them and us was that they were slaves and we were not. We made our own rules and discipline; indeed such rules were a measure of our personal moral fibre. Protestants observed rules, catholics did not. You could see this self-imposed morality or the absence of it in the way parents conducted themselves in the home. In catholic homes the children ran around till midnight or until they fell down asleep on the floor. Parents could be seen on the streets of Dublin at ten or eleven o'clock at night pushing babies in prams and young children blind with sleep. Protestants ordered these things better. I was put to bed at seven or eight o'clock until I was ten years old (and I bitterly resented it). 'Love them and let them be' was not part of my father's ethic. Being five minutes late for a meal, having dirty hands, borrowing money, laziness, lack of desire to succeed, were the categories of sin best known in our house.

And the catholic church was intent on bringing the protestants, whom it viewed as heretics, over to its faith so that they, too, would become supine. Look at its policy on mixed marriages: the non-catholic partner had to bring up the children as catholics, and the catholic partner had to try to bring the members of the other family over to the faith. This in fact happened three times in our family. My sister was the first to fall in love with and marry a catholic. Her future husband was obliged to seek his bishop's permission for such a doubtful marriage. The bishop was the formidable and deeply conservative Bishop of Galway, popularly known as 'Cross Michael' because of his episcopal signature, Michael†, and because of the cross conservatism of his temper. He questioned the 23-year-old catholic man in front of him and asked him why he, a university graduate, had not found a good catholic girl to marry in the catholic university. Billy decided then and there that 'these celibate career churchmen do not know anything of the experience called love'. The bishop questioned him on the strength of his faith, to which the thoughtful Billy replied that it would do until he found a better one. The reply did not help his cause. At the end of the interview, Bishop Browne extended his hand adorned with the episcopal ring to be kissed in the usual kneeling manner, but Billy merely shook it, thus strengthening the impression in the bishop's mind that he was not a good catholic. My father and I attended the marriage service in St Joseph's church in Galway. The ceremony was performed not in the sanctuary, as was usual, but at its steps. There was neither mass nor papal blessing and the parish priest refused to attend the reception afterwards.

After two years of marriage, my sister became a catholic, her conversion owing nothing to her husband's influence, contrary to my father's suspicions. From that time, he kept a stricter eye on me, even forbidding me at one time to go near my sister's home, and quarrels and disputes broke out continually between us because of this prohibition. 'She is very friendly with the jesuits; they are notorious schemers and will try to get you in.' I felt very important: imagine men who had been seventeen years in training trying to convert a mere schoolgirl like me! When I met a jesuit in my sister's house, I felt all the thrill of danger. Nevertheless, there was a change after this change of religion. When my nephew was born, followed by three nieces, I loved to look after them but from all the important occasions of their lives, from baptism, first communion and all those ceremonies which close relatives celebrate together, I was excluded. A mental barrier was erected by the church which separated from one another people who naturally belonged together. (The same happened with the children of my two brothers who married catholics.) I felt all the chill and hurt of this most unnatural divide. The version of Christianity in which I had been brought up was, it seemed, unacceptable.

My sister, forbidden to attend a protestant service, nevertheless was present at her brother's marriage in a Methodist church in the North of Ireland. When she confessed this 'sin' to the parish priest, he told her that it was so grave that it had a special name: it was called 'a reserved sin' and only a bishop could absolve it; so to a bishop she had to go to be absolved. My father was never told of this piece of intolerance for he had enough fuel for his fire without adding to it. 'Look at the way the state takes orders from the bishops!' he declared. 'Everyone knows that the bishops are behind all legislation in the state, not openly, of course, but secretly. They are so powerful that nobody would dare say a word against them.' He saw himself as a man carrying a light in darkness. Never a day passed without his children receiving a great deal of his spleen on the subject. It was a crusade with him and in the manner of all crusades it was charged with passion. George Eliot, who was herself in the middle of a turmoil of religious and anti-religious ideas, said wisely: 'Free thinkers are scarcely wiser than the orthodox . . . they all want to see themselves and their own opinions held up as true and lovely.'

My father's constant inveighing against that abstraction, the catholic church, was very wearisome to our spirits. Hardly a day passed without his coming upon some piece of incriminating evidence: 'Look at this picture in the newspaper, three fat priests being received by de Valera! Look at this advertisement; subscribe to the Golden Book in Liverpool and you will get x years off Purgatory! When this church publishes its accounts, I will take more notice of it!' When we passed one of the many monastic sites in Dublin we knew what would ensue: 'Look at all that wealth and the poor of Dublin without a decent house to live in!' By too much battering his instrument became blunt. We resisted this 'too palpable a design' upon us. Coming as it did from someone with whom we had no instinctive sympathy, it passed us harmlessly by. Our hearts and imaginations remained untouched. Feeling the lack of reaction, he tried harder; he reasoned and expostulated; could we not see? He never understood that argument and explanation cannot create sympathy, either in religion or in anything else. This was the blind spot in an otherwise well-meaning father and it helped further to sour his relations with his children.

Children take on the values and attitudes of their parents through love and respect, and in religion through the familiar formulas of the spiritual which they share with them. Who has been argued into belief, a real, warm, imaginative belief, through reason? Cardinal Newman understood this. In *Grammar of Assent* (1870) he wrote:

Deductions have no power of persuasion. The heart is commonly reached, not through reason but through the imagination, by means of direct impressions... Persons influence us, voices melt us, looks subdue us, deeds inflame us. Many a man will live and die upon a dogma; no man will be a martyr for a conclusion. A conclusion is but an opinion, it is not a thing which *is*, but which we are *quite sure about*, and it has often been observed that we never say we are certain without implying that we doubt... No one, I say, will die for his own calculations: he dies for realities.

Reason, although it may not enable us to love religion, may very well argue us out of it. My father's constant demand for rational explanations of experience, including religious experience, came from his own culture, a culture of enlightenment which saw the light of reason as the only true interpreter of experience. Voltaire and Gibbon were his mentors and behind him was the scientific movement of the nineteenth century and all the brilliant inventions which had been discovered by the operations of reason. Reason was clearly capable of explaining everything including the non-rational, the religious and even evil itself. My father saw with uncomprehending eyes all the outward and visible signs of the catholic religion without understanding anything of its inward and spiritual grace. He had not been brought up with it, his feelings had not entwined themselves around its symbols and its ceremonies and found joy and consolation there. For feelings cannot be commanded; to be deep and sure they must grow slowly over time. One culture can look alien and hostile to another; two people can be divided by different cultures and be very unhappy.

T.S. Eliot wrote, 'We had the experience but missed the meaning.' My father's case was the other way round. He had the meaning (of catholicism) but missed the experience. A 'meaning' extracted from a rich poetic experience may not represent it at all, hence the inadequacy of abstracting 'meaning' from what to others is the poetry of life. The painful divide, the lack of sympathy between two cultures which is everywhere apparent today, is beautifully expressed in *Helbeck of Bannisdale* by Mrs Humphry Ward, an example of the creative writer's ability to help us to picture and imagine experience which is normally impossible for us, or to give depth and understanding to what we confusedly half-know already.

HELBECK OF BANNISDALE
AND THE RELIGIOUS DIVIDE

Helbeck of Bannisdale was published in 1898 when my father was nineteen years old. It was extremely popular and deserves to be so again. The subject, the clash of catholic culture and the free-thinking agnostic, fascinated people at the time and as the clash took place between a man and a woman passionately in love with one another, the interest was doubly intense.

How can two cultures so fashion and form our feelings that they make two people incapable of sympathising with one another, the relationship ending in wound and hurt? That is the burden of the novel. Mrs Ward sets it in the England of her time but the conflict she so vividly describes was very little different from the Ireland of mine. It exists in any country where two seemingly inimical cultures exist side by side. It is still true of Northern Ireland. The Ireland of the thirties, forties and fifties saw many mixed marriages often frayed and worn by the hostility of the families involved, and sometimes difficult to sustain by the partners themselves. I knew all about it.

Why should a religious subject have been so intriguing for the readers of novels one hundred years ago? There was a huge interest in religion at the time; one's very identity was closely bound up with one's religious culture. It is still so in Ireland and in many other parts of the world. Mrs Ward knew the English scene very well. She had been in a devastating clash of cultures in her own family. Both her mother and father were protestants, her mother coming from Huguenot stock and her father being the son of the famous headmaster of Rugby School, Dr Thomas Arnold. Her uncle was the equally famous thinker and poet, Matthew Arnold. Her father, after six years of married life, did an unthinkable thing for such a family: he converted to catholicism. The girls were brought up protestants and the boys catholics according to the common model, an arrangement which gave great pain to the family because of the weight of anti-catholic feeling in England at the time. After several years, her father changed back to his old religion in which he remained for eleven years more. He then espoused catholicism a second time and remained in it for the rest of his life.

The predicament of his daughter, Mary (later Mrs Ward), was particularly painful. She loved her father passionately but was revolted by his new religion. For her mother, it was much worse.

> My poor mother felt as though the earth had crumbled under her. Her passionate affection for my father endured till her latest hour, but she never reconciled herself to what he had done. There was in her an instinctive dread of Catholicism . . . It never abated. Many years afterwards, in writing *Helbeck of Bannisdale*, I drew upon what I had remembered of it in describing Laura Fountain's inbred and finally indomitable resistance to the Catholic claim upon the will and intellect of men.

In fact the situation was so terrible for her mother that she became a kind of permanent invalid from stress and heartbreak. After her death her husband married again, a co-religionist this time.

Mary remained on close terms with her father and when she was in her forties had the idea of writing a novel on the subject. Her personal experience, her intelligence and imagination gave her the authority to write about it and the avid interest in the religious controversy gave her a fascinated audience. She had hit on the spirit of the times. *Helbeck of Bannisdale* was the most famous of her many novels. She consulted her father as she wrote it and got his approval. She wrote to him:

> Of course, my point of view is anything but Catholic. I should certainly want to do what I had thought of doing, with sympathy, and probably in such a way as to make the big English

public understand more of Catholicism than they do now.

If my father had read it, would it have had that effect on him? Alas, I think not. His situation was different in one important way; his was almost a lone voice in the midst of an overwhelmingly catholic, conservative and triumphalist Ireland. He felt far more embattled than did Mrs Ward, who belonged to the majority culture.

Mrs Ward set the novel in the Lake District of England, which she knew and loved. She had spent many holidays there in her grandmother's house, Fox How, near Ambleside. She knew well the old catholic family of Strickland who had lived for centuries in Sizergh Castle. She knew the beautiful Leven's Hall nearby, which she rented while she was writing the novel. A combination of both houses served as the model for Bannisdale Hall. Her self-confessed task was to open up the religious question and to be fair to both sides in such a way as to meet the expectations of the reader for a good story, love and romance, and a serious attitude to experience. How was she to provide such a story? She had to invent convincing characters, place them in interesting scenes and situations, keep the story moving from scene to scene and bring it, finally, to a satisfying end. She did all this in *Helbeck*. She gave me back my own experience of the religious divide, better identified, better understood, better expressed, while all the time keeping me in the grip of the exciting story.

She opens the novel thus:

'I must be turning back. A dreary day for anyone coming fresh to these parts!'

It is very like the opening of *Jane Eyre*. We are in the middle of the action and a new turn of events is promised from the first sentence. We are full of expectation.

So saying, Mr Helbeck stood still – both hands resting on his stick – while his gaze slowly swept the straight white road in front of him and the landscape to either side.

Alan Helbeck is brought to life through poetic descriptions of the landscape, very much as Rochester and Heathcliff are brought to life in the Brontë novels. His is an old and weather-beaten house of a singular character and dignity . . . But the whole structure seemed still to lean upon and draw towards the tower; and it was the tower which gave accent to a general expression of austerity . . . while behind it, beyond some thin intervening trees, rose a grey limestone fell, into which the house seemed to withdraw itself as into a rock, whence it was hewn.

In these descriptions we sense the ascetic, the strong, the private man. We do not so much 'see' Helbeck as 'feel' his being. He is the woman's hero, the man of magnetic authority, sensitive, aloof.

The woman, as she milked, watched him propping the ruin-ous gate with a stone; her expression all the time friendly and attentive. His own people, women especially, somehow always gave him this attention.

We learn that he had been solitary for many years and loved his solitude. He is carrying a devotional book in his pocket which calls on him 'to cast himself at the feet of men for love of Me'. Here we have in an economic way the hint of his religious zeal and that soli-tariness which has drawn him aside from the mainstream of English society.

Mrs Ward plunges us directly into the action. His solitude is about to be broken by the arrival of his sister, Augustina. She had, we learn, 'married out' of the faith some thirteen years before and had been estranged from her brother because of it. Her husband now dead, she has returned to her brother, to the family home and to her old faith. As she is recuperating from illness, she is accompa-nied, most reluctantly, by her stepdaughter, Laura Fountain, a young, beautiful, high-spirited and independent young woman whose prejudices against Alan Helbeck are enormous. He had not spoken to her beloved father during all the thirteen years of his mar-riage to Helbeck's sister because she had betrayed the faith. When we learn that Laura not only is not a catholic but has been deliber-ately brought up to have no religion whatsoever, we have all the makings of a powerful drama. Her father, we learn, was a Cam-bridge don and an atheist who hated – as did my own father – all organised religion as ignorance, superstition and bigotry and who viewed the concept of sin as an invention of priests to keep the people down. He had failed to get promotion at Cambridge, the 'clerical party' had seen to that. Laura had been bred in the liberating atmosphere of doubt and scepticism and her views, like her father's, were directly opposed to Helbeck's certainties.

'For her – for all of us – doubt is misery' [said Augustina].
'Papa taught me – it was life – and I believed him' [said Laura].

It is made clear that the bond between father and daughter had been very deep, so deep that she loved and respected all his values, his scepticism, his love of poetry and of nature. She had been borne along on the current of his sympathies and the great loyalty of her life was loyalty to him. (I wish my relationship with my father had been able to create such a strong and uncomplicated feeling in me.) Here then was Laura coming to be the guest of an extreme representative of the beliefs which her father detested. She was ready for battle and she had no doubt it would come.

Alan Helbeck, we learn, is the last of twenty generations of catholic aristocrats and recusants who had, since the Reformation, lived on the margins of English society and looked after their own. His life had been a life of extreme loyalty to his kind, of exemplary devotion, discipline and self-deprivation. His home was now half-denuded of furniture, sold to help his co-religionists who depended on him for financial aid. He is thirty-seven years old (women novelists of the nineteenth century very often have their heroines fall in love with older men – Rochester and Jane Eyre, Emma and Mr Knightley, Dorothea and Casaubon). This eruption into his quiet, retreated life is the beginning of the drama.

'And tell him, please, Augustina – make it very plain – that I shall never come in to prayers.'

The note of defiance is struck early. The little indicators of strict religious observance – fish on Fridays, abstinence in Lent (which I knew, too) – irritate and exclude.

'He looks hard and bigoted. I suppose most people are afraid of him – I'm not!'

In this house of religious 'slaves', she will be free at least, of this she is quite determined. Mrs Ward captures very well the tone of the 'new woman', the kind of woman that Helbeck had never known of in all the long line of dedicated and pious Helbeck women.

Laura's personality is suggested in the same poetic way as Helbeck's:

A strange nobility and freedom breathed from the wide scene; from its mere depths below her; from the spacious curve of the river, the mountains half-shown, half-hidden, the great race of the clouds, the fresh beating of the wind. The north spoke to her, and the mountains. It was like the rush of something passionate and straining through her girlish sense; intensifying all that were already there.

The vocabulary suggests her passionate inner life, her soul dilating at the contemplation of the natural scene before her. Helbeck's soul 'withdrew' into the house that was his church and sanctuary. Here is the religion of nature, the love of all natural beauty through which 'intimations of immortality' raise the soul in a way we could loosely call 'religious'. My father's greatest superlatives were reserved, likewise, for the natural beauty of sea, sky and land.

Having brought them together at Bannisdale, Mrs Ward's strategy is to invent scenes, situations, dialogue which will do justice to both sides, while at the same time drawing the two together in passionate love. To concentrate the action, she brings Laura to Bannisdale in Lent, a season when the intensest rituals of the church will go on under her very eyes. (My father's temper was similarly exacerbated by the concentration of conservative catholicism of his day.) Laura's soul is revolted by all this obsession with guilt and sin, 'this poison in the blood'. She looks round at all that is holy and familiar to the catholic mind with the cold, critical eye of the outsider. 'God – the Christ of Calvary – in that gilt box upon that altar!'

During Holy Week, when the rituals reach a climax, she writes to her friend in Cambridge:

'After this week . . . I shall always feel kindly towards "sin" – and "the world"! How they have been scouted and scourged! And what, I ask you, would any of us do without them? . . . O

– such a waste of time! Why doesn't Mr Helbeck go and learn geology?'

I might have been listening to my own father: 'Religion wished to crush all the natural human things that bigots are always trampling underfoot.' Mrs Ward is careful to show that this child of the Enlightenment has far too superficial a view of human evil in contrast with Helbeck's profound conviction of it. She was overconfident, as were many in her time, in the power of man to improve his own situation.

> 'Of course there have been *very* great villains – I don't like to think about them. And the people who are born sick and wrong. But by-and-by we shall have weeded them all out or improved the breed. And why not spend your energies on doing that, instead of singing litanies, and taking ridiculous pains not to eat the things you like?'

This is the voice of Voltaire, the voice of my father.

> 'There will be no one to come after,' said Augustina slowly, 'for of course he will never marry.'
>   'Is he too great a saint for that too?' cried Laura. 'Then all I can say is, Augustina – that – it – would – do him a great deal of good.'

It is the comment of uncomprehending common sense upon the sanctities and sacrifices of the soul. When my own father uttered such sentiments, I always recoiled without knowing why. In this unpropitious way, Mrs Ward prepares us for the love story.

In order to be fair to both sides – her avowed intent – the author provides a set of protestant relations on Laura's father's side and has them live nearby, creating scenes in the protestant farmhouse which are vivid and lively. There is Mrs Mason, Laura's cousin, for whom catholics are 'a sort of vermin' and Helbeck 'nobbut a heathen'. She is a vehement, narrow-minded woman and she is shown, ironically, to be as much against the free-thinking Laura as the jesuitical Helbeck. Mr Bayley, a fiercely evangelical parson, is a protestant bigot of huge dimension. Mrs Ward does not like him:

> He was a little man, with a small sharp anaemic face buried in

red hair. It was two or three years of mission work, first in Mexico then at Lima as the envoy of one of the most thorough going of Protestant societies, that had given him his strangely vivid notions of the place of Romanism among the world's forces. At no moment in this experience can he have had a grain of personal success. Lima, apparently, is of all the towns in the universe, the town where the beard of Protestantism is least worth the shaving – to quote a northern proverb. At any rate, Mr Bayley returned to his native land at fifty, with a permanent twist of the brain. Hence these preposterous sermons in the fell chapel; the eager nosing out and tracking down of every scent of Popery; this fanatical satisfaction in such a kindred soul as that of Elizabeth Mason.

Mr Bayley is offset by the farmhand, Daffody, an itinerant preacher who is against all 'paid' clergy but respects all who follow the Spirit. 'I've allus thought mysen' . . . as we'd a deal to larn from Romanists in some ways.' He is the best of the protestants, although the bigoted Mrs Mason is shown to be capable of a dignity and goodness which surprises Laura.

Laura's distaste for extreme protestantism is counterbalanced by her equal dislike for the variety of priest she meets in Bannisdale Hall. Father Bowles is

a priest of the old-fashioned type, with no pretensions to knowledge or to manners. Wherever he went he was a meek and accommodating guest, for his recollection went back to days when a priest coming to a private house to say mass would as likely as not have his meals in the pantry . . . He would blow out a candle on the altar before the end of mass that he might enjoy the smell of it.

Father Leadham is a jesuit, a Cambridge man and a convert who wishes Helbeck to sacrifice even himself to bring Laura into the church. In this way, Mrs Ward reminds us that the jesuits were formed to counter the Reformation. Helbeck increases in stature by the contrast. He is 'an aristocrat to his fingertips'. 'I, too, have never influenced, never tried to influence, anyone in my life.'

For the first half of the book we see everything through Laura's eyes. Helbeck remains remote, private, enigmatic, a mysterious force waiting to be revealed. How will Mrs Ward do this? By a clever device she has Mrs Mason's son, a rather loutish but handsome boy, fall in love with Laura. Although Helbeck is capable of saying shameful things about protestants which diminish him in our estimation and in Laura's, he is shown to be more truly noble and more generous, more gentlemanly in his dealings with her, by contrast. It is inevitable that these two fastidious beings shall be drawn one to the other, beings 'whose passion had no need of caresses. It was deep calling unto deep.' Laura comes and goes between the two houses, exercising ostentatiously her right to think and do as she pleases. This tension mounts between them. There is the power which draws them slowly and inexorably to one another, and the equal power which drives them apart.

Helbeck is amazed to find new and powerful feelings inside himself. He is 'racked with desire for this little pagan creature, this girl without a single Christian sentiment or tradition'. Ironically, it is her very 'pagan' spirit which draws him, inflames him, and her 'innate maidenliness', the parallel to his own fastidious nature, which enthrals him. Scene after scene is created full of powerful hints and suggestions in which the zigzags of their mounting passion are minutely charted. Beneath the irritable chafing of spirit against spirit the real drama goes on. Helbeck is forced more and more into the open, a brutal forcing for his deep and private nature. The struggle for power between male and female – engagement, submission, ascendancy – recalls *Jane Eyre*. Why is Laura drawn to this jesuitical man so apparently unsuited to her? Mrs Ward supplies a possible and intriguing answer: 'In all ages the woman falls before the ascetic – before the man who can do without her'; and 'she had the woman's passion for influence'. Does this explain the attraction to the woman of the celibate priest? I wondered.

Mrs Ward faces her most difficult imaginative undertaking in making Laura, the non-catholic, understand Helbeck's religious passion. Laura's side of the experience is more readily understood and approved of by the great protestant English public, aligned as in her time, or agnostic or indifferent as in our own. Helbeck has to be made to declare himself. His love for Laura, the uncomprehending, finally goads him into explaining the historical necessity which created him.

'A difference that has law and education besides religion behind it, goes deep. Times are changed, but it goes deep still.' [This is true of Ireland.]

'So they lived to themselves and by themselves; they didn't choose to live with their Protestant neighbours – who had made them outlaws and inferiors! And, of course, they sank in manners and refinement. You may see the results in all the minor Catholic families to this day – that is the old families. The few great houses that remained escaped many of the drawbacks of the position. The smaller ones suffered, and succumbed. But they had their compensations!'

And of the spirit of his race, Mrs Ward says:

Their privations and persecutions, their faults, their dumb or stupid infidelities, their very vices even, had been the source in him of a constant and secret affection... He was proud of calamity, impoverishment, isolation; they were the scars on the pilgrims' feet – honour-marks left by the oppressor.

This passage helps us to understand the passionate attachment of persecuted minorities to their culture.

Helbeck struggles to subdue his passion for Laura and although so disciplined in subduing his desires, he fails miserably. The author's comments on his struggle have, I think, a clear reference to Ireland. 'There is something in the Catholic discipline on points of sex-relation that perhaps weakens a man's instinctive confidence in women.' His later revelation to Laura of how he came to 'religion' confirms this. At Louvain, after having read some French sceptical books, he nearly lost his religion. Having recovered it, he nearly lost it again for a woman but 'God in the church' saved him after much extreme spiritual torment. When they finally come together in an ecstasy of surrender, Laura is given a powerful, prophetic insight.

'Will you never, never let me get the upper hand? Make me afraid to mock at your beliefs!' she said passionately, 'make me afraid! – there is no other way.'

She knows that it is his authority over her that subdues and delights her, and that if that authority were to be weakened, their love would fail. It is an authority beloved of the heroine from Jane Austen to Charlotte Brontë. Yet, ironically, she is repelled by his longing to put his own soul under authority to his church and to his God.

Finally, he opens his very soul to her. She listens in awe. 'I was not worthy you should tell me a word', and 'It is the most sacred honour that was ever done me. I thank – thank – thank you.' Mrs Ward has made us imagine with great poetry and generosity his religious experience. But it is to Dr F. of Cambridge, friend of Laura's father and a non-catholic, that she gives her objective assessment of the appeal of that church.

'What does the ordinary Protestant know of all those treasures of spiritual experience which Catholicism has secreted for centuries? *There* is the debt of debts that we all owe to the Catholic Church.'

Laura agrees to become a catholic against all her instincts. The drama intensifies between them. She cannot, on any terms, accept 'the spiritual intrusiveness of Catholicism, its perpetual uncovering of the soul – its disrespect for the secrets of personality – its humiliation of the will . . .' Even love of the highest intensity cannot make his faith acceptable 'to the eyes of this daughter of the modern world'. Mrs Ward knows that our feelings grown from our childhood loves are too powerful to be brutally transplanted. At bottom it was 'those facts of character and of temperament which held them separated! – facts which are always, and in all cases, the true facts of this world'.

Mrs Ward is right. Laura feels deeply unworthy of Helbeck but she cannot make herself feel for his religion as he would wish her to feel. She cannot live with him and she cannot live without him. This is the stuff of tragedy. There is no way out; nobody is to blame; circumstances have brought this about. Sensitively and poetically, Mrs Ward describes Laura's despair, her deliberate act of throwing herself into the river on Helbeck's estate, the river she loved so much.

It is Helbeck who finds her:

He brought her home upon his breast. Those who had come to search with him followed at a distance.

He carried her through the garden, and at the chapel entrance nurses and doctors met him. Long and fruitless efforts were made before all was yielded to despair; but the river had done its work.

In that long agony, Helbeck's soul parted for ever with the first fresh power to suffer. Neither life nor death could ever stab in such a way again.

Persons of shallower feelings than Laura and Helbeck would have found an accommodation.

FRIENDS AND NEIGHBOURS

I did not share my father's view on the catholic church. In fact I did not have any 'views' on any church. The poor catholics around James's Street seemed happy and cheerful in spite of their poverty. Whatever their church demanded of them they gave willingly. They did not look browbeaten or behave any more ignorantly than anyone else. When I walked into the Atticks' room in Bow Lane, I was offered an open, affectionate welcome and an ease and warmth I did not get at home. They did not criticise me for not reaching high standards for they did not aspire to reach them themselves. They simply wanted to survive and their religion helped them to do so. They were never long out of the chapel and they never stopped thanking God for His mercies. They seemed to understand people's difficulties and were full of natural pity for them. 'The lord ha' mercy on him, sure he was half crazed with the drink when he bate her up.' Their patience (inertia to my father) was unbounded. They accepted their state without a complaint.

'Aunt Mamie', Mrs Attick's sister, was a widow when I knew her. She was a large woman, not very good on her feet and was always enveloped in innumerable skirts and shawls. Three of her daughters were married, but one, Mary, lived at home for she had a TB hip and only one kidney. She had a handsome face with the broadest, warmest smile you could see anywhere. She knitted jerseys to make a little money and whenever I saw her, she was sitting in a low chair by the window watching the passers-by, her arms and hands unceasingly at work with wool and needles and a large piece of knitting issuing from under them onto her lap beneath. She could knit a sweater in two or three days. She never spoke of herself save to say that she was going to the hospital for a check-up. She asked me questions about myself, listened sympathetically to my complaints and always defended my father for 'doing so much for you'. He had taken neither to women nor to drink and was scrimping and saving to give us the best education (this view was generally held in the neighbourhood). The moment I came in, the kettle was put on and tea was made and I was gathered up in the warmth of their interest in my little doings. I always felt better when I left that house, my refuge in many times of trouble.

Mrs Attick was the more vivacious of the two sisters. She had a vivid turn of phrase which made us all laugh. 'If that oul' gouger looks sideways at me again, I'll turn him inside out with me knife and he won't know his guts from his brains!' She was afraid of nobody and could stand up for herself in any situation. The only thing she was afraid of was the high railway bridge over the River Boyne at Drogheda. Once a year she took the train to Dundalk to see a friend, and the only way she could face that bridge was to close her eyes tight and swallow a Baby Power before the train took her over it. She knew everybody in the neighbourhood and was always engaged on little missions of unselfconscious charity. No matter at what inconvenient hour I arrived, she never showed any irritation at this protestant child. In this, she and her sisters were natural ladies.

For all this, we were different from them: we were protestants and they were catholics. Everything told us that, in some sense, we were in a foreign land. The catholic church in the thirties and forties had a very public presence all over the Irish state and you could not walk down a street without being aware of it. Our religious observance took place once a week; not so with our catholic neighbours. The doors of the many chapels on Dublin streets were open seven days a week and at all hours. People streamed in and out continually to attend mass or just to say a prayer. As we passed the open doors of the chapels we could see line after line of women kneeling in devotion before pale waxen statues (idols to protestants). They crossed themselves reverently and lips moved silently as they passed the rosary beads one by one through their fingers. Great tiers of candles glowed in the half-darkness and suffering figures of Christ looked down from on high. The image of the Sacred Heart, great drops of blood dripping from it, repelled us. We stared at it all from afar with bewildered incomprehension. Three times a day, at dawn, midday and at six, the bells of the catholic churches rang out over Dublin's streets and at once everyone made the sign of the cross and said a Hail Mary. It was the Angelus reminding catholics of the Virgin Mary. She did not figure in our observances. When catholics passed the many chapels on foot or in the tram, men doffed their caps and women made the sign of the cross. We protestants did nothing.

Priests were greeted with extreme deference. Martha taught me to say when passing a priest, 'God bless you, Father', to which he returned, 'God bless you, child'. In this way I felt less awkward. I was wary and rather frightened of the priests with their blacker-than-black clerical suits, stiff white dog collars, clean scrubbed faces and inscrutable expressions. Our protestant clergy in the same uniform looked more comfortable, more relaxed. Did priests say prayers all day long? I wondered. For, breviary in hand, they even said their prayers in the street – an unthinkable thing for a protestant clergyman. I would not have liked my father or some of my protestant friends to have heard me blessing a priest in the street. We protestants kept our religious feelings, if we had them, strictly to ourselves. The liturgy of the church on Sundays was quite enough to take care of them in a general way without public demonstrations. We were deeply embarrassed by such shows. In that way we were very different from the catholics, who spoke easily and naturally of their religion and who invoked the name of God, Jesus, His Mother and all the saints frequently and emphatically – 'Holy Mother of God, what are ye after doin' on me!'; 'Jesus, Mary and Joseph, did ye ever see the like of it?'; and 'God and His blessed saints have mercy on ye for a dirty liar!' This was, for us, to break the commandment 'Thou shall not take the name of the Lord in vain' and few things marked us off so clearly from our catholic neighbours as our inability to blaspheme.

The chapel in James's Street had a small area in front of it where, during Lent and other special seasons, stallholders sold crucifixes, rosary beads, miraculous medals and holy pictures, all aids to worship conspicuously absent in our practices: to us it looked like the tables of the money-changers whom Christ drove out of the

Temple with such passion. We had nothing but our prayer books and our Bibles. That, we were told, was all we needed. The rest of the week, which brought us only Girl Guides, brought a dizzy succession of ceremonies to the catholics – confession on Saturday evening, benediction every evening, stations of the cross, novenas, retreats, missions, saints' days, holy days of obligation, days of special intention, fast-days, women's sodality, men's sodality, children of Mary. The church was the centre of activity, the co-ordinating authority in everyone's life.

Martha was a child of Mary and walked in the procession. The girls emerged from the side of the chapel in Echlin Street, walking two by two in long blue and white garments, living replicas of the Virgin Mary who adorned the chapel. She was comfortably familiar with categories of sin of which I knew nothing. She talked with easy confidence of 'venial sins', 'mortal sins' and even 'cardinal sins'. She would say 'my mammy says it is only a venial sin' – that meant she did not need to worry about it. Going into a protestant church service, however, was a mortal sin, she darkly proclaimed; on no condition could it be done. A saint was responsible for every human activity, and Martha wore several miraculous medals of saints around her neck to protect her. 'Saint Christopher guides,' she said, 'and Saint Antony finds. Give him a little penny for charity and he will find what you have lost. Saint Jude looks after lost causes.' She taught me how to get rid of a speck in my eye. 'You pull down your eyelid and say, "Blessed mote went in my eye and blessed Virgin Mary take it out", and it will be gone.' I loved these little formulas and wished we used them in our lives. They were strangely comforting. I loved the Dublin habit of offering a blessing on everything that gave pleasure. 'God bless your curly head,' a woman would say and give me a penny. They delighted in my hair for itself without expecting anything back for their money. It was an acknowledgement of the blessings that lay all around them, in spite of their poverty.

Public, too, was first communion. Martha made her first communion when she was seven. I had to wait until I was fourteen. Catholic children were fêted on this occasion; they went from door to door showing themselves off, being given little presents of money. 'What are you going to do with your communion money?' was the question for catholic children. We received none. Weddings, too, were public affairs. All the children of the neighbourhood gathered round the chapel doors waiting for the bride and groom to emerge. They knew that as the couple drove off, the bridegroom would throw a fistful of coins out of the window and they would scramble for them in great excitement. Our weddings were more reticent, more private, less enjoyable for the waiting crowd.

Nuns both fascinated and frightened us. Their strange, exotic headgear, behind which we could just catch a glimpse of shining, blank faces and expressionless eyes, spoke of mysterious people who did not share our human experiences. They were 'in orders'. Martha could tell by their headdresses what order they belonged to. They moved noiselessly about and disappeared behind closed doors into bleak convent buildings. No one saluted them as they saluted priests. One of the more intriguing orders lived in a huge grey building behind high walls in Kilmainham; they were, Martha said, the Little Sisters of the Poor. We watched them go from door to door on the Circular Road, asking for food or money. 'They have no dowry,' said Martha. 'Only poor girls go in there and they have to beg for food.' I wondered how they could bear to beg when they might work instead.

The pervasive atmosphere of the catholic church surrounded me even in a hospital bed. Although Steevens's Hospital was a protestant foundation which endowed bursaries for poor protestant girls to train as nurses, catholic masses were sometimes said in the wards. I would watch as an altar was set up at the end of the room. The nurses draped it with a pure white cloth and placed a crucifix and other objects on it for the priest to celebrate mass. A nurse came to each bed and asked, 'Are you receiving?' I never was. The candles were lit, the priest appeared bedecked in lacy garments and the smell of the molten wax floated down the ward. I looked on as a stranger at the devotion on the faces of the patients beside me, the strange movements of the priest, I heard the sound of the bell on the altar and the murmur of the prayers. I was glad when the mass was over, the altar cleared and the life of the ward returned to normal and I was the same as everybody else.

Martha prepared for Sunday by going to confession the night

before. She always had 'to get confession' before she was free to play with me. Her penance for sins was so many Hail Marys and so many Our Fathers, all of which she bore very lightly. Our preparation was different. On Saturday night we were rubbed and scrubbed to meet the Lord on Sunday. Our inner being had already been purged the night before with senna tea for which we paid heavily on Saturday morning with frequent and painful stomach cramps. In the evening, the big zinc bath was brought in from its hook in the yard and placed in front of the kitchen range, where it was filled with hot water from the shining brass tap on the side of the range. One by one we immersed ourselves in the warm water and scrubbed ourselves with Lifebuoy soap, often omitting our ears and between our toes, which we were exhorted never to forget. As there was never enough warm water for a change of water for each of us, one person had to enter the used bathwater of another, which was the cause of endless fierce disputes. I loved lying in the hot water, my head pushed up against one end of the tub and my feet crushed against the other end, gazing at the glowing coals in the open fire of the range, the door of which was usually kept shut to economise on coal.

The dreaded ordeal of hair-washing followed. It took place over the scullery sink. In spite of the rigorous cleanliness of our household, we picked up lice and nits at school and our heads were under continuous inspection. A fine comb was drawn vigorously through my tight curly hair catching and tugging on its many tangles and making me cry out with sharp pain. My head was hung over the sink and water was cascaded over it from a big jug. Soap was rubbed all over my hair and both soap and water streamed down my face making my eyes smart and running into my nose, giving me the vivid sensation of drowning. After a rough towelling, I had to endure another combing and tugging as my hair was put back into place. The ordeal over, I jumped into clean pyjamas and sometimes I helped myself to a small plate of thin gruel from the steamer on the range, where the porridge was being prepared for the morning.

Sunday morning was special: there was bacon and eggs for breakfast, followed by the excitement of getting into my good Sunday clothes, my good coat, my good shoes which squeaked and my Sunday beret. My father, so unconventional in many ways, was surprisingly conventional in accepting the need for Sunday clothes. Once we were home from church, the Sunday clothes were taken off and put away until the following week. We all went to Sunday School at 10.30 a.m. and I never objected to it. Anything that took us out of the house was welcome. We learned the Catechism by heart: 'What is your name, N or M?' I wondered what those letters stood for but never found out: we were never encouraged to ask questions as children are now. The Devil figured prominently: we promised 'to renounce the Devil and all his works' but he had no reality for us. We repeated our duty towards our neighbour, 'to love him as myself, and to do unto all men as I would they should do unto me'. The parables of Jesus were explained to us; we were told they were 'earthly stories with a heavenly meaning'. We learned our morality from those little stories in a way the Catechism did not teach us. We were required to learn large tracts of the Bible by heart: 'In the year that King Uzziah died, I saw the Lord sitting upon a throne, high and lifted up, and his train filled the temple.' I did not know who Uzziah was but my imagination saw an image of majesty, high in the sky and splendid in the robes of a king. We learned that we were protestants but catholics too, not Roman catholics – we must never forget that – but catholics all the same. Somewhere in the past in an event called the Reformation, the catholic church had taken a wrong turning; it worshipped idols and other wrong things but we had cleansed it of those bad practices and had gone on to be the true church reformed and strengthened.

Morning Prayer began at 11.30 and one morning service comfortably accommodated our modest number of protestants, unlike the chapel where masses went on all morning. When the bell began to toll for service, small drifts of protestants appeared in James's Street and made their way into the church and into their accustomed pews. My father sometimes attended morning service and sat with me halfway up on the right. Frank and Hugh sat under the gallery at the back of the church where they could read the *Hotspur* unseen or draw up a list of players for the following week's Boys' Brigade football match. Olive sang in the choir. The smell of wax polish was familiar and friendly; the big brass eagle with its wings outstretched to support the Bible from which the rector read aloud looked down on us, forever poised for his flight to the skies. The organ was announced by the squeaking and puffing of the bellows, which a little boy worked by hand, and the simple dignity of the office of Morning Prayer began.

We all joined in the General Confession. We were 'miserable sinners and there is no health in us', but we did not feel sinful but rather comfortable and blameless. Then the rector said, 'He pardoneth and absolveth', and we were all absolved. We then were ready for songs of praise. 'O let us sing unto the lord; let us heartily rejoice in the strength of our salvation.' My father never joined in the Creed for he did not believe in it. 'How do they know all that? Who ever heard of the resurrection of the dead? Did anyone ever come back from the dead to tell us about it?' My heart sank if I heard the Litany announced for I knew it went on for page after page in the Prayer Book: 'From fornication and all other deadly sins... Good Lord deliver us.' I did not know what fornication was but assumed that it was another one of the multitude of sins, all unknown to me, which we repudiated in the Catechism.

The sermon was the greatest trial of patience and we fidgeted in our seats as the drone went endlessly on, but sometimes we got an unscheduled laugh. The curate had certain tricks of the trade when delivering a sermon, tricks which we soon found out. Wishing to give the impression of speaking extempore, he hid his notes under the reading shelf of the pulpit and looked down earnestly at the people below him while keeping his eye surreptitiously on his notes. When he wanted to turn the page he leaned forward in the pulpit, his voice swelled on an emphatic note and he dextrously flicked over the page, then leaned back, triumphant, as if to recover from his own rhetoric. We children watched for the moment and giggled when it came. Holy communion was celebrated once a month; more frequent celebration, we were told, led to overfamiliarity. We must not, either, be overfamiliar with the set prayers: every sentence must be thought about. My father never attended communion; all that kind of thing he called mumbo-jumbo.

All the family were confirmed in St Ann's church in Dawson Street. All that Hugh remembered of his confirmation was being told by the rector not to put Brylcreem on his hair in case the bishop got it on his hands. My own confirmation deeply affected me. I made my own white dress for the occasion and borrowed a long, white veil. As we knelt side by side in the girls' pews, we felt as special as little brides, mysterious and shrouded behind our veils. The organ played and we all sang, kneeling, 'Come Holy Ghost, our souls inspire; And lighten with celestial fire'; a profound feeling of holiness came over me. We moved two by two up the aisle to kneel before the bishop, who placed his hand solemnly on our heads, saying 'Defend, O Lord, this Thy child with all Thy heaven-ly grace, that she may continue Thine for ever . . .', and I knew that a solemn rite had been pronounced over me. This special sense of holiness I looked for again when I entered the sanctuary of our parish church and offered my hands at the altar rail to receive the bread and wine. The occasion was so wrapped up in mystery and symbolism that something of its indefinable grace fell upon me but I usually returned to my pew, bent my head and felt guilty for not feeling more exalted.

In spite of the tedium of the church services week by week and year by year, all unbeknown to me then, the great words and rhythms of the Book of Common Prayer and the King James Bible entered my soul and remained with me for ever. 'The strongest part of our religion is its unconscious poetry,' said Matthew Arnold. It was the poetry of spirituality I was taking in, the balanced, weighty and solemn sentences, the imagery of sheep and shepherd, of desert and famine and running water. Impersonal as our rituals were, I was to learn much later the healing power of the impersonal over an-xious souls.

One day, when I was six years old, we witnessed something that exceeded in flamboyance anything we had hitherto witnessed on the streets of Dublin. It was the World Eucharistic Congress which took place in 1932. When we heard that the huge procession was to pass our very gates on its way to the Phoenix Park to celebrate mass, we were very excited. Important people from all over the world were coming to Dublin, Martha said, and the procession would go on for hours and hours. When my father heard that those close allies, the church and state, were to pass the Gate, it was like a red rag to a bull. He forbade us on pain of death to look at the proces-sion. He was not going to give them that pleasure! He posted him-self just outside where he could feed both his eyes and his ire to the full. My brothers, seeing him thus preoccupied, climbed up onto the shed roof of our backyard which looked over Steevens's Lane and pulled me up after them.

Crouching down against the wall so as not to make ourselves conspicuous, we had a magnificent grandstand view of it all. No fairy tale, no kings of the Orient, could have been half so dazzling as that procession. Flamboyant banners, fringed canopies supported on embroidered poles held up by boys in lace aprons, monks in brown habits with white rope around their waists, cardinals, bishops, priests in magnificent garments of purple and red and exotic hats flowed by underneath our fascinated eyes, wave after wave of them, while the sound of bands and choirs and songs filled the air. The smoke of countless censers rose up above the brightly hued raiment and exotic perfumes floated past our nostrils. Sensational and spectacular as was that never-ending colour, sound and smell, we protestants looked on as outsiders to the joy of the Irish people. So vast was the crowd, so intense the pressure of it, that a priest was crushed to death. Hughie told me how amazed he was at this news, thinking that nothing could ever happen to a priest!

We roamed the streets of our neighbourhood, the few protestants among the many catholics, but never encountered any bad feeling. Sometimes groups of catholic boys would shout as we passed by:

> Proddy, Proddy on the wall,
> A half a loaf will do you all,
> A penny candle for a light
> To read your Bible half the night.

(Did the half-loaf refer to the communion service?) And we replied:

> Catholic, catholic, going to mass
> Riding on the Divil's ass,
> When the Divil rings the bell
> All the catholics go to hell.

There was no rancour in these encounters, only good-humoured banter, for neither side really understood what they were saying. They were simply the calls of tribal solidarity which go on all over the world. They were of the same harmless nature as the mild warfare which went on between boys and girls.

'What are ye lookin' at?'

'Not much!'

'Well, I'm lookin' at less!'

'Are ye's out lookin' for fellahs?'

'Well, we're out lookin' for young wans.'

'Come on and get us then!'

And we fled, laughing.

FLAGS AND EMBLEMS

Every household has its flags and emblems, whether the Virgin Mary, a picture of the King of England, a heavily filled drinks cabinet or the biggest television available. A large picture of Queen Victoria hung on our parlour wall. She looked down on us, dour and heavy under her prim lace cap. She might have been the Queen of China for all she meant to us. Opposite her hung a 'classical' picture in black and white of a naked Psyche rising from her bath, one hand gracefully entwining a scarf which flowed discreetly over her lower regions. To my father that picture represented the prestige of Greek culture; to me it represented shame and mortification. I always tried to avoid looking at her and I was embarrassed when any of my friends raised their eyes to gaze at her. My education had not taught me how to understand the art of the nude, and in James's Street the naked body suggested one thing only, sex. We were made to stand around our first little radio, an Interocean, and listen to the solemn tone of the announcer saying, 'The king is sinking fast.' It was George V. He was *our* king, my father said. Alone among the people we knew, my father went to London for the coronation of King George VI. He returned with small red, white and blue souvenirs for his children. We were the only ones in the district who had such things.

Surging steadily around the island of my father's Britishness ran counter-currents which confused and unsettled us. They were in the slogans written on walls such as the one on Kilmainham Gaol where the Irish rebels of 1916 had been shot: 'Ireland unfree shall never be at rest.' They were in the republican songs we heard from some of the maids; they were in the distaste for the northern part of the island; they were in the fierce nationalism of the catholic church. We were, it seemed, the descendants of the Cromwellians who had reduced Irish cities to ruins and murdered their inhabitants.

Yet another symbol of allegiance hung on the bedroom walls of our house, pictures of texts from Scripture as was the fashion then in protestant homes. 'Teach me to do Thy will' and 'Thou shalt show me the path of righteousness' were wrought in faded blue and gold flowers. They must have been put there by my mother. Had she raised her eyes to these texts and been strengthened as she lay dying in the bed below? My father was not given to citing Scripture; he more readily quoted Shakespeare. But one text he favoured and commended to us: ' "Do unto others as you would they should do unto you" – that is all the philosophy a man needs.' A piano in one corner spoke of his respect for music and a bookcase alongside of his love of literature and knowledge. Sunday evenings were dedicated to good 'moral' family gatherings. After tea we had to assemble round the piano under the stern eye of Queen Victoria. We sang hymns to Olive's accompaniment, after which my father read aloud from a good novel, often one of Dickens's novels, which he loved. We were generally morose and inattentive, and I usually fell asleep on the floor. We always finished to the plaintive strains of 'Abide with me, fast falls the evening tide' and quickly made our escape.

Over our kitchen table hung the most important of all my father's emblems. It was a wooden plaque on which was written in blue writing:

> If you think you'll lose you're lost,
> For out in the world you'll find
> Success begins with the will to win,
> It's all in the state of the mind.

In this sentiment he believed with all his heart. The will was the secret of success. In all undertakings, if you willed to succeed you would succeed. It followed from this that failure in anything came from a lack of will; failure to win scholarships and failure to be first in exams lay simply in a weakness of will. No excuse was taken. He showed no understanding of the conflicting pressures of heredity and circumstance to undermine the will. We were captains of our souls and masters of our fate. It was a bracing philosophy and like all such, strengthened those who were already strong. Fortunately, we were all quick and intelligent and won scholarships to good schools which would have been otherwise outside my father's financial reach. My father was pleased with the results of his untiring efforts to educate us. His eldest son became a bank manager, his second son a senior civil servant, his third son an accountant, his elder daughter a secretary in Guinness's brewery and his younger daughter a university teacher. Of all these he was most proud of the bank manager.

The chilling lack of sympathy between ourselves and our father made us feel homeless even in our own home. To his dying day he never understood why we instinctively drew away from him, because, in spite of all his good intentions, he could never imagine the often corrosive effect his words had on our inner being. This is a common story and a sad one. We seldom know why we lose the affection of others. We all long to be understood and are hurt when we are not. An uncomprehending phrase, an insensitive action, and the inner being shrinks, tentative bridges collapse and mute incomprehension follows. How could I have expected my father to be wise simply by being a parent? His own needs, his own frustrations, his own anxieties were dinning in his ears and deafening him to the cries of his children who were, in part, the very source of those anxieties.

Imaginative intelligence, the power to put ourselves sympathetically in another person's place, is one of the highest forms of intelligence and one of the rarest. Its importance is seldom understood. It is often equated in the popular mind with 'romantic' or silly fantasies, feminine oversensitivity, silly vaporising, ego-indulgence or escapism and is thought to have only an enfeebling connection, if any, with practical living. Nothing could be further from the truth. We can be taught to argue, to debate, to analyse, to calculate, to learn the processes of engineering, the pathology of disease, to understand the laws of nature or the laws of the land but who can teach us how to understand and to respect another person's feelings? In this the beginning of the third millennium we are bombarded with information on every aspect of work, living, the self, how to develop our potential. We are offered skills of all kinds – bonding skills, interpersonal skills, assertiveness skills, the management of human resources *inter alia,* and the very abstract non-human language is itself chilling. The very word 'technique' suggests an acquired skill rather than an inner imaginative sympathy. If you only acquired skills you could end up being, in Carlyle's phrase, 'a pair of spectacles behind which there are no eyes'. The danger is that skills and the language in which they are expressed could be taken for the real thing. I do not believe that my father would have been wiser had he read a book on 'parenting skills' or that the information offered therein would have changed the basic urges of his emotions.

T.S. Eliot warned at the beginning of the century of the dangers of mass education and mass information diffused wholesale through sophisticated technology:

Where is the life we have lost in living?
Where is the wisdom we have lost in knowledge?
Where is the knowledge we have lost in information?

The knowledge he speaks of is, in Wordsworth's phrase, 'felt in the heart and felt along the blood'. Shelley says that poetry enables us 'to imagine what we know'. *We always know far more than we can imagine.*

When I was a student at Trinity College I believed that reason and debate would lead me to the truth of things and we students sat over interminable cups of coffee in Bewley's café, walked around College Park or tramped the Wicklow Mountains. We talked and argued about God, the meaning of life, justice, rights and the possibility of platonic love. I believed then that if ever I were given convincing reasons for not believing in Christianity, I would have to give it up. My 'feeling' for it would have to fall before the invincible truth of a logical conclusion. I believed that feeling was inferior to thought and that the two were quite separate. I would discover truth from the books of wisdom the university offered me and learned professors would help me to understand it. I listened to debates, I read books, I went voluntarily to philosophy lectures but it seemed as if one set of convincing arguments could be contradicted by others just as convincing. It was all very confusing.

What road should I take? I found myself always arguing for the good, as my father always argued for the bad that was in people and institutions. We were both finding arguments to support our own temperamental leanings. I puzzled over this for a long time, doubting reason in a see-saw of uncertainty.

Years later, when studying Wordsworth's famous preface to the *Lyrical Ballads*, I came upon the following startling insight:

> For our continued influxes of feeling are modified and directed by our thoughts, which are indeed the representatives of all our past feelings . . .

A shock of revelation ran through me, one of those profound revelations which dramatically changes the way we think. So thoughts and feelings were not separate but were intimately connected? It was not thoughts which created our feelings but *feelings which formed our thoughts.* This insight gave a new and extraordinary importance to the life of the feelings, an importance I had never understood before. Feelings had been thought to be bad for you on the whole, liable to carry you away, get out of control, become mere emotionalism; we must always control and conceal them. I could see that we could not wallow in our feelings – that danger was too obvious, that was to confuse feelings with indulgence-in-feeling, sentiment with sentimentality, strength with weakness. I could see that thought was necessary to 'modify and direct' the feelings but equally I could see that thought itself could not create feeling. You could not argue a mean man into being generous. My father, a man of strong and changing moods, always believed himself to be supremely rational but I could see that it was his feelings which drove him on and that he bent argument to justify those feelings. This was a new and exciting way of thinking about human experience and it gave me an important clue to myself and to other people.

GEORGE ELIOT
AND THE LIFE OF THE FEELINGS

Wordsworth's profound insights opened up new areas for the novelists who came after him. George Eliot acknowledged her debt to him. She worked out in *The Mill on the Floss* this connection between thought and feeling which so fascinated me. She tells the story of an English family, the Tullivers, the father, mother, their son Tom and daughter Maggie. They have deep roots in rural England, roots which go back for centuries. It is a land so known and loved, so carried unconsciously in the blood that they are 'familiar with forgotten years'. She begins the story with a description of the childhood of the brother and sister for she knew how intense are our first childhood impressions and how they feed and shape the adult. Wordsworth summed up this vital connection in the famous phrase 'the Child is father of the Man'. Eliot shows us how the feelings entwine themselves around the known and the familiar, nourishing the soul and directing its way, confidently, in the world. She wrote:

> We could never have loved the earth so well if we had had no childhood in it ... What novelty is worth that sweet monotony where everything is known and *loved* because it is known.

Love and long familiarity encourage growth and deep feeling, not intrinsic merit.

She deliberately chose to tell the story of a quite ordinary family,

> to see the pathos and the poetry, the tragic and the comic lying in the experiences of a human soul that looks out through dull

grey eyes and that speaks in a voice of quite ordinary tones.

This is in tune with Wordsworth's aim to show 'that people who do not wear fine clothes can feel deeply'. Eliot's feeling for the poetry of the ordinary well suited my idealistic nature. At the centre of the novel is the story of Maggie's growth from childhood to adulthood, a subject well suited to enthral me. I read the story with joy, appetite and tears.

Maggie Tulliver lives in the mill by the river. 'I am in love with moistness,' she says, a phrase which made me review poetically my own experience of the Irish climate. She is surrounded, unlike myself, by aunts, uncles and cousins who take a close and critical interest in the goings-on of the family. Maggie, like Jane Eyre, is ten years old when the book opens. She has inherited her father's impulsive, generous temperament. She is lively and intelligent, the despair of her conventional mother and the apple of her father's eye. She adores her brother and playmate Tom. In beautiful scenes of childhood George Eliot reveals how Maggie's feelings develop, how she 'builds up the being that she is' (Wordsworth). She gets into trouble, she cuts off her hair, she runs away; Tom quarrels with her and devastates her young heart. Her need for love and affection is paramount. 'I'll forgive you anything as long as you love me, Tom.' Tom loves his sister dearly but he is clear in his mind that she must do as he tells her since, as a boy, he has more sense of what is right and what is due to the family than a mere girl. He accepts without qualification all the codes and values of the society in which he lives. He is, like his mother, a Dodson, and has a strict sense of what is his due as an upright and hard-working boy.

The scenes between the aunts and uncles and the Tullivers provide some of the finest comedy in English as well as being a powerful portrayal of protestantism as it then existed in provincial England. I recognised the judgemental aspect of that religion in the protestant Ireland of my own time. 'Their religion was of a simple, semi-pagan kind, but there was no heresy in it – if heresy properly meant choice – for they didn't know there was any other religion, except that of chapel-goers, which appeared to run in families like asthma.' Their traditions were:

obedience to parents, faithfulness to kindred, industry, rigid honesty, thrift, the thorough scouring of wooden and copper utensils, the hoarding of coins likely to disappear from the currency, the production of first-class commodities for the market, and the general preference for whatever was home made. The right thing must always be done towards kindred. The right thing was to correct them severely ... (they) would be frankly hard of speech to inconvenient kin but would never forsake or ignore them ... would not let them want bread, but only require them to eat it with bitter herbs.

In the midst of all this family solidarity, Maggie is different. She

was a creature full of eager, passionate longings for all that was beautiful and glad; thirsty for all knowledge ... with a blind, unconscious yearning for something that would link together the wonderful impressions of this mysterious life, and give her soul a sense of home in it.

I knew exactly how she felt. Maggie wanted her life to be full of poetry as I did mine. Maggie always blamed herself for quarrels as I blamed myself. Maggie always wished she had done something different, as I did. Tom was like my father: he would always do the same thing again, firm in the conviction of his own right-mindedness. Both children pass into adulthood learning to deal with the compromises and choices that adulthood forces upon them.

We learn to restrain ourselves as we get older. We keep apart when we have quarrelled, express ourselves in well-bred phrases, and in this way preserve a dignified alienation, showing much firmness on the one side, and swallowing much grief on the other.

Poor George Eliot knew all about this painful façade. She had a heartbreaking experience of alienation from one she loved dearly, her brother Isaac. They had been inseparable companions as children (like Tom and Maggie) but as an adult Eliot had done something for which Isaac never forgave her. After a long period of nursing her father through illness, her life changed. Quite exceptionally for a provincial girl at the time, she had educated herself to a high degree and was able to mix on equal terms with interesting intellectual people near her house in Coventry and travel abroad with them. Eventually she decided to settle in London and live by her pen. She became assistant editor of the prestigious *Westminster Review* and an important figure in the literary world, but her need to be loved was not fulfilled until she met Henry Lewes, an intellectual like herself. By the time she came to know him, his marriage had been broken by his beautiful wife's infidelity and her departure to live with another, leaving him with their three boys. As both he and his wife believed in 'free' love a divorce was impossible.

George Eliot's deeply passionate nature found complete satisfaction with Lewes, whom she viewed as being morally, if not legally, free to marry. (She says of Maggie that 'the need of being loved would always subdue her'.) She went to live with him as his wife, called herself Mrs Lewes and commanded all her friends to do the same. This was an enormous act of courage on her part given the contemporary view on such irregular unions. She knew she would be ostracised and she was. Her beloved Isaac said he would never see her again and he kept his word. The union was blissfully happy but she paid for her happiness with social isolation. Into *The Mill on the Floss* she put all her understanding of the pattern of feelings which made Isaac and herself take such different moral attitudes. In the novel we get to know both brother and sister and their long habits of feeling so well that when they are brought to sorrow and suffering as adults, we are convinced by what they see and do.

George Eliot was passionately concerned about the moral life; her own scholarly studies had led her to conclude that the text of the Bible could not be relied on as the divine word of God, and as the Bible was almost the sole authority for protestants she had, with great reluctance, to give up her belief in Christianity. She remained, however, deeply convinced of the absolute obligation of making our own moral choices. She once said, 'God, Immortality, Duty, how inconceivable the first, how unbelievable the second and yet how peremptory and absolute the third.' Hers was an agnosticism steeped in the moral life and fed and watered by her love of the Bible. She believed that 'we must do without opium and live through all our pain with conscious, clear-eyed endurance'. In *The Mill on the Floss* she shows that duty is a *feeling* or it is nothing.

George Eliot's purpose is to put Tom and Maggie to the test by placing them in difficult situations. Their happy childhood comes to an end when their father is made bankrupt and is forced to become a tenant in the mill he once owned, his landlord being the lawyer Wakem, whom he hates. In a spasm of uncontrollable rage Mr Tulliver horsewhips Wakem, has a seizure and dies. The family has to leave the mill and face poverty and the pity of neighbours. Both brother and sister are severely tested by suffering and the difference in their temperaments drives them painfully apart. Tom must find work, pay his father's debts and buy back the mill so that he can hold his head high in the world again. He tells Maggie, the girl, what she should do and is unequivocal that she must give up seeing Wakem's son, Philip, with whom her starved emotional and mental life has found solace. Poor Maggie gets the only work open to her as a seamstress in a school, monotonous and suffocating bondage. All her hopes of joy are crushed in this endless soul-destroying life:

> She wanted some key that would enable her to understand, and in understanding, endure the heavy weight that had fallen on her young heart.

She turns to *Imitation of Christ* by Thomas à Kempis, that wonderful book which has strengthened so many people to find peace in self-sacrifice. But self-sacrifice is rejected by George Eliot as it was rejected by Charlotte Brontë. She has Philip tell Maggie:

> 'You are not resigned: you are only trying to stupefy yourself... You will be thrown into the world some day, and then every rational satisfaction of your nature that you deny now, will assault you like a savage appetite.'

Maggie is seeing Philip unbeknown to Tom and when he finds out he is furious. He judges her from his 'righteous' standpoint, having no imaginative capacity to understand her. George Eliot sums him up:

> A character at unity with itself – that performs what it intends, subdues every counteracting impulse, and has no vision beyond the distinctly possible – is strong by its very negations.

Carlyle called this 'the completeness of limited men'. Maggie accuses him of being a Pharisee.

George Eliot now prepares the real assault on Maggie's nature, of which Philip has warned her. Lucy, her loving cousin, anxious to relieve the terrible poverty and monotony of Maggie's life, invites her to stay for some months. In her house, full of comfort, music, colour and love, she meets Lucy's intended husband, Stephen Guest. The quite unexpected happens. Stephen, who had patronisingly expected to meet 'a fat, blond girl with round blue eyes who will stare at us silently', finds instead a woman, strange, unconventional, independent, a woman whose like he has never before encountered, and he falls passionately in love with her. Maggie, in her turn, is drawn irresistibly to this good-looking, cultured, masterful man. In scene after scene between them, George Eliot shows that a writer does not have to mention the words 'sexual attraction' for it to be powerfully felt. As the magnetism grows, Maggie is thrown into a terrible moral dilemma to which the author has deliberately brought her. If she returns Stephen's love it will be treachery to Lucy and treachery to Philip, to whom she has almost promised herself. She does everything in her power to avoid what she most desires, Stephen, but he manoeuvres to have her to himself, distracted by his passion for her. They embark on a boat down the River Floss and a dreamlike enchantment descends on Maggie 'from which memory was excluded'. Stephen provokes a declaration of love from her. Eliot warns us against facile judgement:

> Such things, uttered in low broken tones by the one voice that first stirred the fibres of young passion, have only a feeble effect – on experienced minds at a distance from them.

Little by little, despite the blinding passion, old habits of feeling assault Maggie as she sees the situation and the choices before her. Memory is her attachment to the bonds of affection forged in the past and it will not let her rest.

> And a choice of what? O God – not a choice of joy, but of conscious cruelty and hardness; for could she ever cease to see before her Lucy and Philip, with their murdered trust and hopes? Her life with Stephen could have no sacredness: she

must forever sink and wander vaguely, driven by uncertain impulse; for she had let go the clue of life – that clue which once in the far-off years her young need had clutched so strongly.

And that clue? It is faithfulness to *feelings*, faithfulness to those with whom she had passed her life. She could not live with herself if she took her own happiness at the expense of others. This feeling is as strong in her as her love for Stephen. To Stephen, George Eliot gives the modern argument for personal happiness based on natural law.

> We have proved that it was impossible to keep our resolutions. We have proved that the feeling which draws us towards each other is too strong to be overcome: that natural law surmounts every other; we can't help what it clashes with.

If they can give up one another, then their passion is not strong enough: nature has provided the most powerful argument. Powerful arguments indeed and sweet to the modern mind. Maggie's feeling for Lucy and Philip is too strong to be overcome:

> There would be a warrant for all treachery and cruelty – we should justify breaking the most sacred ties that can ever be formed on earth. If the past is not to bind us, where can duty lie? We should have no law but the inclination of the moment.

Unwelcome and devastating to Stephen, murderous to her own happiness, this feeling for past loyalties grows stronger in Maggie; it is a feeling we have come to know in her through her childhood years. She cannot hurt those to whom she is already bound. Struggle agonisingly as she will, it is this feeling which cannot be overcome. There is no way out.

The author ends the book as tragically as did Mrs Ward in *Helbeck of Bannisdale* and for the same reason: there was no way out. But George Eliot has a last reconciliation between Tom and Maggie before they both go under in a flood of water that envelops the mill: 'In their death they were not divided.' Was Maggie right to make this choice? Can we believe in her heroic struggle? Only those capable of such a struggle will believe in it, said Eliot; only those with feelings as deep and sure as Maggie's. George Eliot here shows that duty is a feeling or it is as 'cold as charity'. No one can argue us into loyalty.

The Mill on the Floss had a profound effect on me. It made me more aware of people's needs, it gave me a horror of hurting others. I could never build my happiness on someone else's hurt. And Wordsworth was to show me that kindness, generosity and loyalty are habits of feeling rather than commandments, and as such can be weakened by other habits, by social pressures, by personal ambition, by the appetite for material things and by the all-consuming belief in personal happiness.

JOHN STUART MILL
AND THE LIFE OF THE FEELINGS

I could see plainly that my father and Tom Tulliver had much in common. There was the same work ethic, the same horror of being under an obligation to anyone, the same emphasis on the will, the same certainty of their own right-mindedness, the same inability to imagine the feelings of another. I knew that in my father's case these qualities came partly from his temperament and partly from his early puritanical upbringing but I did not know how much of it was his inheritance as a British Victorian. The ethos which ignored the feelings and valued the education of the rational faculty and the stiffening of the will existed in Great Britain and the North of Ireland long before it was imposed on us children in Dublin. It was many years before I discovered how representative my father was in this respect.

It was John Stuart Mill's *Autobiography,* published in 1873, which told me this. I did not expect to enjoy the book (I was reading it as background to the nineteenth-century novel while in Trinity) for I knew that Mill wrote on political and economic theory, both of which I viewed as 'dismal sciences'; but I was wrong. An ageing man when he wrote the book, Mill was looking back at his emotional and intellectual development. His early education as described in the opening chapters was, in some important respects, very like my own. Like me, he lost his mother early and was brought up without any softening feminine influence. Like me, he was subjected to the unceasing educational attention of his father who, unlike mine, was a well-known political thinker and historian. Both fathers were brought up in the Scottish presbyterian faith, both gave it up (Mill's father was a licensed minister but he never practised) and both came to dislike all institutional religion as bigoted, superstitious and aggressive. Neither believed in God on the rational grounds that a benevolent God could not have created such a suffering world. Mill was brought up without any religion at all. 'I am one of the very few examples in this country who has not thrown off belief but who never had it.'

My father sent us to church and to church schools, partly because it would have been scandalous at the time not to bring up your children in the Christian religion and partly because he expected financial and moral support from the church in which his wife had been a teacher. If we had refused to go to church on the grounds that we did not believe in God, he would have supported us. Mill's father did not trust anyone to educate his son, Oxford and Cambridge universities he viewed as the haunts of priests and bigots, and being a scholar, he took his son's education into his own hands. Although leading an intensely active intellectual life, he devoted a large part of every day to his son. The rigorous training of the mind, the prodigious reading and learning of Greek, Latin, history and the natural sciences which he put his son through from the age of three were extraordinary. Mill wrote:

> I have no remembrance of the time when I began to learn Greek, I have been told that it was when I was three years old. My earliest recollection on the subject, is that of committing to memory what my father termed vocables, being lists of common Greek words, with their signification in English, which he wrote out for me on cards. Of grammar, until some years later, I learnt no more than the inflexions of the nouns and verbs, but, after a course of vocables, proceeded at once to translation; and I faintly remember going through Aesop's Fables, the first Greek book which I read. The Anabasis, which I remember better, was the second. I learnt no Latin until my eighth year. At that time I had read, under my father's tuition, a number of Greek prose authors, among whom I remember the whole of Herodotus, and of Xenophon's Cyropaedia and Memorials of Socrates; some of the lives of the philosophers

by Diogenes Laertius; part of Lucian, and Isocrates ad Deonicum and Ad Nicoclem. I also read, in 1813, the first six dialogues (in the common arrangement) of Plato, from the Euthyphron to the Theoctetus inclusive: which last dialogue, I venture to think, would have been better omitted, as it was totally impossible I should understand it . . .

In my eighth year I commenced learning Latin, in conjunction with a younger sister, to whom I taught it as I went on, and who afterwards repeated the lessons to my father: and from this time, other sisters and brothers being successively added as pupils, a considerable part of my day's work consisted of this preparatory teaching. It was a part which I greatly disliked; the more so, as I was held responsible for the lessons of my pupils, in almost as full a sense as for my own . . .

From about the age of twelve, I entered into another and more advanced stage in my course of instruction; in which the main object was no longer the aids and appliances of thought, but the thoughts themselves. This commenced with Logic, in which I began at once with the Organon, and read it to the Analytics inclusive, but profited little by the Posterior Analytics, which belong to a branch of speculation I was not yet ripe for. Contemporaneously with the Organon, my father made me read the whole or parts of several of the Latin treatises on the scholastic logic; giving each day to him, in our walks, a minute account of what I had read, and answering his numerous and searching questions.

His father drilled him remorselessly in reasoned argument and debate for he believed that the right arguments would influence people and change society for the better. The young Mill learned to categorise and classify, analyse, synthesise, take false arguments to pieces and construct better ones. The philosophy which Mill senior held forth to his son was that created by Jeremy Bentham, the philosopher of utilitarianism. The young Mill called his education 'almost a course in Benthamism'. Bentham is scarcely heard of now but his ideas had a huge influence on British thinkers and British institutions throughout the nineteenth century and right up to my own youth. Like Mill, he was devoted to the improvement of society and worked incessantly to that end. It is, unfortunately, not enough to be well intentioned and devoted to prescribe for society: one must first have imagination and know a great deal about human nature, its needs and satisfactions. Bentham believed that man had one overriding interest – self-interest. But how could the clash of individual self-interests be reconciled? How could each man be made to serve the common good? Bentham believed that encouragement or discouragement would do the trick, and by creating a system of rewards and punishments 'the greatest good of the greatest number' would be achieved. Men would accept, he believed, the reasonableness of their punishments.

> It were strange if men grew not every day more virtuous than on the former day. I am satisfied they do, satisfied they will continue to do so, till, if ever, their nature shall have arrived at its perfection... There will be no moral enigmas by and by. (*Deontology*)

With hindsight, such naivety is staggering. But to contemporaries it seemed a beautiful, mechanical system for regulating society. When the young Mill first looked into it, he recorded:

> It burst upon me with all the force of novelty... the feeling rushed upon me that all previous moralists were superseded, and that here, indeed was the commencement of a new era in thought... as I proceeded further, there seemed to be added to this intellectual clearness, the most inspiring prospects for practical improvements in human affairs.

So it must have seemed to those ardent idealists who read *The Rights of Man* in 1791 or *The Communist Manifesto* of 1848. The dazzling completeness of a self-contained system is always beguiling: it seems to explain away all former weaknesses in social organisation and to herald a hitherto unknown theory for the regeneration of human society. All that has to be done is to put it into practice...

The young Mill was allowed no holidays 'in case the habit of work should be broken and a taste for idleness acquired'. My own father accused us constantly of the vice of idleness. Mill was 'constantly meriting reproof by inattention, inobservance and a general slackness of mind'. His father's 'senses and his mental faculties were always on the alert, he carried decision and energy of character in his whole manner and into every action of his life'. It might have been a description of my own father, who exhorted us to 'be on your toes', 'look sharp about it', 'quick's the word and sharp's the action'. Children's books were not encouraged nor play with boys of his own age which would have helped to make Mill easier, socially. Poetry was excluded entirely from his programme of education. This is not surprising given the views of both Bentham and Mill senior on language. They had a strict literal approach to language and dismissed both religion and poetry as 'misrepresentation'. My father would have agreed with them on the so-called mysteries of the Christian faith which, they believed, were not answerable to sovereign reason and were invented by 'wonder working priests who deprived the intellect and cherished superstition' (Bentham). Along with the supreme trust in abstract reasoning in Mill senior went a deep suspicion of all show of feeling:

> For passionate emotions of all sorts, and for everything which has been said or written in exaltation of them, he professed the greatest contempt. He regarded them as a form of madness. The intense was with him a bye-word of scornful disapprobation. He regarded as an aberration of the moral standard of modern times, compared with that of the ancients, the great stress laid upon feeling.

And, like my father, he was deficient in tenderness of feeling for his children.

> He resembled most Englishmen in being ashamed of the signs of feelings, and by the absence of demonstration, starving the feelings themselves.

Mill was to discover just how harmful was this starvation when he grew up. At the time he did not notice it nor did he feel the want of a spiritual dimension to his life. 'It was enough to do good' and 'I had what may truly be called an object in life, to be a reformer of the world.' When he was twenty years of age the totally unexpected happened: he had a severe nervous breakdown.

> I was in a dull state of nerves, such as everybody is occasionally

liable to; unsusceptible to enjoyment or pleasurable excitement; one of those moods when what is pleasurable at other times, becomes insipid or indifferent . . .

In this frame of mind it occurred to me to put the question directly to myself: 'Suppose that all your objects in life were realised; that all the changes in institutions and opinions which you are looking forward to, could be completely effected at this very instant: would this be a great joy and happiness to you?' And an irrepressible self-consciousness distinctly answered, 'No!' At this my heart sank within me: the whole foundation on which my life was constructed fell down. All my happiness was to have been found in the continual pursuit of this end. The end had ceased to charm, and how could there ever again be any interest in the means? I seemed to have nothing left to live for.

A black depression of spirits engulfed him. He had no joy in learning, no joy in living of any kind. No matter how he urged himself to recover, he could not. He could feel nothing. Thinking and wishing were unable to create the feelings that were lacking. He was in that state of mind which 'intellectuals can so easily find themselves in by overcultivation of the mind at the expense of the feelings'. Like Casaubon in George Eliot's *Middlemarch*, he was 'highly educated but unable to enjoy'. He did not see how he could continue living in this death-like state. As in my case, the person to whom it would have been natural to turn for help was the last person who would have been capable of giving it. 'Everything convinced me that he had no knowledge of any such mental state as I was suffering from.' At nineteen years of age, while at university, I too had a nervous crisis. It was an anxiety state which I was unable to understand but which frightened me. I was hardly able to eat or sleep for many weeks. I hid it as best I could from my father, knowing how little he would understand my condition. 'What', he would say, 'have you to be worried about? Haven't you had a good education, plenty to eat and drink and a good constitution?' Our maid, alarmed, finally alerted him. All he could think of to account for my condition was 'she must be expecting a baby!' I was humiliated by this gross piece of insensitivity. I knew even more clearly than before that there was no hope of real communication with my father. We continued to talk to each other over the years on harmless topics but never on any subject that really mattered.

Mill recalled:

> I was thus, as I said to myself, left stranded at the commencement of my voyage, with a well-equipped ship and a rudder but no sail... no delight in virtue or the general good, but also, just as little in anything else.

He managed to continue in this near-suicidal state for almost a year. One day he was idly turning over a book of memoirs when he came upon a moving description of a scene between a son and his dying father. He felt a tear come to his eye, and was immensely relieved by this sign of feeling in himself. 'I was not a stock or a stone.' Then, another day, he just as idly took up a book of the poetry which had been proscribed by his father: the poems of Wordsworth.

> This state of my thoughts and feelings made the fact of my reading Wordsworth for the first time (in the autumn of 1823) an important event in my life. I took up the collection of his poems from curiosity, with no expectation of mental relief from it... But Wordsworth would never have had any great effect on me, if he had merely placed before me beautiful pictures of natural scenery... What made Wordsworth's poems a medicine for my state of mind, was that they expressed, not mere outward beauty, but states of feeling, and of thought coloured by feeling... which I was in quest of. In them I seemed to draw from a source of inward joy, of sympathetic and imaginative pleasure, which could be shared by all human beings.

Slowly Mill recovered. He now realised something very important, that *abstract ideas* about happiness were not the same as the *feeling* of happiness and that thought alone cannot create feeling; feeling must come first. ('The analytical faculty can do nothing to rouse the generous emotions,' wrote Wordsworth.) Wordworth's poems showed how *habits of feeling* can be created and sustained, but if blocked, deadened or devastated, can overflow even to madness.

And it was in the verses of another poet that Mill read the exact description of his depressed state: in 'Ode to Dejection', Coleridge wrote:

> A grief without a pang, void, dark, and drear,
> A stifled, drowsy, unimpassioned grief,
> Which finds no natural outlet, no relief,
> In word, or sigh, or tear –

Mill felt even more bound to Wordsworth when he discovered that he, too, had gone through a long period of desolation of spirit and had come out of it in the same way as he was now teaching others to do. Wordsworth had been an ardent idealist like Mill when a young man. He, too, longed for justice and equality for all men. He met intellectuals like William Godwin (the father of Mary Shelley), took part in passionate debates about theories and systems for the improvement of society. He was nineteen years of age when the French Revolution took place and the great ideas of Liberty, Equality, Fraternity burst upon the world. Wordsworth's hopes were enormous. He later wrote:

> Bliss was it in that dawn to be alive,
> But to be young was very heaven!

He crossed to France in 1790 and spent three months meeting and talking with revolutionaries and royalists. He returned in 1791 and spent almost a year there but in 1793 France declared war on England and his visits had to come to an end. A friend, Beaupuy, a French revolutionary soldier, had convinced him that human nature was reasonable and that the revolution would triumph. But in the summer of 1793 all these theories, together with all his hopes, turned empty and hollow when the terror broke out and in nine months, sixteen thousand people were guillotined in the whole of France. As happens so often, the liberators had become the new tyrants. Wordsworth suffered a nervous collapse at the fall of all his hopes for humanity and he remained in a desolation of spirit for almost two years. He recovered slowly, partly because of his new friendship with the brilliant young poet Coleridge, but above all because of the loving support of his beloved sister Dorothy. Like Mill, he learned from this terrible experience: he learned not to look for wisdom in intellectual systems alone but in deep-seated habits of feeling for fellow human beings, in what he called 'the natural pieties'. And the life of the feelings was the subject of all his poems. '*Poetry,*' he said, '*is the history and science of feeling.*'

Mill, after his recovery, spoke to his friend Roebuck about the importance of poetry. 'It was naturally very difficult for a fellow Englishman to comprehend this change of heart,' he says. He induced Roebuck to read Wordsworth's poems, which Roebuck had always thought of as the poetry 'of flowers and butterflies' with nothing at all to do with practical living. But Mill knew that Roebuck was not a philistine:

> Roebuck was in many respects very different from the vulgar notion of a Benthamite or Utilitarian. He was a lover of poetry and of most of the fine arts . . . But, like most Englishmen who have feelings, he found his feelings stand very much in his way . . . he wished that his feelings should be deadened rather than quickened. And, in truth, the English character, and English social circumstances, make it so seldom possible to derive happiness from the exercise of the sympathies, that it is not wonderful if they count for little in an Englishman's scheme of life . . . [he] saw little good . . . in any cultivation of the feelings, and none at all in cultivating them through the imagination, which he thought was only cultivating illusions.

Mill attributed this deficiency to Englishmen and he considers it a weakness. Jane Austen in *Emma* (1816) also notices this absence of demonstration of the feelings in Englishmen but she notices it with approval. Mr Knightley and his brother John meet after a long interval:

> 'How d'you do, George?' and 'John, how are you?' succeeded in true English style, burying under a calmness that seemed all but indifference the real attachment which would have led either of them, if requisite, to do everything for the good of the other.

Both Mill and Jane Austen notice how differently the English and French deal with their feelings. Mill, who spent many years in France, approves of the French style, and noted the contrast between the frank sociability and amiability of French personal intercourse, and the English mode of existence in which everybody acts as if everybody else (with few, or no exceptions) was either an enemy or a bore. In France, it is true, the bad as well as the good points, both of the individual and the national character, come more to the surface, and break out more fearlessly in ordinary intercourse, than in England: but the general habit of the people is to show, as well as to expect, friendly feeling in everyone towards every other, wherever there is not some positive cause for the opposite. In England it is only of the best bred people, in the upper or upper middle ranks, that anything like this can be said.

I was glad that it was natural for me to express my feelings freely. In this I saw myself to be a true Irishwoman. Having lived for a time in both England and France, I was convinced that it was in Ireland alone that a stranger was always to be regarded as a possible friend unless he positively proved himself an enemy!

CHARLES DICKENS
AND THE LIFE OF THE FEELINGS

When John Stuart Mill was writing his autobiography, his childhood was long behind him and he could look back and place it in the curve of his life. But years before he told the world about his childhood, Dickens knew all about it and the disastrous effect it had upon him. He knew the utilitarian principles on which Mill senior had formed his son and he hated them. He had seen the results of these principles in schools, factories, workhouses and prisons and knew that they were dry, insensitive and degrading, shaped by people who knew nothing about human nature. Dickens knew about contemporary institutions. As a boy he had visited the Marshalsea prison in London, where his father had been imprisoned for debt, and at the age of twelve he was put to work in a blacking factory labelling bottles at six shillings a week. These two experiences haunted him all his life. As an adult he worked as a criminal reporter in the Old Bailey, where he heard appalling stories of crime and violence and the terrible punishments meted out for them, punishments especially cruel and insensitive to hapless children. Into his novels he put his passionate protest against all the ideas, theories, institutions, greed, cant and hypocrisy which debased human beings. My father loved his fantastical, satirical humour and gloried in his eccentric and idiosyncratic characters.

Appalled by the utilitarian system of Bentham, Dickens decided to deliver a powerful satire against it in a new novel which he called *Hard Times* – hard times for schoolchildren, hard times for factory workers whose bosses professed utilitarian principles of laissez-faire to justify the exploitation of their workers, hard times for young men and women reaping the rewards of an ignorant and degrading system of education. Unlike Mill's autobiography, which was read by the educated public only, Dickens's novel would be read by a huge popular audience in Britain and America, by readers who loved his exciting stories and his unforgettable characters. Everyone knew and savoured Uriah Heep, David Copperfield, Oliver Twist, Sarah Gamp and Mr Pecksniff. Even those who never read a word of Dickens knew that Oliver Twist had asked for more. They laughed and they cried over his characters and over his extraordinary zest for the English language, which he played in as expertly as a dolphin plays in water. 'I am stunned with work,' he wrote, 'I am three parts mad and a fourth delirious with rushing at *Hard Times*.' He finally brought it out in 1854, a full nineteen years before Mill's *Autobiography*.

He tells with marvellous energy the story of a sister and brother, Louisa and Tom, who are subjected to a strict utilitarian education and shows that what happens to them as adults is a direct result of their early education. It is a cautionary tale for our own times. When you read the story, you might think that Dickens exaggerates wildly when describing the children's education but David Craig in the introduction to the Penguin edition (1969) claims that

> the first two chapters of the novel are an almost straight copy of the teaching system in schools run by two societies for educating the poor. In the Manchester Lancastrian School a thousand children were taught in one huge room, controlled by a kind of military drill with monitors and a monitor-general, and taught by methods derived from the Catechism.

My father told me that his schooling in Newtownards at the end of the last century consisted entirely of question-and-answer sessions as if every aspect of the world was a matter of ascertainable fact and all known to the teacher. The pupils were required to recite the principal cities of every country without, in the least, knowing anything more about them than their names. In the 1930s and 1940s in Dublin I was required to learn by heart the causes of the Penal Laws and the five causes of the French Revolution. David Craig says that as late as 1959 he was 'present in a Scottish school when one of HM

Inspectors spent twenty minutes trying to get the boys to define a table. As he was about to leave he turned and asked them to repeat the hard-won definition. Not one of them could remember it!'

Dickens calls the father of the children in *Hard Times* Mr Gradgrind; he is an easily recognisable variant on James Mill, father of John Stuart Mill, and Dickens makes him not only an educationist and a father but a Member of Parliament, thus cleverly suggesting that the system had government approval. He links him in friendship with Mr Josiah Bounderby (Dickens is wonderful at creating names), a self-made, self-important factory owner, and shows that the utilitarian philosophy can be just as well invoked to justify maltreating workers as to educate children. Jack Yeats, artist brother of the poet W.B. Yeats, called this union of piety and thrift 'sanctimonious commercialism' and claimed that its last stronghold was the North of Ireland!

Dickens opens the novel, significantly, in a schoolroom. Mr Gradgrind is questioning the 'little vessels' in rows of desks in front of him.

'Now, what I want is, Facts. Teach these boys and girls nothing but Facts. Facts alone are wanted in life. Plant nothing else, and root out everything else. You can only form the minds of reasoning animals upon Facts: nothing else will ever be of any service to them. This is the principle on which I bring up my own children. Stick to Facts, sir!'

The tone is dogmatic, bullying.

The scene was a plain, bare, monotonous vault of a schoolroom, and the speaker's square forefinger emphasised his observations by underscoring every sentence with a line on the schoolmaster's sleeve. The emphasis was helped by the speaker's square wall of a forehead, which had his eyebrows for its base, while his eyes found commodious cellarage in two dark caves, overshadowed by the wall. The emphasis was helped by the speaker's mouth, which was wide, thin, and hard set. The emphasis was helped by the speaker's voice, which was inflexible, dry, and dictatorial. The emphasis was helped by the speaker's hair, which bristled on the skirts of his bald head, a plantation of firs to keep the wind from its shining surface, all covered with knobs, like the crust of a plum pie, as if the head had scarcely warehouse-room for the hard facts stored inside. The speaker's obstinate carriage, square coat, square legs, square shoulders – nay, his very neckcloth, trained to take him by the throat with an unaccommodating grasp, like a stubborn fact, as it was – all helped the emphasis.

In another brilliant scene he reduces to absurdity the utilitarian belief that only literal language can convey the truth. (There are people who still believe this.) Mr Gradgrind calls for the definition of a horse from girl number twenty, Sissy Jupe. She is the daughter of a circus worker and knows all about horses but she is 'thrown into the greatest alarm by this demand'. She cannot bring out a word to describe what she knows so intimately.

'Girl number twenty unable to define a horse!' said Mr Gradgrind, for the general behoof of all the little pitchers. 'Girl number twenty possessed of no facts, in reference to one of the commonest of animals! Some boy's definition of a horse. Bitzer, yours.'

Bitzer answers:

'Quadruped. Graminivorous. Forty teeth, namely, twenty-four grinders, four eye-teeth, and twelve incisive. Sheds coat in the spring; in marshy countries, sheds hoofs, too. Hoofs hard, but requiring to be shod with iron. Age known by marks in mouth.' Thus (and much more) Bitzer.

'Now girl number twenty,' said Mr Gradgrind. 'You know what a horse is.' The point is skilfully and economically made: information is not knowledge but is frequently taken for it. Theories, analyses, percentages, statistics can look authoritative, scientific and final but they may be completely divorced from real knowledge, and when professed by people who have power to direct our lives, can be very dangerous. (Bitzer, who has successfully studied the system, is to do very well for himself but he knows neither loyalty nor gratitude.)

Mr Gradgrind tries hard to show the little vessels in front of him the hard realities of fact:

'Now, let me ask you girls and boys. Would you paper a room with representations of horses? ... I'll explain to you, then ... why you wouldn't paper a room with representations of horses. Do you ever see horses walking up and down the sides of rooms in reality – in fact? Do you? ... Of course, No ... Why, then, you are not to see anywhere, what you don't see in fact; you are not to have anywhere, what you don't have in fact. What is called Taste, is only another name for Fact!'

Dramatically and wittily, Dickens has shown the absurdity of the literal men – and they are always with us – who deny the language of metaphor and imagery, the expressive language of the imagination, because it is not literally true.

Mr Bounderby is the counterpart in industry of Mr Gradgrind in education, but he is less honest and less well intentioned. In fact he is a deep-dyed hypocrite who makes himself out to be much more of a self-made man than he really is – he falsely claims that his mother abandoned him in a ditch – so that his business acumen and success will look all the more impressive. He has pulled himself up by his braces, so to speak. He invokes the self-help principles of laissez-faire utilitarianism to justify sanctimoniously the heartless conditions he has created for his workers. It suits him not to believe in imagination.

'When a man tells me anything about imaginative qualities, I always tell that man, whoever he is, that I know what he means. He means turtle-soup and venison, with a gold spoon, and that he wants to be set up with a coach-and-six.'

I often heard my father say this kind of thing: 'Haven't they got enough food and clothing and a roof over their heads? What more do they want?' The flamboyant hypocrisy of Bounderby, his stupid dogmatism, his unrepentant self-righteousness, his utter philistinism are made hugely funny by Dickens's language which is the opposite of literal. He lived

in a red house with black outside shutters, green inside blinds, a black street door, up two white steps, BOUNDERBY (in letters very like himself) upon a brazen plate, and a round brazen door-handle underneath it, like a brazen full-stop.

Mr Bounderby is very interested in the beautiful but very bored Louisa, who is thirty years his junior. He asks for her hand in marriage and Mr Gradgrind sees no objection to this union as he judges only by material criteria. Bounderby is a good match. Mr Gradgrind's reasoned approach might have come straight from my father. I never knew how to answer this logic but the knowledge of something vital that was missing, something I could not quite grasp, almost suffocated me. My father would have thought, like Gradgrind, that there was no feeling that could not be overcome for material advantage, particularly in women. Louisa's brother, Tom, will later say of his sister's loveless marriage to Bounderby, 'she's a regular girl. A girl can get on anywhere', and 'girls can always get on, somehow'. In these little phrases lay the humiliations of many a girl's flesh and spirit.

Louisa looks through the window at the smoking chimneys of Coketown. She makes a startling remark:

'There seems to be nothing there but languid and monotonous smoke. Yet when the night comes, fire bursts out, father!' She answered, turning quickly.

'Of course I know that, Louisa. I do not see the application of the remark.' To do him justice he did not, at all.

My father knew full well what the fire was but, in the manner of the times, he carried on as if these fires did not exist either for himself or for his children. His only reference to the fire was his advice to me on going to Paris for a year on a French government scholarship: 'Remember, my child, Dublin is not Paris.' I could make what I liked of that.

Louisa marries Bounderby, for no one thing matters more than another, and becomes an icy princess. She is profoundly bored but apparently in complete control of herself. Dickens then brings into her life an apparent gentleman of taste and sensitivity. Dickens's purpose is to show what happens when feelings, long suppressed and twisted, finally erupt and fire breaks out. Beauty is to be aroused from a death-like trance by the beast. James Harthouse is another measure on Dickens's barometer of feeling. Like Louisa, he is very bored. He had come to Coketown to try his hand at politics, having been everywhere and done everything and 'having found everything to be worth nothing [was] especially ready for anything'. His carefully cultivated gentlemanly manner misleads; he is not a man who hides his feelings for he has no feelings to hide. He becomes curious about the relationship between the icy princess and the coarse, stupid bully. She is a challenge and he determines to get her in his power, 'is there nothing that will move that face?'

He says to Louisa:

> 'The result of the varieties of boredom I have undergone, is a conviction (unless conviction is too industrious a word for the lazy sentiment I entertain on the subject), that any set of ideas will do just as much good as any other set ... What will be, will be.'

This attitude exactly suits Louisa: it justifies her bored and barren life. She, too, has missed nothing for there is nothing to miss. Cynical people need to be reassured in the same way that everything is, at bottom, dust and ashes. They, too, have missed nothing and, what is more, they have the great satisfaction of knowing it. My father had a habit of dismissing generous motives, preferring to see them as self-interested. My soul revolted against this contempt which was in fact the other face of his disappointed idealism. Oscar Wilde's phrase about cynics, that they know 'the price of everything and the value of nothing', sums up both the contemptuous and the lovers of facts.

Dickens charts the movements of Louisa's heart with the utmost poetic sensitivity. The shallow Harthouse is playing a dangerous game with the deep-feeling Louisa. 'To be sure, the better and profounder part of her character, was not within his scope of perception; for in natures, as in seas, depth answers unto depth ...' This assumption of honesty in dishonesty is dangerous indeed. He manoeuvres to find her alone so that he can declare his passion. He speaks of his adoration, sure of a happy reception. 'My dearest love ... what could I do? Knowing you were alone, was it possible that I could stay away?' She urges him to go, 'but she neither turned her face to him, nor raised it'. He is sure of his prey. 'Shall I ride up to the house a few minutes hence, innocently supposing that its master is at home and will be charmed to receive me?' Louisa refuses the artifice, and breaks from him promising a later meeting. She flies, instinctively, to her father and confronts him with her pain.

'Father, you have trained me from my cradle.'
'Yes, Louisa.'
'I curse the hour in which I was born to such a destiny.'
... 'Curse the hour? Curse the hour?'
'How could you give me life, and take from me all the in-appreciable things that raise it from the state of conscious death?'

But Mr Gradgrind and his philosophy are as incapable of helping Louisa as James Mill was incapable of helping his son and as my father would have been incapable of helping me.

'All that I know is, your philosophy and your teaching will not save me. Now, father, you have brought me to this. Save me by some other means!'
He tightened his hold in time to prevent her sinking on the floor, but she cried out in a terrible voice, 'I shall die if you hold me! Let me fall upon the ground!' And he laid her down there, and saw the pride of his heart and the triumph of his system, lying, an insensible heap, at his feet.

'I shall die if you hold me!' is a sure touch. It was just as impossible for me to hold my father in my arms as he lay dying. The embarrassment, even *in extremis*, would have been too great. The barriers of years cannot so easily be crossed. Our feeling for one another, genuine as it was, had to remain unexpressed. He turned his eyes towards me, all that he was able to turn in his weakened state; they were bright and full of expression, of affection, of gratitude, the nearest he ever got to expressing his real feeling for me. Mr Gradgrind is allowed to learn, at this terrible price, the errors of his system, for he meant well; but Bounderby remains encased in his brazen hypocrisy.

Dickens's readers expected and wanted a happy ending. Louisa had suffered enough; make her happy now! But Dickens's instinct was true: he knew that feelings so thoroughly damaged in childhood cannot fully recover. He does not allow her to remarry.

Herself again a wife – a mother – lovingly watchful of her children, ever careful that they should have a childhood of the mind no less than a childhood of the body ... Did Louisa see this? Such a thing was never to be.

It is Dickens's purpose to show that the healthy feelings of love, loyalty, sympathy are found deep and sure in the 'unsuccessful' Sissy Jupe; it is she who cares for Louisa and becomes a loving sister to her and it is she who dismisses Harthouse, much to his mortification. Although Dickens makes her uneducated, her heart is shown to be supremely tutored to all that matters. Sissy – unable to define a horse – is the proof that 'a man of clear ideas errs grievously if he imagines that what is seen confusedly does not exist'.

I knew this to be true. I knew that all the little kindnesses I had received in the street around the Lodge had had nothing to do with formal education.

AT SCHOOL IN DUBLIN
DURING THE WAR

My brothers went from Mount Brown National School to Mountjoy School as scholarship holders. My sister had won a scholarship to the Church of Ireland Diocesan School for Girls and I was to follow in her footsteps. Most of the pupils of our primary school would leave at fourteen years of age to become shop assistants or tradesmen. I was told to prepare for the entrance examination and not to fail to win a scholarship. No excuse would be taken. Frank and Hugh were ordered to prepare me for it. Neither brother savoured the task but they knew they could not refuse: there was no arguing with our father. After a school day followed by rugby or cricket, they were faced with me and my exercise book. Frank was to teach me Irish and Hugh mathematics. English I would have no difficulty with. Frank was much too impatient to be a good teacher and after a busy day and a full meal his patience was particularly thin. He would ask me some questions and if I could not answer he would fling the book back at me and tell me to learn the rules and report to him later. He then usually fell into a deep sleep in front of the kitchen range and I dared not wake him. Hugh was more conscientious: he drew up a chair beside me at the big kitchen table, explained the problem, wrote out examples and rules and put me through the exercises. I enjoyed working with him and understood his teaching so well that I think he would have made a very good schoolteacher.

If I failed, my father said, it would be the factory for me. I was more afraid of his anger than of the factory floor and as the time drew near for the examination and I was to be taken to the other side of the town to a school and teachers I did not know, I became very apprehensive. The day came, my stomach was churning and I felt hopeless. The papers were put in front of me and I turned them over and ran my eye over the questions; that special form of torture was to be repeated many more times in my scholastic career and I never got used to it. Thankfully, apprehension in my case, although intense, was never as bad as the reality. I forgot everything but the effort of understanding and answering the questions asked. At the end of every examination I ever did, I was nervously drained and suffered from indigestion. When, a few weeks later, news came that I had not only passed the examination but won a scholarship, I was delighted with myself. My sense of justice, however, was outraged when my father presented Hugh and Frank with five shillings each for having coached me, but to me, the successful candidate, he gave only two and sixpence!

I was to start in Diocesan in September 1937. That summer passed lazily by. There were many hours of wearisome boredom when Martha did not come to play or my father was in a bad mood, making the present hours a desolation. Then Martha turned in through the Gate and all was happiness again. We took off on our bikes to the Park and to any form of fun and mischief we could find or manufacture. In August, a letter arrived from Diocesan listing the dress requirements for the new pupil – a dark green school tunic, cream blouse, striped tie, gym-shoes and gym-bag with my initials attached. The seriousness of all these new vestments deeply impressed me. I had never had a uniform before. Solomon in all his glory could not have been half so much in love with himself as I was when I embarked for my new school in beautifully pleated gym-frock with girdle carefully arranged in a casual way and my tie knotted by the expert hands of Frank. I loved wearing the uniform; it gave me a feeling of belonging. That tunic grew shiny, thin and almost threadbare and in the six years I spent at Diocesan I had only one other tunic.

The transition from the friendly neighbourhood school to Diocesan was, at first, bewildering. We were given a timetable, something I had not heard of at Mount Brown School, and all sorts of new subjects appeared on it – French, Geography, Art, Science and

Domestic Science (for some unknown reason I was not allowed to do Science, something which still rankles with me). And we were to have different teachers for each subject instead of the comfortable one teacher for everything. I would not even know how to find the different rooms we were to move to throughout the day.

The headmistress, Miss Latimer, addressed me in the corridor soon after the beginning of the term: 'So you are Edith Gaw. I hope you will do as well as your sister here. And how your poor dear mother will be pleased to watch you working hard and behaving yourself.' I was shocked and confused by this pious mention of someone who had been absolutely dismissed from my consciousness. What had my mother to do with it? And 'watching me', what an uncomfortable and even nauseating idea. I hoped the headmistress would never mention that name again. She did, once more. I had been the organiser of a harmless piece of mischief – hiding the school bell in a sack of waste paper – when I was discovered. Miss Latimer called me to her office, viewed me with solemn and reproachful eyes and said, 'If your poor dear mother could see you now, how ashamed she would be of her little daughter.' The tears welled up in my eyes and ran down my face, not, as she thought, from contrition, but from deep and profound embarrassment. That name which was on nobody's lips had been on hers, she who knew nothing about me. I could not understand my horribly painful emotion.

The teachers in long black academic gowns looked much more impressive and much more remote than the kindly, gownless Miss Barnett who had mothered us all. They were teachers and we were pupils in the given order of things. We never thought of criticising their academic ability or teaching methods as we had no standards of comparison and we were used to accepting authority. Miss G—— was our algebra teacher; her gown bedraggled, chalk-strewn, half-on, half-off, matched her grey hair which was roughly drawn back from her face into an undisciplined bun, and all, like her teaching, dull and disorganised. Her weak commands for us to stop talking never succeeded. I was one of the worst offenders. We never thought of her as a human being with her own personal hopes and fears: she was simply a teacher, anonymous, rootless, crossing our visual and mental horizons five times a week. But she was the first person to tell me that W.B. Yeats was a great Irish poet. She had been brought up in the Sligo countryside and often visited Lissadell House, where his friends, the Gore-Booths, lived. And he was buried in a little churchyard which hardly anyone had heard of. She told us that her father was a clergyman and knew the churchyard. Daughter of a clergyman? We were not surprised, for to us, clergy were all dull and boring.

My art teacher I can remember very well. She was young, just out of art school and full of new ideas. She watched us mixing yellow and blue paint in our paintboxes so as 'to make green', the standard rule. 'Why not mix the colour straight onto the paper?' she said. 'Put one on top of the other and see what comes out. Half-close your eyes and try to paint the impression of a scene. Forget what you think *ought* to be there and paint what your eyes tell you.' It was exciting. We were released from the restrictions of perspective, hard outlines, representationalism and deadness. She helped to form my delight in the visual world, a delight which has remained with me.

My bicycle, second-hand as it was, was my Rolls-Royce, my magic carpet, my transporter to seaside and mountain, my wings of Mercury to fly down the two-mile hill of the main road in the Phoenix Park. Not many poor people in James's Street owned bicycles. I cared for mine like a treasure, cleaning and polishing each individual spoke of the wheels until they gleamed, and every now and then, with the touch of a paintbrush, transfiguring it into a shining new model. Dynamo lamps were then all the rage and I dreamed of having one on my bicycle, but they were expensive and out of my reach. My father had only recently changed from an acetylene lamp which had to be lit with a match and which hissed like a gas jet, so there was no use applying to him. There was one way, however, of acquiring a dynamo without money and it was a hard and long way. Wills's cigarettes Sweet Afton gave away one miniature playing card with each packet of cigarettes. If you collected a complete pack of these miniature cards you could take them to Wills's tobacco factory on the South Circular Road and be given a real pack in return. If you collected seven of these miniature packs you could get a dynamo lamp.

Martha and I began the seemingly impossible task of collecting them. Nobody in the family smoked, so we had to beg, borrow and bargain for them. We stopped strangers in the street and asked if they had a card to give us; we picked up discarded cigarette packets from the gutter, hoping to find a card in one; we bought cards from youngsters at six for one penny; we swapped cards and we did deals. Every now and again we laid out our cards on the kitchen table and counted and computed. At long last we had seven packs each. We cycled to Wills's factory, laid our packs on the counter, each one neatly secured with a rubber band. The showcases all around displayed wonderful articles which you could acquire with the unthinkable number of fifteen, twenty, thirty packs... We watched our cards being counted out and checked, and with an affirmative nod the assistant handed each of us a box with a dynamo inside it. For many weeks thereafter we waited for dark to descend, then jumped on our bikes, leaned forward in a professional manner, pressed our dynamos to the front wheel and watched proudly as the big, white beam lit up the road in front of us.

I usually chose to cycle to school by the canal. It was quiet and leafy and I could easily do a little reading of a book in my bicycle basket if I found it exciting. Besides, there was always plenty on the canal to see – immaculate swans gliding in and out of dirty sedges, ducks with gleaming blue-green necks, an occasional rat, or a heavy barge being pulled slowly along by a poor tow-horse. We children loved to watch the barges going through the locks, to be allowed to stay on the footboard of the big double-deck lock gates while the lock-keeper turned his wheel to force open the gates and let the great weight of green-brown water surge over the retaining wall and fall thundering into the hollow bottom below.

I kept to the right-hand side of the canal, pedalling effortlessly along on the flat, past the bridges which brought Dubliners into work from the suburbs. There were occasional small Georgian houses on the other side of the canal, rubbish dumps of twisted metal, the grey building of the Griffith army barracks and the handsome Portobello House. Over Rathmines and Ranelagh bridges, cyclists, cars and well-dressed people poured into work. I passed to the other side of the canal over Ranelagh bridge and turned right into Harcourt Terrace where the once stylish period houses were peeling and dilapidated. In front of me lay a long rectangular building of red brick – our school where I was a pupil for six years.

I was almost thirteen years old and I had completed two years at the school when something happened to disturb the even tenor of our lives. War broke out between Britain and Germany. Even in faraway Dublin the resonances were profound. My father made us all gather round our crackling little wireless to hear Neville Chamberlain make his fateful announcement that Britain 'is at war with Germany'.

'What does that mean, Daddy?' I asked, puzzled.

'It means a long terrible war ahead, far worse than the first war. Whoever wins will be the poorer for many years afterwards.'

I could not understand that paradox.

'There will be bombing, thousands will be killed, food will be hard to come by. If Hitler wins, God help us all.'

Frightened by this bleak scenario, I asked, 'Will we have to take to the mountains, Daddy, and live in tents? What will happen to our house and furniture? How will I get to school?'

'We don't know yet what will happen,' said my father. 'We don't know if this damned country will go in with the Allies or not.'

Ireland remained neutral, much to my father's disgust. Nothing happened for a time. Three times a day, coinciding with mealtimes, my father listened to the radio news and we did not dare stir. News came of disasters in Europe, the evacuation of Dunkirk, ships sunk by German U-boats, aeroplanes shot down and pilots missing. I came to dread the news, not because of the losses reported for I could scarcely, at my age, take them in, but because of the black mood of irritability which would seize hold of my father and overflow onto us.

The distant war became suddenly less distant when we Girl Guides were summoned to the Mansion House to help assemble gas masks for the citizens. They must be expecting us to be bombed, I thought, and I might be killed . . . We tried to laugh off our fears as we put on the masks and looked at each other in our pig-snouts and goggle-eyes. Martha and I climbed to the top of the big chestnut tree which we called the King Tree, which was outside our kitchen window, to discuss the impending disaster. We made a plan of campaign: should the big air raid sirens go off, we would run to the endless acres of the Phoenix Park and hide there till the raid was over. We found a tin box, put two apples and some biscuits into it and hid it in the higher branches of the tree, ready for emergencies. I arranged with Martha to warn her if I heard startling news on the radio (Martha's family had no radio) by running to the top of Bow Lane and signalling with my bicycle lamp S-O-S, S-O-S, aiming at a piece of silver paper she would put in her window to catch the light. If necessary, we would live on haws, bread and cheese and wild mushrooms. There was always some alarm in those early days; newsboys dashed around the streets with bunches of newspapers yelling 'Stop press! Stop press!' and everyone rushed to read the latest sensational headlines.

All at once there was no coal to be had. 'The British government can spare no ships from the war-effort to carry coals to Ireland,' said my father. Luckily there was a plentiful Irish substitute – turf. The demand was so great that turf was cut from the bogs and delivered to the shops without being given time to dry out. It went straight to the fires and ranges where it spluttered, hissed and expired in a cloud of steam and smoke. 'Call me when the turf comes to the boil' was a common joke. Worse was the shortage of coal for making gas to supply the countless black gas cookers which were the centre of every home for making tea, the national drink. The Gas Company was obliged to ration the supply of gas to three one-hour sessions each day but it was unable to completely cut off the gas in between times, and the small amount which remained could be ignited to make a tiny flame. This was known as the 'glimmer'. It was strictly forbidden to use it under pain of having your gas supply cut off altogether, but everyone did. The Gas Company recruited an army of 'glimmermen' to surprise culprits. A network of neighbours constituted a watch committee and word flew from house to house if a glimmerman appeared in the vicinity. The hot rings and bars were rushed under cold water by one person while another tried to keep him talking at the door. All sorts of jokes were current. Question: 'What did the blonde say when she opened the door to the glimmerman?' Answer: 'Come in and we'll have a bit of gas' (gas – fun). Petrol became almost unobtainable. Cars could be seen in Dublin with great bags of gas attached to the roof like giant travelling mushrooms. Horses and carts multiplied. Bicycles, always a popular form of transport, became so thick on the roads that a car could scarcely pass them. Unemployed men with entrepreneurial skills set up bicycle parks in O'Connell Street and guaranteed to mind your bike for a few pence a day.

Another emergency was the shortage of coal to fire the trains. There were tales of passengers having to descend from the carriages, dig turf out of the bog and throw it into the engine. The long-distance bus, the usual conveyor of country people, conveyed everyone, everywhere. Olive, now married, was living in Galway. Billy, a reservist in the Irish army, had been called up in September 1939 and Olive was alone. I manoeuvred with my father to get away and spend a week or two with her. It took all day to cross Ireland in the bus. As the Galway bus left Aston Quay at 8.00 a.m., I had to be in the queue at 7.00 a.m. and that meant having to leave the house at 6.30 a.m. on my bicycle as city buses did not run at that hour of the morning. I strapped my suitcase to the back carrier, and with one hand behind me, I tried to steady it as it lurched from side to side, while trying to steer with the other. I checked my bike in to a bicycle park in O'Connell Street and joined the queue. How cold it was at that time of the morning with the wind whipping up along the line of the Liffey! As always, there was a joker or two in the pack who made us all laugh. At 7.30 a.m. the bus drew up and we clambered aboard, men, women, children, babies, bags, sacks, parcels and other diverse objects. The driver ran up and down his little ladder loading bicycles, prams and sacks onto the roof and when all was secured we were off on our journey across the central plain of Ireland.

After a couple of hours, the bus drew up outside a public house and the driver shouted, 'Fifteen minutes here!' The fifteen minutes up, there was no sign of driver or passengers. After another fifteen minutes the driver returned and sounded the horn to warn the stragglers. Ten more minutes passed. The driver got out, went into the pub and reappeared with the missing passengers. There was now a distinct odour of Guinness in the bus. Twice more we went through the same procedure. No one complained for all knew that it would be the height of bad manners to complain when men were enjoying themselves. At 8.00 p.m., two hours behind schedule, we drew into Eyre Square in Galway, weary and stiff, and I was borne off in Olive's car to her new home in Salthill.

I was very happy there. I helped Olive in the house, went for long walks by the sea and occasionally was taken for drives to Connemara. Bowling along in all the pleasurable luxuriousness of a car, gazing, entranced, at the infinitely changing patterns of sky, water and mountain, I was in heaven.

In April 1941 I was delighted when Babs Newman, my mother's cousin, invited me to spend a week with her parents and herself in Belfast. I had never been to the North, that mysterious Black North which people spoke of rather glumly. I had to persuade my father to let me absent myself from home. This time he had a good reason for letting me go. The South, although not at war, had to impose rationing for some foods, and two ounces of sugar a week and half an ounce of tea was a mortal blow to a nation addicted to sweet tea. We had been reduced to digging up dandelion roots, roasting them and making an abominable drink out of them. My father suffered particularly as he began his day at 6.00 a.m. with tea and ended it with the same at 11.00 p.m. Butter, eggs, bacon, short in the North, were plentiful in the South and a steady stream of smugglers passed up and down across the border with the prohibited goods. My father saw his chance. He provided me with two pounds of butter and two of bacon to give to the Newmans with instructions to bring back as much sugar and tea as I could lay my hands on. Before I got to the border, I was to put one pound of butter under my cardigan, the other pound in my case and the bacon in the small of my back. Everyone in the train spoke of their contraband, told stories of heroic passages of arms with customs men and how they were going to best them again. One man had a small ham in his suitcase which he intended to pass from his hand outside the window to his friend in the next compartment at the very moment when the customs men moved from one compartment to the other. Everyone enjoyed talking about this national sport.

The train came to a halt at Gorraghwood on the border between the South and Northern Ireland and on came the dreaded inspectors. They entered our compartment, gave each one of us a penetrating look and asked to see the contents of our suitcases. I began to tremble, seeing myself being discovered, shamed and removed from the train between two customs men. One of them opened my case, put his hand in and tumbled the contents about: he did not find the pound of butter so I could breathe again. A priest in the window seat was not even questioned, for all priests were, of course, above suspicion.

My 'Uncle Jim', as I called my mother's first cousin, was a head constable in the police. Though kindly, he found it very hard to communicate with others and I was afraid of him. He was a fine figure of a man with a small moustache which he waxed regularly. His hands were always occupied twirling the ends into two points. He was a southerner, Church of Ireland like my mother but puritan and austere. He said his prayers so loudly in his bedroom at night that we could all hear the steady drone through the walls. Ironically, his wife, the northerner, smoked, laughed and loved to play a hand at poker for money when her husband was out. Husband and wife did not get on. I was confirmed in my conviction that one must be very, very careful before one married.

The fact of war was more real in Belfast than in Dublin. As in Dublin, a blackout was imposed so that not even a crack of light could escape from windows. Babs and I went for a walk in the nearby Holywood Hills, slipping out from the dark kitchen into the darker night. A huge object suddenly loomed up in front of us. It was only a barrage balloon, Babs said, ready to lift off and prevent enemy aircraft form descending too low over the city. Enemy aircraft . . . I did not like the idea of that. Then 'Who goes there?' rang out in the darkness, terrifying me. 'Don't worry,' said Babs, 'it's only the Home Guard.' The fright provoked an instant desire to relieve myself. I stepped aside onto the grass verge and fell, bare-bottomed, into a bed of nettles. Not even the threat of enemy aircraft and Home Guard could prevent me from yelling out with the pain of a hundred stings on my tender flesh.

A few days afterwards a terrible undulating wail sounded through the streets. It was an air raid warning. I looked down from my bedroom window over Sydenham airport and saw men running in all directions and aircraft taking off. Uncle Jim called out, 'Come down at once and go to the cellar and stay there till the all-clear sounds.' I shot down the stairs and joined Babs and her mother in the cellar, which had been made into a shelter and filled with blankets, candles and tins of food. This was the real thing. Why had I ever come to Belfast? Would I ever see the Lodge again? Would we all be buried under tons of rubble? After what seemed many hours but which was only a short time, the steady note of the all-clear sounded and we were able to emerge. It had only been a 'reconnaissance', Uncle Jim told us. The next morning, at breakfast, looking stern, he told me that I would have to return to Dublin. He could not be responsible for me in present circumstances. I was put on the train with half a pound of tea and four pounds of sugar in my suitcase. The day after my departure, on 15 April, German planes unloaded over one hundred tons of bombs over Belfast, killing at least 745 people in one night. A bomb fell just outside the Newmans' house, creating a huge crater. Nineteen days later 204 German aircraft returned to the city and dropped 95,000 incendiary bombs on the harbour and shipyards just below their house. I had had a near escape. I felt that I had seen war and I did not like it. I was glad to be finished with it. But I was wrong.

Olive, who was expecting her first baby the following June, moved to Dublin for 'the Duration'. I often cycled over to Clontarf and spent the night with her when Billy was away. On the night of 30 May we were awakened by a strange noise. We listened intently, straining to identify it. It got nearer and nearer, a low throbbing noise, then faded slowly away into the distance. I leaped out of bed and ran to Olive, who was decidedly nervous. I then flew downstairs and out of the front door to see what was happening. The sky was all lit up by great pathways of light crossing and recrossing one another while green lights, like fireworks, sped up into the sky and down again. All the neighbours were by now outside, questioning, wondering. 'Surely it can't be German planes mistaking us for an English city? Surely they know we're neutral! Or is it the English warning us not to hand over the ports?'

Another wave of sound swelled in the sky, pulsating, sinister. I ran indoors to find Olive in near-hysterics. What would I do if her baby was born with the fright and I had to manage the birth myself? I had no idea of how a baby came into the world. I prayed hard, 'O God, don't let it happen!' That sound again ... silence ... then the thick thud and thump of an explosion. Before we had time to take in what was happening, there was another violent thud, then another and another, followed at once by terrific explosions from the direction of the city centre. Terrified now, we huddled together in the cupboard under the stairs. Would one of these bombs fall on us next? We prayed fervently, flinching in the darkness until all was quiet. We risked a sally into the kitchen to soothe our nerves with tea, then crept back again under the stairs. About 6.00 a.m. the milkman appeared and told us that half of Dublin had been wiped out and hundreds of people killed. We were aghast. An hour later, we learned over the radio that parts of Amiens Street and North Strand had been levelled by German planes and thirty-four people killed. It seemed we were in the war now. Like London, Belfast and Coventry we could be bombed again . . . but we never were.

Frank came home on leave from the Air Force from time to time but never in uniform. He was the best-looking in the family and I was always proud to be seen with him. He always took me to Cafolla's ice cream parlour in O'Connell Street with an invitation to order what I liked. This was a dream come true! I always ordered Knickerbocker Glories but could manage only two. Hugh was living in Belfast working in the civil service. When he could afford it, he came for the weekend to see his Dublin girlfriend so I saw little of him. I was often, now, quite alone with my father. All through 1941 when the war was going badly for the Allies, his mood was black. 'The Board of Admiralty regrets to announce the loss of HMS *Hood*, *Ark Royal*, *Repulse*, *Prince of Wales* . . .' 'Ships are having a far worse time than they did with us,' he said. 'Those Arctic convoys are frightful.' I melted away to avoid his nervous irritation. It was all far away and unreal for a schoolgirl like me. I once caught sight of 'the enemy'. They were German internees walking behind barbed wire fences in the Phoenix Park. I was surprised to see that they looked just like everybody else.

ROMANCE

In the spring of 1943, after nearly seventeen years working at St Patrick's, my father had a row with the hospital authorities and left the Lodge. He was in a state of unusual emotional turmoil over this decision and, for the first time in his life, he appealed to one of his children for support and justification, an appeal that was deeply unsettling to a child who had only known him strong and self-assured. He confided in me: he had never liked the hospital; he had taken the job to support his wife and children; he would be glad to be free of the servility he believed to be demanded of him; he had his naval pension and some savings and we two would find somewhere to live in peace and quietness together.

Just at that time, my Aunt Jenny found herself in financial difficulties and decided to sell her house in Drimnagh Road and move to rented accommodation in nearby Crumlin village, where she was a teacher. My father bought the house and arranged to move in the following autumn. In the intervening period, we could stay with Olive and Billy and their two children in the north of the city. Our furniture was put into store and with a couple of suitcases each, we left the Lodge for good. I have never liked leaving anywhere or anybody I have known long, even when I do not feel very affectionate towards them. My emotions wind themselves round what I know and the shock of severance, if it comes, is felt all along my nervous system. I had known no other home but the Lodge, no other locality but James's Street, no other father but the one who minded the Gate and wore hospital uniform. Now all that was to be changed. My emotions see-sawed rapidly between the extremes of relief and regret. When we walked out of the porch and through the Gate for the last time, I wept uncontrollably, I hardly knew why.

Living with Olive and Billy in a tree-lined road in the suburbs was the nearest I ever got to a 'normal' life. The bustling household, the comings and goings of family and friends, the fun and chatter, the wheeling of prams and telling of stories, filled the days with a happy inconsequence that was new to me. No longer could my father demand that his meals be served up on the dot of the hour; no longer could he command in a household where he was not the boss; no longer could he keep his eye solely on me. I became less prone to the nervous indigestion which had long plagued me. My father's mood became more constantly cheerful as he found himself obliged to go with the flow of a household where, as he said, meals were movable feasts and there was no fixed bedtime. His catholic son-in-law, subject of his earlier resistance, proved, to his surprise, to be a congenial companion who thoroughly enjoyed his father-in-law's trenchant Ulster humour. Every now and again, my father's voice was raised in excited argument as he expounded his views on his son-in-law's church. Billy loved an argument, enjoyed baiting my father and enjoyed seeing him take the bait but, at heart, he, too, was very critical of the church. When my father finally understood this, he was convinced that he himself was the instrument of his son-in-law's enlightenment and savoured his victory. He was so far carried away as to pay for himself and Billy to have a continental holiday!

Diocesan School brought its pupils to the State Intermediate Certificate taken at sixteen years of age. The majority of girls then went on to secretarial training, nursing or clerical jobs but two or three girls a year moved to the well-known Alexandra College to spend a further two years preparing for the Leaving Certificate. I was to be one of these and was to win a scholarship as my sister had done before me. Failure was not an option. Luckily I was successful and the next stage of my education was secured. The move to Alexandra in 1943 was a move in an upward direction in every sense, academically, socially and culturally. I felt the difference at once. The very buildings were bigger and handsomer; there was a large garden behind the school and there were vases of flowers in the hall and landing. A big assembly room with stained-glass windows was lined with hundreds of books and there were tables where girls could read or work by themselves. The headmistress, Miss Holloway, spoke with a cultured English accent; she was queenly, gracious and extremely remote. The teachers were more interesting and more energetic than those at Diocesan: history with Miss Armstrong emerged from its lists of reasons and became possibilities and hypotheses, and mathematics with the dynamic Miss Brooks took us into seas of thought which we had not known before. The college was so well endowed that it could attract women of the highest calibre as teachers, some with first class degrees from Oxford and Cambridge. Distinguished speakers (I remember especially A.L. Rowse) were brought over from England to give us lectures on subjects of special interest. The orchestra, the flowers, the hall, the library, all gave me a taste of refinement I had never known before.

Socially, I was less at my ease. Unlike the lower-middle-class girls of Diocesan School, boarders came up from the big houses in the country, and the daughters of clergy – who benefited from reduced fees – came from educated rectories all over Ireland. My address was even more embarrassing at Alexandra than it had been at Diocesan. Invitations to the richer suburbs of Dublin were impossible to return. I was overwhelmed to be asked to spend a whole weekend with a friend, Christine Matthews, in Fort Royal House in Donegal, where Field Marshal Montgomery had been a frequent visitor. How could I ask girls to James's Street and let them see my father in hospital uniform? Social snobbery was overt. 'Was your father an admiral?' 'Oh no, not so high as that.' 'A vice-admiral then?' 'No, a captain,' I answered, chancing the lie. I was sure that nothing less than a captain would be acceptable in Alexandra. I was aware of being viewed by some girls as a Leaving Certificate class drudge, forced to sit the state exams and to learn the obligatory Irish. We would have to earn our living, poor things. I ducked and dived on the social issue but held my own academically.

Right opposite the college was the handsome long façade of University College which catered for catholic students. It might as well have been in a distant country so closed was it to us and we to it. I was never once inside it. Once a year, on Rag Day, we had a dramatic encounter with its students. Dressed as girls, with hairy legs showing under gym-frocks and collecting boxes in their hands, they besieged the college, which, no doubt, they thought of as being full of prim protestant girls and starchy teachers. The doors were barred against them but they always succeeded in getting in, to our immense delight. They swirled the teachers off their feet, kissed the girls, jumped on the desks and took to their heels before the police could be called.

All this time, underneath my external occupations, my real life was going on, secretly and silently inside me. The adolescent agony of doubt and self-absorption was mine in full measure. Who was I? How did I appear to others? Was I worthless? Unlovable? I went over and over conversations, seeking to discover nuances of affection or lack of it. I often felt let down, even betrayed, without a single person to love me. At other times I was exuberantly happy. There was no middle road. I sometimes daydreamed during lessons but it was at night when I climbed into bed and turned out the light that I gave myself up to an orgy of introspection. Could anyone ever love me? The need for affection overwhelmed me and often sent me to sleep weeping. When my father quarrelled with me or was grossly insensitive I felt worthless and diminished. So I turned to my loving Father who had spoken so tenderly to me through the Bible at Sunday School and at church and talked to Him. The lovely words and rhythms of the Bible were a balm to my anxious spirit. 'Weeping may endure for a night but joy cometh in the morning.' 'Let not your heart be troubled neither let it be afraid.' 'They that wait upon the Lord shall renew their strength.' He was speaking directly to me; I felt comforted, stronger, lighter in being. I talked to Him every night and received His healing words into my soul.

I came upon a book which seemed as if sent to me: it was a series of essays by A.C. Benson called *From a College Window*. Benson was a lonely, introspective Cambridge don whose questions and answers mirrored my own soul-searching. He talked of belonging to 'the City', the inner city of God into which I felt myself drawn. He warned of the dangers: 'One may become humble and develop a complacency about it which is really a dangerous form of pride in disguise.' Was this my state? Was I deceiving myself? I was trying to be trusting and humble but I was not. I was proud of my own sensitivity. I wrote in my diary, 'My poor self, I almost feel sorry for you, battered and cross-examined as you constantly are.' Sometimes I felt so alone that I wondered if there was a God at all. Had I been inventing a consoling father-substitute for myself? When I told Martha of these doubts she said that she had had the feeling of faith in God for so long that it had become a part of her; she never doubted. Would I have been better to have been born and bred a catholic? I asked myself.

Haunting all my dreams and doubts was an image, the image of the man who would one day love me, a Rochester who would gather me up in his arms and protect me. The shadowy images which flitted across my consciousness all came from books. Characters in books were my intimate friends and haunted my imagination. I wanted to be like Maggie Tulliver, sensitive, loyal, independent. I wanted to be morally beautiful like her. I wept when I thought of the way she had sacrificed the man she loved because he was promised to another. I hoped I would never be asked to make such a sacrifice but if I had to do it, I would. I understood instinctively how Maggie could not live with herself if she had been the cause of pain in others. I was in love with self-sacrifice as an idea. I would, naturally, reserve myself pure and undefiled for my Rochester as did the heroines in books. Their purity was the most beautiful thing about them. I knew how terrible, how unspeakably awful, was the sin of unchastity, how nothing worse could have happened to blight the life of Tess of the D'Urbervilles. Everyone in Dublin knew about this most terrible sin, the Fate-worse-than-Death. It was so bad that it could only be whispered in the mouths of grown women and never told to children.

I was a puritan, with a romantic puritanism formed from books and built on ignorance. I thought women who drank sherry were decidedly 'loose' and women I saw slipping into the snug of Reilly's pub already 'lost'. A young woman in Dame Street, drunk and staggering, fell on the pavement in front of me; in one split second I caught a glimpse of black underwear. With shock and horror I knew I had seen 'one of them', for only prostitutes wore black underwear. I was embarrassed by any show of physical love between man and woman and when I passed the Hollow in the

Phoenix Park, well known for its courting couples, I averted my eyes. I knew very little about the facts of life, and my own passage into womanhood frightened and bewildered me. The little I knew was picked up from girls at school; notes passed along the benches and sniggers erupted. I hated 'dirty talk' but at the same time was overcome with curiosity to know what it was about. One of the notes ran:

> Green, white and yellah
> My mother had a fellah,
> The fellah died, my mother cried
> Green white and yellah.

The very idea that anyone's mother could have a 'fellah' was shocking. My heart burned with the shame of it.

All unknown to ourselves, a chemistry was working inside us driving our curiosity. We were often moody, restless, eager to find quarrel in a straw. My friend Sylvia and I went about with our arms around one another and hugged each other. I knew so little and was so desperate to know that I came home one day and furtively looked up the word 'breast' in the dictionary. It seemed that this part of the anatomy was mysteriously important. We were all emerging from flatness into roundness and it was too embarrassing to look at myself in a mirror. I dreaded in case anyone would notice my developing figure and I always kept my arms folded across my chest. Girls talked continuously of boys they fancied, who had been kissed and so on. And often, when we came out of Guides, we laughed and talked with the boys from the church – laughter always shot through with something else, we hardly knew what . . . A tall boy I knew and secretly admired put his arm round my waist, authoritatively moved me close to the wall and placed his mouth abruptly on mine. It was a kiss! The delicious sensation I had read about in books had not been delicious after all.

What kind of girls were we? We probed one another on the way home from school. Who is beautiful? Who is not? How would we rate with the opposite sex? I knew I was not beautiful with my curly hair, round face and my home-made clothes. 'But you have personality, you are very attractive,' they said. But I put no value on these tepid qualities. Beauty was what books talked about and beautiful was what I wanted to be. I had a deep sense of failure. If only I could be like the actress Ingrid Bergman; her beautiful face was full of soul. I cried so much during her films that I could not trust myself to be seen, red-eyed, when the lights went up and I had to wait, snivelling, until everyone passed out before me. Self-sacrifice for the man you loved, that was the noble ideal. The vague spectre waiting in the future would be older, experienced; he would appreciate a girl like me. None of those downy-lipped boys for me! Like all romantic girls, I believed that love was made in Heaven, that one man was destined from all eternity for one woman. The idea of a widow or widower marrying again was an affront to the purity of that ideal. I would be faithful unto death; anything else was unthinkable. (When, older, I revised my ideas on this subject, it was one of the biggest mental turning points of my life.)

During my teens and early twenties I nourished myself with these romantic, unrealistic dreams which I had found in books. I loved dancing. Occasionally, I went with Billy's younger brother and his friends to tennis club 'hops'. The girls all sat along the wall – 'wallflowers' waiting and hoping to be asked 'up'. It was humiliating. But once you were led onto the dance floor, swung into the pattern of the dance, an arm around your waist guiding you this way and that, spinning you around and around in a balanced delirium of controlled movement, the exhilaration was magical. We all knew that we were expected to pay for our pleasure. 'Can I leave you home?' was the question from whoever had strategically planned to be your partner for the last dance. A goodnight kiss was the least you might be asked for. And you wondered how you might avoid the embrace of someone who did not particularly appeal to you . . .

I was nearly nineteen years old when I was invited to my first dress dance. This was a huge rite of passage for us girls. It meant we were grown-up, being taken seriously. Pat, an Irish army officer and a friend of Billy's whom I had often met casually at his house, wrote me a short letter. 'We are having a formal dance at the barracks in Arbour Hill. I do not know anyone to ask. Would you like to oblige?' I imagined my father's reaction were I to tell him that I was proposing to go to a dance with an Irish army officer! Still, I was tempted and soon decided to accept, to make up an excuse to mislead my father and to manage the whole thing without being found out. I knew Pat; he was gentle and shy and I felt sure no return would be expected. He had had no other choice but to ask me to be his partner. But what was I to wear? Long dresses, off the shoulder, were then de rigueur for formal dances and I neither possessed one nor had any hope of buying one. I would have to borrow one, so I applied to my ever-obliging friends whose solidarity in these matters was constant. An emerald green taffeta dress was found which, with a few tucks here and there, would look well on me. It was decidedly off the shoulder; no, I could not go to a dance bare like that – I was not even sure that it would stay up. Another friend Joan said that her mother's white ermine shoulder cape would be just the thing to put over it, really chic; she would sneak it out of her mother's wardrobe. Trying the clothes on in the security of my bedroom, I looked at myself in the mirror and was amazed at the sophisticated vision looking back at me. If only I had long hair instead of curls . . .

On the day before the ball, I told my father I was going to a birthday party and would be back by midnight by which time I knew he would be fast asleep. My father never gladly saw me go out for an evening although he could never bring himself to say so. He enjoyed the feeling of domestic cosiness (which he was never able to create himself) when I sat sewing or knitting beside him. We were, by this time, living in a small suburban house in Drimnagh Road and I had my own front door key. The dress and the cape were already deposited in Sylvia's house so that my father could have no inkling of my real destination. Pat was to call for me at Sylvia's house in a taxi. Prompt to the minute, he arrived looking very tall and handsome in his army uniform. His eyes showed how impressed he was with the vision before him. As we sped across Dublin in the luxury of a taxi I felt like a character in a novel.

We alighted at the barracks. Pat led me into a building and into an atmosphere which were both completely strange to me. A band was playing and men in uniform were standing about, waiting for their partners to emerge from the cloakroom. I joined the women in the cloakroom, unsure of myself, embarrassed and awkward. I did not know a single person. Everyone chatted easily to everyone else in Dublin fashion.

'God, what will I do if my hair falls down?'

'Would you ever lend me a bit of your lipstick?'

'Who are you with tonight? Pat? God, he's lovely. But keep an eye on the whiskey!'

Everybody had taken off their wraps and had exposed bare shoulders. I slipped off my cape and could hardly bring myself to look over the heads of those who were adjusting their toilette in the mirror. How could I emerge among all those men undressed like this? Emerge I had to. Pat was waiting to lead me off into the hall to join his party. He introduced me to his friends; the women smiled at me and put me at my ease. I was sure they were wondering where Pat had got this girl. I hoped they would not find out I was a protestant. I had always tried to keep this fact dark when in a catholic group for fear of being thought different. It seemed more polite to pass myself off as one of the crowd.

'What will you have to drink?' asked Pat, ordering a round.

Sherries, gins and whiskeys were requested, and I, feeling gauche, whispered, 'A soft drink, please'. I knew this was a bad start. The men ordered round after round as the evening progressed but the women rarely took more than two drinks each. I made my orange juice last an unconscionable length of time. Pat stood up and asked me to dance. We moved into the beautiful, poised measures of the slow waltz, calculated to make anyone feel romantic. Pat was a lovely dancer and we moved this way and that in a solemn, flexible ritual that was immensely satisfying.

At midnight I whispered to Pat, 'I will have to go home now or my father will kill me.'

'What!' said Pat, who by now had consumed many whiskeys. 'The night is just beginning and nobody will think of leaving here before two.'

I could see that, in his present mood, I was powerless to influence him. I would be 'murdered', that was sure. At 2 a.m. the last dance was announced, and Pat escorted me onto the floor. The lights were dimmed, the band played a haunting tune and couples moved closer to one another. Pat held me very tight and we finished the dance in a giddy whirl, exhilarated and laughing. Then the national anthem was struck up, everybody stood rigidly to attention and I smiled, inwardly, at the thought of my father seeing me now, standing respectfully for the Irish anthem by the side of an Irish soldier. Pat was swaying slightly on his feet, his face flushed.

My cape thankfully retrieved, we went out to find a taxi and off we sped through the empty streets. The 'goodnight' was getting near, but as Pat was very quiet I felt reasonably safe. Suddenly he leaned over and put his arm around me and kissed me. It would have been a pleasant sensation except for the smell of whiskey. I would settle for that, I thought, and felt sure there would be nothing to follow. Then he said in a grave voice, 'I want you to marry me. Why do you think I took all those whiskeys tonight? To give me courage to ask you, of course, what else? I could never ask you otherwise. No one else will do for me, I'm telling you fair and square.' I tried to laugh it off as a joke, but he was in deep earnest. We had now drawn up to a few yards from my house and I tried to go but he held my arm. 'If you do not say "yes" I will get out and bang like the devil on the front door until I bring your father down!' I would have agreed to any marriage to save myself from that. I could see my father descend, raging at being violently awoken, to see his daughter in a long dress with an Irish soldier, the worse for drink. Instantly I agreed to marry him. 'We will choose the ring next week,' said Pat, 'the biggest and most expensive diamond you can lay your eyes on!'

With a last embrace I jumped out of the taxi. I turned the key in the lock with the utmost caution, and waited, panting, inside the door to hear the taxi move off. I sank onto the bottom stair, overcome by the emotions of the evening and particularly of the last half-hour. Then, step by wary step, I climbed the stairs, past my father's room, to my own bedroom. Afraid to make a click by turning on the light, I flung the dress and cape onto a chair and collapsed into bed. The next morning, what was my horror on seeing the white ermine cape with a large yellow stain on its immaculate surface! It had fallen against a loosely fastened bottle of hair oil. I was distraught; what was I going to do? The problem of my 'engagement' to Pat was as nothing compared to this new problem. How was I going to tell Joan? How was Joan going to tell her mother? My mind, ever inventive, ran over the possibilities. A new one would cost at least £50 – I might as well think of £1,000. Could I remove the stain myself? I squeezed it into paper, put a towel over the stained portion and sat on it. Still the yellow stain looked obstinately back at me.

That afternoon I cycled over to Joan's house and made my confession. She was as worried as I. 'We'll try the dry cleaners,' said she, 'they are great at getting out stains.' We laid the offending garment on the counter. Yes, he could get it out but it would cost fifteen shillings! Even five shillings was beyond our combined resources. We racked our brains for a solution. Then I thought of Olive. I knew she would lend me the money, and she did. All was well again but for Pat. What was I going to do about him? He might well arrive at our house to claim me and I must prevent that at all costs. I took pen and paper and wrote to him, thanking him for the lovely evening he had given me and releasing him from his most 'imprudent' engagement, the product of too much whiskey. 'Don't worry,' I wrote, 'I won't hold you to it, I have no intention of getting married but I enjoyed the joke.' I did not see Pat for many years after that: he was still single, still shy and still drinking . . .

I was in my last term at Alexandra when the war ended. It was May 1945. The news flashed around the classrooms – 'The war is over!' Many girls had fathers and brothers in the forces and were elated by the news. Frank would be coming back to us; he would not be killed. Although we had not experienced the war as Britain had done, I felt the importance of that day. As we walked through the Green after school our euphoria was slightly manufactured. At the top of Grafton Street we merged into a crowd of people making their way to the city centre to see what, if anything, was going to happen. We were borne excitedly along in the crowd towards the front of Trinity College, where I was soon to be a student. Suddenly all heads were turned upwards towards the roof of the college. 'Look! Look up at the flags!' At first I could not see why they were attracting such attention until I realised that there were six flags on the mast – the Union Jack, the Stars and Stripes, the Hammer and Sickle, the French Tricolour and the Irish Tricolour in that order, and a crowd of students standing alongside them on the roof. The strains of 'God Save the King' and 'It's a Long Way to Tipperary' floated down.

The crowd below began to object, insulted by the position of the national flag. 'British arrogance from a British institution' came from beside me. Slogans and insults were shouted and then a surge towards the gates of Trinity swept us forward. A number of civic guards, batons drawn, rushed at us and we were pushed backwards, stumbling and swaying. We were half frightened, half elated by our situation. We looked at one another in excitement: we were in a fight – it was terrific! Someone shouted that 'they' had set fire to the Irish flag, that it was blazing on the roof. I could see nothing. The people around me were laughing and uttering witticisms and I encountered no real ugliness of mood. There is little the Irish savour so much as a confrontation with authority and here we were in the midst of one. So little frightened were we that we came back into town that evening, hoping we would once more be charged by the police and have 'a bit of gas' and we were and we did. Trinity remained securely locked for several days after this incident, and an armoured car was stationed just inside the gates to fend off a possible assault. The college authorities were furious that a few students had behaved so badly and they were severely reprimanded. Such was my Victory in Europe day.

We had heard many terrible stories of Nazi atrocities during the last years of the war but we did not believe them. No one was capable of being so inhumanly cruel, we were sure of that. It was 'only propaganda'. During my last week in school that summer, I walked down Grafton Street as usual with my friends and as we came to the Grafton cinema we noticed that a documentary on Belsen was showing. 'Shall we go in and see it? Seats are cheap in the afternoon.' We sat down in the dark to *enjoy* ourselves but what we saw was too terrible for words; human skeletons piled high like rubbish with here and there a limb still twitching; living dead with great hollow eyes unable to take in their liberation; children like withered old men. It was my first sight of real evil and I was sick into my handkerchief. Why all this hatred of jews? I knew many jewish girls at school; they sat beside me in class and were just like everyone else except that they did not come in for prayers, but the few catholics in the school did not come in either. I had a special friend Vera Fine, a plump, jolly jewess who invited me to her birthday parties in Terenure. She was always laughing; who would want to murder her?

★

The war, for me so distant and unreal, had ended in 1945, but two years later a very real piece of its debris was washed up unexpectedly on our shores. In that year the Red Cross brought two hundred destitute children from the big cities of devastated Germany to Ireland and appealed to Irish people to take them in. Olive and Billy, touched by the plight of these innocent victims, offered to take one and bring him up with their own children. A young boy of six years of age from Dusseldorf was assigned to them. Illegitimate, he had somehow survived the bombing and starvation by foraging in cellars and bombed-out buildings. A man from the Red Cross brought Friedhelm into Dublin from its centre for German children in the Wicklow Mountains, there to meet his new 'father' who was to take him on to his home in County Galway.

Billy asked me to go with him to meet the little boy as both of us could speak a little German and this would put the child at his ease. I was very curious to see him. There he was suddenly before us, this piece of jetsam left behind by the brutalities of war, a strong-framed, stolid child thinned out now by hunger, a hunger which made his distinctly German jaw look excessively elongated. His broad forehead was overhung by short blond, lustreless hair. His poor little jacket and trousers supplied by the Red Cross hung drab and lifeless on his thin body and a defiant, obdurate expression was firmly set on his features, like a dog which had long been ill-treated but which retained a fierce self-respect in spite of it. Under his arm he grimly clutched his only possessions, two brown paper parcels, *zwei Paketen* containing a few clothes and toys supplied by the Red Cross.

Eager to use my German, I leaned towards the little boy and said, 'Wie geht es Ihnen?' No reply from the set face. Then, remembering how ridiculously formal this construction was, I tried again: 'Wie gehts, Friedhelm?'; and this friendlier, familiar phrase drew from the fixed expression a weak smile which moved slowly across the mouth but avoided the eyes. In this way the little bewildered German child entered the life of my sister's family and my own life. He was to remain with her for nine years, at the end of which time, at fifteen years of age and with a strong Irish accent, he was sent back to Germany to be rehabilitated into his own country and to learn his native language anew. There he has remained ever since, upright and hard-working and with an undying loyalty and devotion to his Irish 'mammy' and 'daddy', whom he comes to see once a year and on all important family occasions.

For some time the child's expression remained quietly defiant, his body taut. As soon as we got him to Galway, Olive and I put him into a bath and rubbed and scrubbed him all over while uttering tender phrases in a language he did not understand. To my German 'Zu heisz, Friedhelm? Zu kalt, Friedhelm?' he merely nodded or shook his head. He was applying himself to uncomprehending endurance. His skin had a yellowish, unhealthy tinge and was covered in scabies. His hair was dry and dull from poor nutrition. We applied an ointment to his little body and dressed him up in fresh clothes, shoes and socks: it was like a rite of passage to another life.

Wary of the children and unused to play, he gradually, very gradually, came to join in their games. At the end of the day, however, nothing could induce him to go upstairs with them to bed: he knew that only downstairs was there shelter from the bombs and explosions that had torn open his night. His bed was brought downstairs but it was almost impossible at first to get him to part with his day clothes for pyjamas, and for nothing in this world would he part with his *zwei Paketen*. Only when they were securely stowed under the pillow and his two hands placed firmly over his ears to cut out the screams of the bombs would he consent to go to sleep. It was only very slowly that he allowed himself to lower these defences and to feel secure in the warm bustle of the household. He even began to allow himself the occasional smile, when he looked like any mischievous youngster.

Friedhelm was very difficult to manage at first. He stole money and cheques which were turned down in the local shops; he disappeared, he broke things. He hated school and with his German accent and broken English was often the target for laughter. Obliged by law to learn Irish when he could scarcely speak English, he frequently mitched from school and spent hours with the gypsies who were encamped nearby. He was always in trouble and sometimes beaten but his strong physique and prematurely toughened nature sustained it all without a murmur. His schooling passed over his head like an irksome interlude in the day but his English, spiced with racy Galway expressions, grew better and better with every week that passed. He was strong now as nature meant him to be, and his natural intelligence, so repressed at school, showed itself in his powerful hands; whenever a car needed to be fixed or a machine mended Friedhelm was always ready and willing for the job. With the first money he stole from my sister, he bought her a present, an attempt at buying her affection. As time went on, he gave as an offering not chocolates or sweets but his time and attention. He was always at hand to offer to do some little thing for her. In spite of his toughened exterior his heart was full of tenderness.

When the time came for him to go back to Germany (he had a natural mother) everybody was sad to see him go; he had become part of our lives. He recalled later the fateful moment when he was about to leave Germany, which he had not understood at the time. In Dusseldorf a Red Cross worker had held two sticks out towards him: 'Choose one of these, Friedhelm,' she ordered. He pulled one from between her fingers. 'You are to go to Ireland,' she said, 'the other one is for Switzerland.' 'That,' said Friedhelm with passionate sincerity, 'was my lucky day!'

TRINITY COLLEGE DUBLIN

M ay 1945, VE Day, the end of the war in Europe, was a turning point in the history of the world. It was also a turning point in my personal history. It was the month in which I decided, quite unexpectedly, to go to Trinity College and become a university student.

I had never once entertained the idea of going to university, nor, indeed, had any of us children. University degrees did not figure in the expectations of people like us. We already knew that we had, educationally, far outstripped the usual expectations by attending private schools until the age of eighteen with every prospect of a good job and a pension at the end of it. As our disappointments are always in strict ratio to our expectations, we were not disappointed. It was the teachers in Alexandra College who first opened up the subject: I was expected to do well in the Leaving Certificate, especially in English, so why not try for Trinity? I could take Modern Languages and combine English with French, for which I had a flair. I was amazed by this suggestion. Me? Go to Trinity? What an extraordinary idea! It would be ridiculous! My father would never hear of it. I tried to dismiss the idea from my head, but a sort of subterranean excitement seized hold of me and unsettled my days. I put all the powerful reasons against it to myself. How could I go on for another four years being dependent on my father for every penny? How could I put up with his moods with the prospect of blessed independence just opening up in front of me? Alone among my friends, I would have neither job nor money. But at the same time an image of myself as a university student, walking as of right through the great doors of Trinity College where Burke and

Goldsmith had been students, grew daily more and more attractive. I thought of the learned men and women I would meet, historians, linguists, scientists. For four years I could read and study.

Finally I brought myself to mention the idea to my father. I felt certain that I knew what he would say – that he had done enough for me, more than enough, that he had slaved to give me a good education and brought me to the chance of a good job. To my extreme astonishment he did not immediately scoff at the idea, but asked about the fees. I told him they were ten pounds a term, the same as Alexandra College, that I could continue to cycle to and from home, that I would have to buy some books, nothing more. A few days later, he spoke: 'You can go to the university if you want; I can see nothing against it.' I puzzled over his decision. At first I thought he was attracted by the idea of having a BA in the family, the crowning of all his efforts for his children. But what really attracted him, I discovered, was the possibility of keeping me at home for company. He once told me that he would prefer to have the company even of someone he disliked than to live alone. And so we lived on together in Drimnagh Road, my father's moods and temper as uncertain as ever.

My Leaving Certificate results being good, I applied to Trinity to be accepted for the degree of BA (Honours) in Modern Languages, English and French. Trinity accepted me on condition that I passed its entrance examination in Latin, which was then a compulsory subject. Having only had the opportunity to learn Latin for two years at Alexandra, I had not yet reached the required standard and I would have to swot up Virgil and Cicero during the summer holidays and take the examination in September. Meanwhile, a friend of Olive's who had a business making nuns' clothing offered me a part-time holiday job as I was handy with a needle. I was delighted to earn a little money and intrigued by the thought of making clothes for these strange enigmatic women – me, a protestant! I reported for work, up two flights of stairs and into a workroom where girls were already positioned before large tables cutting into vast quantities of black cloth while others sat at sewing machines passing the cloth under the needle.

I was assigned to the cutting out and sewing up of knickers. Instructions were precise: Reverend Mother had ordained that all garments had to be so many inches from the ground, so many inches below the knee, and knickers were to be long and voluminous. Nuns came and went during the day, always accompanied by a superior who did the talking and gave the orders. Healthy, scrubbed country girls with pink complexions disappeared behind screens, came out again, went away, eyes downcast, submissive. I gazed at them in wonder. I thought of the skin underneath those black draperies, underneath the strings of rosary beads and heavy crucifixes suspended from the waist; it must be very white. And what about the hair? Martha had told me that the hair was cut off when they made their vows. What a shock it would be to see the shaven heads underneath those rigid, all-concealing headdresses!

All that summer, I swotted in the evenings at Latin, an English translation propped up beside me as I worked. I learned as much as I could by heart, knowing how shaky were my grammar and vocabulary. In September, I entered for the first (but not the last) time the imposing and frightening Examination Hall of Trinity College to sit my written paper. This was followed a few days later by the viva voce examination. I had never had a viva before and even the term was new to me. I was very nervous as I took my place with the other candidates at the back of the hall and looked around me. Several aged professors in long, black gowns were sitting on the platform and calling up the candidates in turn to examine them. I had already heard of these professors, elderly clergymen, most of whom, it was said, hated women being allowed into the college and were never satisfied until they had made a female candidate cry. One of them, it was said, had even failed a candidate for writing in green ink.

'Miss Gaw!' came ringing down the hall from the platform. My neighbour leaned over and whispered, 'You've got Sir Robert Tate: he's awful!' My nervousness grew decidedly worse at this alarming piece of news. I determined that I would not cry whatever happened. Bullying never made me cry. I mounted the platform and took the seat before him. I looked up at the grey head and black gown, intimidated.

'You are Miss Gaw, are you not?'

'Yes, sir,' I replied.'

'So you think you know some Latin, do you?' And he waved my

written exam paper back and forth under my nose. I could see that it was liberally covered in red ink.

'I hope I know enough, sir,' I answered apprehensively.

'Well, you will need to know a lot more than you have displayed here,' he continued, moving my paper before me, 'if you hope to pass this examination!' At this, my heart fell and I knew that he was going to fail me. 'Translate this passage, Miss Gaw!' he ordered, the finger pointing, the eyes staring coldly over my head into the distance. I could scarcely get a word out. 'Speak up! Speak up! If you cannot be heard you fail the examination!' Stung as I always was by rudeness, I recovered myself. 'But sir, you are making me nervous!' A complacent smile passed over his austere features. 'Pray, make a start!'

I began slowly and fumblingly to translate and in a short while, happily recognising the passage as one I had learned by heart in translation, I managed it very well. A passage from Cicero followed which I managed less well but before I had finished speaking, he had called out the name of the next candidate and I was left, confused and embarrassed, to get up and make my way back down the hall and into the air outside to cool my indignation. If this was Trinity, did I want to be part of it? A short time later, I learned that I had passed the Latin examination and was accepted to study for a BA.

My next task was to find a 'tutor' who would advise me as to the regulations, academic courses and so on. I asked for Mr Godfrey whose reputation as a friend of students was well known and who, it was said, would even fight for you with examiners if your results were shaky. I found him in a small, narrow room in No. 1 Front Square, totally immersed in bundles of seemingly uncontrolled papers. He was a small, dapper, round man in a dark suit with a smudge of a moustache and a habit of tilting his head to one side when he talked. I relaxed as he told me in his rather ceremonious manner of the regulations, the opportunities, the hurdles.

'Yes, you are Miss Gaw, of course, of course, you have passed the Latin entrance examination, you say. A very important language, Latin; we cannot do without it. Very clever of you, very clever, goodness gracious me! So you will take advanced Maths instead of Latin in Little-Go?' (This was the general exam for all students at the end of the second year.) 'How clever, how very clever; few girls take it, you know, goodness gracious me!'

He explained that women, as they were not allowed to live in rooms in the college as men did, had No. 6 Front Square put at their disposal and there they could have a locker, could change and brush up. Women were not allowed to dine in 'Commons' in the ancient dining room for this privilege was reserved to men. Nor were they permitted to attend services in the college chapel, or to join the Historical Society or the Philosophical Society (which had comfortable rooms in the Graduates' Memorial Building). Further, if a woman wished to read in the Reading Room after 6 p.m., when all women had to be out of college, she had to sign a book at the porter's office on arrival and note down the time, walk the 200 yards to the Reading Room, sign again and again note down the time. The two times would be compared by the Junior Dean, who allowed several minutes for this hazardous journey. If the time gap was longer, hanky-panky would be suspected and the culprits pursued and punished. Decidedly, women were neither welcomed nor trusted in Trinity.

An undergraduate's gown must be worn, Mr Godfrey said, and he directed me to where I could find one, second-hand. Clad in my gown and very self-conscious, I assembled with the other junior freshmen (first year students) outside the Examination Hall, where we were to be addressed by the senior tutor. A tall, stern, aged clergyman in black gown and mortar-board stood on the steps above us and in a tone of great authority told us what was expected of us, our behaviour, our loyalty, our obedience, in this venerable institution to which we had been graciously admitted. He was A.A. Luce, professor of philosophy and distinguished critic of Bishop Berkeley, the famous eighteenth-century Irish philosopher. Beside him stood another aged clergyman, his tall figure slightly bent, a large hearing-trumpet at his ear which he directed towards the crowd below him. This, I learned, was R.M. Gwynne, one of the many Gwynnes associated with Trinity (there were so many of them that it was known as 'Gwynnity' College). Trinity seemed full of ancient clergymen, and I promised myself to keep well clear of them . . .

Trinity was an extraordinary experience from the beginning to the end. My years there changed my life intellectually, socially, personally. No other four years were so concentrated, saw such an acceleration in the rate of change of my thinking, none ever again so crowded with congenial company, none so emotionally overwhelming.

The college stood, four-square, handsome, symmetrical, right in the heart of the city. Ordinary people streamed past its doors on their way to work in shops and offices without ever penetrating inside. When you passed through the porch, you were in an exclusive, all-sufficient intellectual world where, if you were male, you could live, sleep and eat and have your being without ever moving outside its walls. The two worlds were quite distinct and I was always glad that I could move easily between them without ever being isolated in either. I cycled the four miles from home and arrived in Dame Street, right opposite the entrance to Trinity, to find my way barred by a continual stream of traffic passing in front of it. A large, red-faced policeman with a heavy Cork accent usually controlled the traffic and as soon as he saw me, he held up his hand in both directions, stopped the traffic and waved me across. We always exchanged the same greeting: 'How's every bit of you this mornin', gurr-el?' to which I replied 'Grand, thanks, and all the better for seeing you!' And I sailed across like a queen. (I liked Dublin policemen who were always ready for a chat even when they held you up for being without a light on your bicycle. I usually finished our chat by making a date to see them at a dance in the AOH hall in Parnell Square the following Saturday. Neither of us believed I would keep it but we liked the pretence.)

I put my bicycle outside No. 6, went in, put on my gown and, very self-consciously, emerged as a student. Coming as I did from an all-girls' school, even the thought of sitting beside boys in the same lecture room was ridiculously thrilling. Every crossing of the square, every walk to a lecture room was crammed with promise of exciting encounters, leisurely conversations which but thinly disguised the fascination of fencing with the opposite sex. And there were so many young people to meet . . . a few protestants from the Irish provinces, some students from England, an odd one from France, Germany or the USA, but the majority of students in the Arts Faculty came from the North of Ireland. It was my first real encounter with northerners. What distinguished my years in Trinity after the war was the presence of mature men and women who had just been demobilised from the forces and had come to Trinity on government grants. Beside these experienced people, the rest of us looked like schoolchildren. Some of these ex-forces people were from the North, where they had volunteered for war service.

The most intellectually gifted pupils in the North's protestant schools at that time went on to Trinity as a matter of course. Having then no right to government grants, they had stayed on for an extra year at school to prepare for scholarships and exhibitions. They had learned to work on their own, could fillet a book rapidly and serve it up well garnished in examinations. They knew their way around the library, a difficult task then for freshmen for Trinity had a copyright library and no students could enter the stacks of books and browse. You had to consult the heavy, leather-bound catalogues in the Reading Room, hope you had hit on a likely book, fill in a form which the desk assistant sent to the Long Room in the adjacent library. In a few minutes, the book came across by underground passage and you could take it to your seat, but no books were allowed out of the Reading Room.

I had no idea what to look for or how to manage my studies and very little help was offered by the lecturers. The change from school had been abrupt and brutal. A huge programme of reading was prescribed in both English and French (you were not then allowed to study one language only, for which I shall always be grateful). Lectures were few, boring and unhelpful and there were no tutorials. I soon saw that it was a case of sink or swim. I felt myself drowning in a sea of unconnected books and impossible, unknown expectations. I began by taking copious notes in lectures, hoping to make sense of them afterwards, but soon gave that up as unprofitable. I became so panic-stricken in the first two terms that I contemplated withdrawing altogether. It took me two full years to catch up with those clever northern students, but from then on my confidence grew and with it my marks rose until they reached their best in the final examinations.

An intense spirit of competition marked off the northerners from us, the more easygoing southerners. A first class degree was what most of them aimed for and intended to get. I recognised in them my northern father's belief in the will. I was overawed by their confidence, having, realistically, only modest ambitions myself. Confident intellectually, they were much less so socially and emotionally. Some were gauche and awkward, the boys often very disturbed by the proximity of the opposite sex; they did not know how to go about romance yet longed for it to happen. Some retired from the struggle behind a superior stance of wit and irony; some never entered it at all being too shy to make any overtures. The intellectual promise of a few crashed in the ferment of unsettling and unsatisfied emotions and they did not achieve their promise. One boy, a northerner and scholar of the college, 'fell in love' with a friend of mine and to prove his superiority forced her to give up her studies in her last year to marry him.

Like most Dublin girls, I found it easy to talk, banter and tease but I felt deeply insecure about my appearance. A spot on my face spelt tragedy for days and I scarcely dared lift my eyes from the ground in case I should be noticed. I thought myself unattractive and badly dressed. I admired other girls to my own disadvantage, and wished I were smart and sophisticated like the girls in the Dramatic Society. I felt it impossible that any man should be interested in me. If anyone did show interest, my idealistic nature was grateful, and this gratitude got me into many scrapes which I learned to avoid only by experience.

Then how we all talked, explained, accused, excused by the hour together. We sat on the steps of the French Department after lectures and talked, reluctant to disengage from one another. We walked round and round College Park and talked again. We never tired of trying to find the answer to the Big Questions, of trying to find the truth about one another and about ourselves. At night, we sat in the Reading Room, each one isolated before a book and under the pool of light thrown by the green-shaded reading lamp, yet all of us joined in one common intensity of concentration. Every now and again eyes were lifted from books to encounter other eyes, notes were passed along tables to 'come out for coffee at nine', and we put away our books and slipped out of the silence and into the bustling streets outside, into the cafés which served as the mixed common rooms, missing inside the college. There we lingered, making one cup of coffee last for hours and never harassed by the kindly waitresses, who understood our financial situation.

The lack of good teaching and the lack of contact with the lecturers, which threw us entirely on our own resources, was accepted philosophically, for there was so much else to compensate for it in our college life. We loved the ancient buildings set among squares of grass and we loved moving about among them as if, for those few precious years, we were ourselves owners and possessors of this wonderful place. This impression of ownership was reinforced by the complete absence of any visible bureaucracy or administration: there was nobody to tell you to do this or not to do that, and if we wanted information about courses or examinations we had to hunt for it. (In my last year, I had great difficulty locating the academic in charge of the diploma in education which I considered taking. I gave up the hunt when I heard that only the month before he had sent somebody for an interview for a teaching post which had been filled three years previously.) The delicious feeling of living in a free and undirected world was reinforced, too, by the number of eccentrics who inhabited its corners and backways, seemingly unaccountable to managers and directors. There were men who gave one or two lectures a year on some abstruse subject yet managed to hang on to rooms in the college, men who would not last long in a modern 'managed' university. It was said that if the place was ever burned down, we would be astonished at what crawled out of the debris!

Our professor of English, H.O. White, lived in a couple of bachelor rooms in New Square. He glided though the college, arm above his head in a kind of genial benediction on all, for *he* was a man who had known the poet Yeats! Professor R.B. McDowell, brilliant Irish historian, lived in a set of rooms in Front Square and never emerged, even for five minutes and even in the hottest weather, without being engulfed in a long, black, woollen overcoat, flat hat pulled well down over thick-bespectacled eyes and neck completely bound up in a heavy, woollen muffler. He muttered continually to himself as he went along like someone surprised to find himself out in the daylight. From the professor of German, Maximilian Liddell, I attempted to learn Anglo-Saxon so that I could try for a scholarship, but as he had no idea of beginning, middle and end, it was in vain: he addressed himself only to those students who had half-mastered the language already. If a student said 'in my opinion' he was at once corrected: 'It is your business to *know*, not to have opinions.' When he offered an opinion himself, he took off his gown for a moment to signal that he was not speaking *ex cathedra*. Professor A.A. Luce, whose philosophy lectures I attended for two years, was feared for his abrasive style. At the end of a lecture on Berkeley, he asked for questions and a student asked one about a modern philosopher to which he replied: 'If you want to know the answer to that question, you will have to pay more fees!' Anything you said to R.M. Gwynne, senior lecturer of the college, had to be delivered at close quarters into a brass trumpet the size of a saxophone.

One of the many eccentrics who hung about the college was a small, high-coloured man with a limp, impecunious, the worse for wear but courteous and well-spoken: it was said that he had been a senior judge whose time on the bench was cut short when he attempted to fine a man one million pounds! A male student named Florence boasted of the fact that he was the only man to have joined the all-female Elizabethan Society. A Belfast student who lived on the same stairway as Professor McDowell used to study far into the night before examinations while taking pot-shots with his shotgun at the rats which emerged from a hole in the corner of his room. The porters in the Lodge at the Front Gate were everybody's friends; they heard many a personal story, arranged rendezvous, passed on messages, could tell you who had passed in or out and generally facilitated the social and human traffic of the day.

Although women's freedom within the college was so very restricted, we could accept an invitation to a man's rooms during the day. They were usually cold, very plainly furnished with a table, an old armchair which had been sold on from one occupant to the other, a chest of drawers, a wardrobe and a bed. You might be offered a cup of tea brewed up on an old gas ring together with a delicious piece of toast done to a turn on a metal contraption over the same ring. There was no running water except from a communal tap on the landing. Communal, too, were the toilets which were found in several places in the college and communal were the baths which were overseen by Mr Ussher, a protestant from our part of Dublin. I envied the men the chance of living inside the college and having it all to themselves when the great doors were closed at night and the bustle of the town was excluded.

I had been bothered by the snobbery I met in Alexandra and loved this new, liberated atmosphere: it did not matter *who* you were to these students, it was *what* you were that counted. And what were we? That was what we were trying to find in all this fascinating interminable talk. We were not ashamed to admit our love for books, for poetry, for ideas. One student talked of the influence on him of the German poet Rilke, of his introspective verse, of his mysticism; another of the French poet Baudelaire, of the rich and sensuous heaviness of his lines and rhythms expressing the ecstasy and horror of experience. I loved the English poet Keats, gave myself up to the mesmeric authority of syllable, cadence and sensation, and repeated like a mantra:

> My heart aches, and a drowsy numbness pains
> My sense, as though of hemlock I had drunk,
> Or emptied some dull opiate to the drains
> One minute past, and Lethe-wards had sunk . . .

Then I discovered his letters; I discovered his struggle to understand the paradoxes of his experience, his efforts to grasp that experience and to hammer it into words and rhythms. He had an extraordinary capacity for receiving impressions: 'If a sparrow comes before my window I take part in its existence and pick about the gravel.' He called this attention 'negative capability' (its greatest exemplar is Shakespeare). His fine-tuned senses felt the beauty of the world to a point that his nervous system could scarcely bear. He was tempted to give himself up in verse to the luxuriousness of sense impressions and to 'fade far away, dissolve, and quite forget', but he had too much iron in him for that. He knew that the poet's business was with all human experience, with 'the weariness, the fever, and the fret'. He wrote that

> scenery is fine but human nature is finer. I find earlier days are gone by. I find I can have no enjoyment of the world but continued drinking of knowledge. I find that there is no worthy pursuit but the idea of doing some good in the world . . . The way lies through application, study and thought. I will pursue it and for that end purpose retiring for some years. I have been

hovering for some time between an exquisite sense of the luxurious and a love of philosophy . . .

He was, in T.S. Eliot's words, trying 'to school an intelligence and make it a soul'. This put into words exactly what I, in my confused and haphazard way, was trying to do myself. Keats gave powerful form and content to my search and I saw myself more clearly because of his letters.

Pascal, of whom my brother-in-law had talked to me as a schoolgirl, appeared on my list of prescribed books. Here, at Trinity, I was asked to study his literary aspect. He was not only a man about town, but a brilliant mathematician and scientist who rediscovered many of the propositions of Euclid when only a schoolboy and invented the first calculating machine. After a dramatic mystical experience, he determined to give himself up to a religious life and retired to the Jansenist monastery of Port Royal near Paris. There he made notes for a book which would vindicate Christianity against sceptics, his *Pensées* as they are called for he never finished the work, dying at thirty-nine years of age. He brilliantly diagnoses man's condition, his greatness and his littleness. Man is 'ni ange ni bête', he is 'un roseau pensant'. He opened up extraordinary insights: 'Habit is a second nature which destroys our original nature'; 'The heart has its reasons which reason knows nothing of'; 'All man's misery comes from not being able to sit quietly in a room alone'; and (something which struck me with immense force) 'you would not be looking for Me if you had not already found Me'. The combination of philosophy with a natural religious devotion and a fine, lucid, concentrated and elegant style was exactly what suited my own instinctive preferences. The *Pensées* had a profound and lasting influence on me.

If the northern students were a new experience for me, so were the English. Never having been out of Ireland, I had only previously made their acquaintance in books. Martha and I used always to take for English people those Anglo-Irish we overheard in the street or in the bus who spoke in loud, confident and imperious tones. We imagined that only English people would speak like that. At Trinity I was to make my first acquaintance with the real thing, although that acquaintance was to be deepened and enlarged when, three years after taking my degree, I married and went to live and work in England. English students were attracted to Trinity by its cosmopolitan reputation, by the fact that it was as old and venerable as Oxford and Cambridge and operated the same system, and because it was situated in Dublin, a lively and relaxed capital city. Some of these English students had been at public schools or in the forces during the war or were the children of Irish parents in the British colonial service.

I was immediately struck by their greater confidence of manner, which I envied, and the air they gave of having discovered who they were already, of being at ease with themselves and being relatively free from social awkwardness. They were polite and courteous and when I went out for the evening with one of them, I was made to feel important and flattered. They were not loquacious like we southern Irish nor shy and inhibited like some of the northerners. They seemed to have no wish to shine, to be noticed, no wish to add to the gaiety of nations which was an Irish imperative: they were sensible, tolerant, comfortable, not given to giddy turns like us. Their reserve was striking. They did not seem to want to talk about what impassioned them, were careful not to show their feelings or be carried away by them. It seemed tantalisingly impossible to find out what they really thought and felt under the outward manner. Perhaps they did not feel anything passionately at all?

Years later, I was to find out how misleading was this surface impression, how little I had penetrated a manner that was the result of two centuries of cultural fashioning. I was also to discover how my own Irishness had been passed on from generation to generation by the same cultural process. Books were largely responsible for the phenomenon in both cases.

JANE AUSTEN
AND THE LIFE OF THE FEELINGS

At the heart of every novel by Jane Austen is a heroine: she it is who carries the experience of the book, who makes mistakes and learns by them and who, in the end, because Jane Austen's novels are in the comic tradition, is rewarded with a husband whom she can love and respect. What, I wondered, was the image of womanhood which Jane Austen had inherited from her predecessors? Joseph Addison was probably the most influential of earlier writers. In 1711–12 he published his vastly popular *Spectator* papers. These were not newspapers, for they contained no news, but were essays of instruction and entertainment which appeared six times every week. The exclusion of political news at a time of high political tension between Whigs and Tories not only was safer but made for a larger circulation as the papers cut across or ignored party lines and divisions. Instead, the great topic to be discussed by 'Mr Spectator' – as Addison called himself – was the common question of how to live. Moderation in all things, especially in politics and religion, was the underlying point of all the papers. Addison talked good sense on manners and morals, and in a tone that combined gentle mockery with good humour he implied that displays of passion or strong feeling of any kind were dangerous, ridiculous and in bad taste. (Here is the well-known image of the Englishman who rarely shows his feelings.)

A large part of Addison's originality lay in his wish to include women or (as he frequently called them with characteristic condescension) 'the Fair Sex' among his readership. Jane Austen found his patronising tone intolerable. And with what derision must she have read his claim to rescue women from 'the trivialities of their lives' and to make them fit to converse with men at the tea table! The narrator in *Northanger Abbey* gives this devastating satiric reply to the Addisons of this world:

> She [Catherine Morland] was heartily ashamed of her ignorance. A misplaced shame. Where people wish to attach, they should always be ignorant. To come with a well-informed mind is to come with an inability of administering to the vanity of others, which a sensible person would always wish to avoid.

In *Pride and Prejudice* Mr Bennet warns his daughter Elizabeth:

> 'Your lively talents would place you in the greatest danger in an unequal marriage. You could scarcely escape discredit and misery. My child, let me not have the grief of seeing *you* unable to respect your partner in life.'

Wit and intelligence were dangerous and unwelcome in women. Intelligence in women frightened the Irishmen of my day as much as it did the Englishmen of Jane Austen's. Much better to play the helpless female in need of protection if you wanted male attention. My friend Joan knew all about this trick of the trade: intelligent and artistic, she chose to hide her ability in the presence of men. At tennis dances together, she prepared the field. 'Edith is so clever, you know. She wins all the prizes at school and she is marvellous at sport, while I am no good at anything.' And the young men swooned towards her and I was left, offsided, ill at ease, burning with indignation, but unable to do anything about it. I could not shake off the feeling that I must be distinctly unfeminine, unattractive and muscular. When I attacked her about it, she said, disarmingly: 'But that is the way to get them interested, and I know you do not mind because you are not a terrible flirt like me.'

This image that women were delightfully helpless was deeply engrained in men's consciousness: my brother warned me as I was about to enter university: 'Watch out, now! Men do not like intellectual qualities in women; they prefer feminine ones.' I must be prepared to hide my mental energies, it seemed, and keep a low intellectual profile even inside an intellectual institution. But it was not so at all. Being at university was a most liberating mental experience. Not only was it permissible to talk about ideas with men, it was welcome and exciting. There was a lot of intellectual show, of course, but that came from men, eager to impress, and was solemn and boring. The people I liked best to be with were those who joined intelligent discussion with wit and laughter.

That is why I loved the novels of Jane Austen; in them I found the play of high intelligence with brilliant irony and laughter. It was many years after I left the university before I read her last novel, *Persuasion* (1818). She wrote it during her final illness at just over forty years of age, but did not have time to do the more careful re-drafting that was customary with her. It is both more fiercely satiric and more tender than her other books, and contains a passage which was to startle me and set me thinking in a new way about human experience. Anne Elliot, the heroine, quite exceptionally in Jane Austen, turned down the man she loved before the book even begins. More than seven years before we meet her, she has been 'persuaded' by her only friend that the match was imprudent as the man in question had 'nothing but himself to recommend him, and no hopes of attaining affluence, but in the chances of a most uncertain profession' (the navy). She is now twenty-seven years old, an age of which Marianne in Austen's *Sense and Sensibility*, says:

> 'A woman of seven and twenty . . . can never hope to feel or inspire affection again, and if her home be uncomfortable, or her fortune small, I can suppose that she might bring herself to submit to the offices of a nurse, for the sake of the provision and security of a wife.'

For seven years Anne Elliot has tasted an alternative to the risk of marriage and the taste has been sour and tedious. She has tasted the stultifying boredom of a woman whose life gave her nothing significant to do, the humiliating dependency on the most vainglorious and empty-headed father in all Jane Austen, the company of a complacent, stupid and snobbish sister, and the unsettling knowledge that she was of no importance to anybody at all. She has lost her bloom, her hopes, her purpose in life. 'She must now submit to feel that another lesson in the art of knowing our own nothingness beyond our own circle, was becoming necessary to her.' As for her father, Sir Walter Elliot:

> Be it known then, that Sir Walter, like a good father (having met with one or two private disappointments in very unreasonable applications), prided himself on remaining single for his dear daughters' sake. For one daughter, his eldest, he would really have given up any thing, which he had not been very much tempted to do . . . His two other children were of very inferior value. Mary had acquired a little artificial importance, by becoming Mrs Charles Musgrove; but Anne, with an elegance of mind and sweetness of character, which must have placed her high with any people of real understanding, was nobody with either father or sister: her word had no weight; her convenience was always to give way; – she was only Anne.

Into this mortifying life of stagnation, Jane Austen brings back the man she loves, now a successful naval captain retiring to the countryside after the end of the wars with France in 1815 and eager to marry. To Anne's habitual suffering is added mortification and embarrassment for she has been told that Captain Wentworth, still wounded and smarting from her earlier refusal of him, found her so altered that 'he would not have known her again'. Austen gives us a very significant conversation between Anne and Captain Harville. Harville laments the case of his friend, Captain Benwick, who has suffered terribly by losing his fiancée through death. Now happily he has found another love. He adds, 'Poor Fanny, she would not have forgotten him so soon.'

Anne agrees that women's feelings are more enduring than men's:

> 'We certainly do not forget you, so soon as you forget us . . .
> Your feelings may be the strongest . . . but . . . ours are the most tender.'

She points out that men are allowed to work, are more active than women:

> 'Neither time, nor health, nor life, to be called your own.'

Captain Harville counters this argument by saying:

'. . . all histories are against you, all stories, prose and verse . . . I do not think I ever opened a book in my life which had not something to say upon woman's inconstancy. Songs and proverbs, all talk of woman's fickleness. But perhaps you will say, these were all written by men.'

'Perhaps I shall. – Yes, yes, if you please, no reference to examples in books. Men have had every advantage of us in telling their own story. Education has been theirs in so much higher a degree; the pen has been in their hands. I will not allow books to prove any thing.'

It was true! The roles for women had all been created by men, and women accepted them and tried to conform to them. The great writers up to Jane Austen had all been men – Chaucer, Spenser, Shakespeare, Milton, Addison, Defoe, Richardson, Fielding. Had no woman spoken for women? Hundreds of women took up the pen before and during Austen's lifetime, earning a slender living by writing novels to fill the popular circulating libraries, but their works were derivative and ephemeral and did not seriously challenge the stereotype created by men.

What, I wondered, would the gimlet-eyed Jane Austen have to say about men, in particular about the English gentleman? One hundred years had passed since Addison had written his *Spectator* but the word 'gentleman' appeared on almost every page of her novels. Much had changed in England in that hundred years but very little in the condition of women. Austen belonged to the old eighteenth-century world, to the last generation of the settled, leisured, rural class, unchanged in essentials for centuries but which was about to see its power transferred to the towns and the new business classes created by the Industrial Revolution (Charlotte Brontë, only thirty years after Jane Austen, sets one of her novels, *Shirley*, in an industrial town amidst the Luddite riots – Keighley, next door to the village of Haworth). Austen, unlike Addison who lived in London, spent nearly all her life in rural Hampshire. People lived in small communities, rarely moved far from home and were dependent on a few families for entertainment and comfort. A new arrival in such a community was the signal for great curiosity and speculation (Darcy and Bingley in *Pride and Prejudice* cause a sensation by coming to settle in the neighbourhood). Manners were still tightly prescribed and there was great pressure to conform to accepted standards of behaviour, especially for women of the upper and middle classes.

This is the society Jane Austen records in her novels. In one of her letters she writes: 'A few families in a country village is the very thing to work on.' People met together in groups. Unmarried women were seldom alone with men so that in her novels we see women meeting together with men in sitting rooms, balls, assemblies, picnics where conversation was an important medium for discovery and concealment. (She is excellent at making the reader feel several presences at once even though only one person is talking.) Jane Austen had sat in many such groups, registering every nuance of meaning and what she calls 'the little zig-zags of embarrassment' at play beneath the words. Her concern in all her novels is the position of the sensitive, intelligent, single woman. Underneath the irony and the laughter, their position is hard; society for women is tedious, mercenary, snobbish. When Elizabeth Bennet says, 'There are few people whom I really love and fewer still of whom I think well', she is speaking for all the heroines and for Jane Austen herself, as we can see in her letters. Her heroines must endure a great deal of stupidity, vanity and insensitivity.

When the unmarried Anne Elliot goes to stay at Uppercross with her married sister, Mrs Musgrove, she knows that

> the Mr Musgroves had their own game to guard, and to destroy; their own horses, dogs, and newspapers to engage them; and the females were fully occupied in all the other common subjects of house-keeping, neighbours, dress, dancing, and music. She acknowledged it to be very fitting, that every little social commonwealth should dictate its own matters of discourse; and hoped, ere long, to become a not unworthy member of the one she was now transplanted into. – With the prospect of spending at least two months at Uppercross, it was highly incumbent on her to clothe her imagination, her memory, and all her ideas in as much of Uppercross as possible.

The irony is so understated that it might even be overlooked.

Elizabeth Bennet has to endure the stupidity and vulgarity of her mother, the silliness of her sisters and the vacuity of her neighbours, the Lucases.

On a coach journey:

> Sir William Lucas, and his daughter Maria, a good humoured girl, but as empty-headed as himself, had nothing to say that could be worth hearing, and were listened to with about as much delight as the rattle of the chaise. Elizabeth loved absurdities, but she had known Sir William's too long. He could tell her nothing new of the wonders of his presentation and knighthood; and his civilities were worn out like his information.

Mothers are not held in high esteem by Jane Austen. Lady Middleton,

> a fond mother, though in pursuit of praise for her children, the most rapacious of human beings, is likewise the most credulous. Her demands are exorbitant but she will swallow anything.

Fathers do not fare much better. John Dashwood

> had not much to say for himself that was worth hearing, and his wife had still less. But there was no peculiar disgrace in this, for it was very much the case with the chief of their visitors, who almost all laboured under one or other of these disqualifications for being agreeable – Want of sense, either natural or improved – want of elegance – want of spirits – or want of temper.

Emma Woodhouse, 'handsome, clever, and rich', has to put up with much tedium and she is more unwilling than the other heroines to do so. Her rudeness to the boring Miss Bates, 'neither young, handsome, rich, nor married', brings her into heavy disfavour with Mr Knightley. Anne Elliot goes out to dine:

> It was but a card party; it was but a mixture of those who had never met before, and those who had met too often – it was a common-place business, too numerous for intimacy, too small for variety.

Emma's lively mind must endure the rituals

where the children came in and were talked to and admired amid the usual rate of conversation; a few clever things said, a few downright silly, but by much the larger proportion neither the one nor the other – nothing worse than everyday remarks, dull repetitions, old news and heavy jokes.

What were the hopes for happiness for the intelligent young woman in such a restricted society? Her one and only hope for changing her life was marriage; that was the only 'profession' open to her and it was rarely a free choice. Property, connections, money, all played a part in the choosing of a husband and were jealously guarded or sought after by the men of her family. John Dashwood counsels his sister, Elinor:

'A very little trouble on your side secures him. Perhaps just at present he may be undecided; the smallness of your fortune may make him hang back; his friends may all advise him against it. But some of those little attentions and encouragements which ladies can so easily give will fix him, in spite of himself.'

A young woman married 'to advantage' or 'to oblige her family'. If she had money she was well placed; if she had beauty as well, she could get away with less of the former. Failing any of these, she became a failure, an 'old maid', still known and still treated patronisingly in my youth. Charlotte Lucas in *Pride and Prejudice* is a realist.

Without thinking highly either of men or of matrimony, marriage had always been her object; it was the only honourable provision for well-educated young women of small fortune, and however uncertain of giving happiness, must be their pleasantest preservative from want.

On the first page of *Mansfield Park*, Jane Austen sums up with brilliant irony the choices open to women.

About thirty years ago, Miss Maria Ward of Huntingdon, with only seven thousand pounds, had the good luck to captivate Sir Thomas Bertram, of Mansfield Park, in the county of Northampton, and to be thereby raised to the rank of a baronet's lady, with all the comforts and consequences of an handsome house and large income. All Huntingdon exclaimed on the greatness of the match, and her uncle, the lawyer, himself, allowed her to be at least three thousand pounds short of any equitable claim to it.

However, her sister,

at the end of half a dozen years, found herself obliged to be attached to the Rev. Mr Norris, a friend of her brother-in-law, with scarcely any private fortune... Sir Thomas being happily able to give his friend an income in the living of Mansfield... Mr and Mrs Norris began their career of conjugal felicity with very little less than a thousand a year.

Her second sister married for love.

But Miss Frances married, in the common phrase, to disoblige her family, and by fixing on a Lieutenant of Marines, without education, fortune, or connections, did it very thoroughly.

Jane Austen understands, if she does not approve, the plain and penniless but educated girl who married for a home to escape parental dependency. Charlotte Lucas in *Pride and Prejudice* accepts the hand of the most fatuous man in all the novels, the Reverend Mr Collins. When her friend Elizabeth Bennet hears of this, she exclaims: 'Engaged to Mr Collins! my dear Charlotte, – impossible!' Charlotte replies:

'I am not romantic you know. I never was. I ask only a comfortable home; and considering Mr Collins's character, connections, and situation in life, I am convinced that my chance of happiness with him is as fair, as most people can boast on entering the marriage state.'

When Elizabeth, full of curiosity, goes to visit Charlotte in her married home, she finds that 'when Mr Collins could be forgotten there was really a great air of comfort throughout, and by Charlotte's evident enjoyment of it, Elizabeth supposed he must be often forgotten'. She speaks for all women who have endured tedious husbands for a home of their own in the ironical sentence:

To work in his garden was one of his most respectable

pleasures; and Elizabeth admired the command of counten-
ance with which Charlotte talked of the healthfulness of the
exercise, and owned she encouraged it as much as possible.

There is an even worse fate in store for the accomplished, educated young woman without family or money. More accomplished and more educated than Emma, Jane Fairfax can only hope
to maintain herself by working as a governess; and Austen's comment on that profession is unusually fierce. Jane says, in response to
Mrs Elton's patronising offers of help:

> 'When I am quite determined as to the time, I am not at all
> afraid of being long unemployed. There are places in town,
> offices, where inquiry would soon produce something –
> Offices for the sale – not quite of human flesh – but of human
> intellect.'
>
> 'Oh! my dear, human flesh! You quite shock me; if you
> mean a fling at the slave-trade, I assure you Mr Suckling was
> always rather a friend to the abolition.'
>
> 'I did not mean, I was not thinking of the slave-trade,' re-
> plied Jane; 'governess-trade, I assure you, was all that I had in
> view; widely different certainly as to the guilt of those who
> carry it on; but as to the greater misery of the victims, I do
> not know where it lies.'

We have to wait for the Brontë sisters to give us powerful descriptions of that slave trade, descriptions born out of their own mortifying experience of it. W.H. Auden's poem 'Letter to Lord Byron'
(1937) sums up the marriage market in Jane Austen's novels:

> You could not shock her more than she shocks me;
> Beside her Joyce seems innocent as grass.
> It makes me feel uncomfortable to see
> An English spinster of the middle class
> Describe the amorous effects of 'brass',
> Reveal so frankly and with such sobriety
> The economic basis of society.

Addison stressed the importance of social cohesion; Jane Austen
stressed the price that must be paid in *personal feeling* for that

cohesion. It is marriage that brings the social and the personal together in the most acute form for women and marriage is the focus of all her novels. Society had a measure for everything except the feelings. How were girls to deal with their feelings in marriages not cemented with love? And there are many marriages still without that cement. *Sense and Sensibility*, an early novel, puts this central dilemma for women; in spite of the mockery and the laughter, it is a painful story. Jane Austen gives us the two Dashwood sisters and their widowed mother. Marianne, at sixteen and a half, is impulsive and sensitive, wanting her life (like Jane Eyre) to be full of vividness and poetry. Elinor too, at nineteen, is sensitive but more sensible and level-headed than Marianne. By making them dependent on their half-brother for a livelihood, Austen puts the women in a very vulnerable position. John Dashwood means to keep his promises to his late father to be generous to these women, and the scene in which his wife argues him into reducing his proposed sum of money into a mere fraction of the original is one of the funniest as well as the most enlightening on self-deception in all literature.

Marianne falls in love with the handsome and romantic Willoughby. They glory in their common tastes and in each other. Elinor cautions Marianne to be more decorous in her behaviour, but Marianne burst forth:

'. . . is this fair? is this just? are my ideas so scanty? But I see what you mean. I have been too much at my ease, too happy, too frank. I have erred against every common-place notion of decorum. I have been open and sincere where I ought to have been reserved, spiritless, dull, and deceitful . . .'

No, she will not accept this reprimand. We, on the other side of the romantic divide with its ever-increasing demand for personal happiness, are on Marianne's side. But Jane Austen, like Elinor, is a realist: she knows her society. She knows how dangerous it is for the unmarried woman to show her feelings. She knows that she must conceal them among people who would quickly condemn her for any imagined misdemeanour and even help to render her unmarriageable. Prudence must be her watchword. Jane Bennet, Elizabeth's beautiful sister, knows this instinctively: 'She united with great strength of feeling, a composure of temper and a uniform cheerfulness of manner which would guard her from the suspicions of the impertinent', from what Austen called in *Northanger Abbey* 'a neighbourhood of voluntary spies'.

Willoughby later abandons Marianne for a mercenary marriage (Jane Austen understands 'the mortifying conviction that handsome young men must have something to live on as well as the plain'). Marianne's sufferings are terrible and her illness almost kills her. Elinor, unknown to Marianne, is also in love and also believes herself betrayed. She suffers equally with Marianne but in order to spare her mother and sister she controls her feelings and is shown to be morally stronger by this effort. 'Marianne was without power because she was without command over herself.' Command over the expression of the feelings is a woman's only power in a powerless world. It is her only dignity, her only defence, but her thoughts remain free. Elinor says:

> 'My doctrine had never aimed at the subjugation of the understanding. All I have ever attempted to influence had been the behaviour.'

Marianne will learn this hard lesson 'by that which only could convince her, a better knowledge of mankind'. Jane Austen had not a romantic view of human nature. For the unmarried woman the only heroism is silence, and solitude the only place to indulge the emotions. 'Elizabeth Bennet found herself alone and was then at liberty to think and be wretched.' Poor, impulsive Marianne is married off at the end of the book to the decent but dull Colonel Brandon who wears a flannel waistcoat. This is reality, implies Jane Austen, but it is hard, very hard on Marianne.

In the seven years and three novels which intervened between *Sense and Sensibility* and *Persuasion*, Austen had changed her mind. Anne Elliot, at twenty-seven, is not a romantic immature Marianne but a mature woman. At nineteen, she had been 'extremely pretty, tender-hearted, intelligent', but because of disappointment in love, 'her bloom vanished early'. She had learned before the book opened what Marianne had to learn in the whole course of *Sense and Sensibility*. In the interim, Jane Austen has lost patience with the values of her society. The Big House, so long the symbol of what was best in England, is now tarnished; it is not worth sacrificing the personal life to consolidate it.

> How eloquent could Anne Elliot have been, – how eloquent,
> at least, were her wishes on the side of early warm attachment,
> and a cheerful confidence in futurity, against that over-anxious
> caution which seems to insult exertion and distrust Provi-
> dence! – She had been forced into prudence in her youth, she
> learned romance as she grew older – the natural sequel of an
> unnatural beginning.

It is the navy with its risk, initiative and bravery which now represents the future for England. (Two of Jane Austen's brothers, without influence or connections, rose to be admirals.) By the grace of
the author, a beautiful story of the rediscovery of love opens before
us and we see Anne reunited to Captain Wentworth.

> She gloried in being a sailor's wife, but she must pay the tax of
> quick alarm for belonging to that profession which is, if possi-
> ble, more distinguished in its domestic virtues than in its na-
> tional importance.

The cohesion of the old prudent society of Addison is not worth the
sacrifice of its most sensitive and tender-hearted daughters. But in
practice, they continued to be sacrificed for many years to come.

Jane Austen, witty and lively herself, is very suspicious of charm
in men – a quality much prized in Ireland. In every one of her novels, she introduces a charming gentleman who very nearly de-
ceives the heroine be she ever so intelligent. Elizabeth Bennet is
taken in for a time by Wickham:

> His appearance was greatly in his favour; he had all the best
> part of beauty, a fine countenance, a good figure, and very
> pleasing address. The introduction was followed up on his side
> by a happy readiness of conversation – a readiness at the same
> time perfectly correct and unassuming . . .

The overconfident and intelligent Emma is also taken in by Frank
Churchill, by the grace and easy charm of his manners, and fancies
herself in love with him only to find out that he has simply flirted
with her while being secretly engaged to Jane Fairfax. Anne Elliot
is, like Lady Russell, at first deceived by the mercenary Mr Elliot,

her cousin.

> He was quite as good-looking as he had appeared at Lyme, his
> countenance improved by speaking, and his manners were so
> exactly as they ought to be, so polished, so easy, so particularly
> agreeable, that she could compare them in excellence to only
> one person's manners. They were not the same, but they were,
> perhaps, equally good.
>   He sat down with them, and improved their conversation
> very much. There could be no doubt of his being a sensible
> man. Ten minutes were enough to certify that. His tone, his
> expressions, his choice of subject, his knowing where to stop,
> – it was all the operation of a sensible, discerning mind.

But it is in *Mansfield Park* that Jane Austen gives us her most
serious lesson in how to differentiate style and personality from true
character. She brings Henry and Mary Crawford from London to
stay with their sister in the country, where their style and charming
manner enchant everybody.

> Mary Crawford was remarkably pretty; Henry, though not
> handsome, had air and countenance; the manners of both were
> lively and pleasant, and Mrs Grant immediately gave them
> credit for every thing else.

Mary's conversation is brilliantly rendered, witty, sophisticated,
knowing:

> 'If you can persuade Henry to marry, you must have the ad-
> dress of a French woman. All that English abilities can do, has
> been tried already. I have three particular friends who have
> been all dying for him in their turn; and the pains which they,
> their mothers, (very clever women,) as well as my dear aunt
> and myself, have taken to reason, coax, or trick him into mar-
> rying, is inconceivable! He is the most horrible flirt that can be
> imagined. If your Miss Bertrams do not like to have their
> hearts broke, let them avoid Henry.'

She is captivated by Edmund, with whom the plain Fanny Price
is secretly in love, and intends to marry him until the day she finds
out that he is to be a clergyman.

'But why are you to be a clergyman? I thought *that* was always the lot of the youngest, where there were many to choose before him.'

'Do you think the church itself never chosen then?'

'*Never* is a black word. But yes, in the *never* of conversation which means *not very often*, I do think it. For what is to be done in the church? Men love to distinguish themselves, and in either of the other lines, distinction may be gained, but not in the church. A clergyman is nothing.'

Edmund, seeking to defend the clergy, says:

'And with regard to their influencing public manners, Miss Crawford must not misunderstand me, or suppose I mean to call them the arbiters of good breeding, the regulators of refinement and courtesy, the masters of the ceremonies of life. The *manners* I speak of, might rather be called *conduct*, perhaps, the result of good principles; the effect, in short, of those doctrines which it is their duty to teach and recommend; and it will, I believe, be every where found, that as the clergy are, or are not what they ought to be, so are the rest of the nation.'

Here Jane Austen makes the important distinction between manners and morals, but Mary, though socially very sensitive, is not morally sensitive enough to understand this distinction.

'You really are fit for something better. Come, do change your mind. It is not too late. Go into the law.'

'Go into the law! with as much ease as I was told to go into this wilderness.'

The moral coarseness of her mind is made clear, 'darkened yet fancying itself light'. Yet Edmund, right up to the end of the novel, feels her power. For Austen knows full well the devastating power of beauty, personality, charm and energy. But she is suspicious of charm and ease, in men especially, and she can more easily forgive the lack of it than the absence of a gentlemanly heart. Darcy has no social ease.

'I certainly have not the talent which some people possess,' said Darcy, 'of conversing easily with those I have never seen before. I cannot catch their tone of conversation, or appear interested in their concerns, as I often see done.'

He appears rude and proud, but because his heart is good, he is capable of being corrected. Mr Knightley declares, 'I cannot make speeches', although he is the best talker in the book. He is, indeed, suspicious of too much talk. He says to Emma, 'If I loved you less, I might be able to talk about it more.' William, a good brother to Fanny, is 'worn out with civility. I have been talking incessantly all night and with nothing to say.'

Reading is a requirement for a true gentleman. Mr Darcy has a large library and is always sending to London for new books. 'I cannot comprehend the neglect of a family library in such days as these.' Mr Bennet is seldom out of his library but that is a defect: he shelters there from his silly wife and from the moral responsibility of educating his daughters. Sir Walter Elliot reads one book only, *The Baronetage*, always open at the letter E. Mr Knightley does not talk about books or reading, nor is his library mentioned, but Emma declares 'when he is at home, he is either reading to himself or settling his accounts'. We know that he values a well-informed mind for he reproves Emma for her inability to motivate herself to a course of reading. He says with indulgent irony:

> 'Emma has been meaning to read more ever since she was twelve years old. I have seen a great many lists of her drawing up at various times of books that she meant to read regularly through – and very good lists they were – very well chosen, and very neatly arranged – sometimes alphabetically, and sometimes by some other rule... But I have done with expecting any course of steady reading from Emma. She will never submit to any thing requiring industry and patience, and a subjection of the fancy to the understanding.'

Of all the gentlemen, flawed or redeemable, who walk through the pages of her novels, there is one only who answers the ideal. Jane Austen makes us fully aware that Mr Knightley represents the best that English culture can produce. His name is subtly allegorical; he is the knight of England, the true gentleman who behaves in a knightly fashion, and the Christian name that Emma cannot bring herself to use, George, is the name of the patron saint of England. The qualities which Austen selects and admires she sees as English. Mr Knightley is non-intellectual but intelligent, sensible and practical. (The English still have little patience with intellectuals.) He is manly and upright, rational and unaffected. He has Addison's cheerfulness, a great social quality; the hypochondriacal Mr Woodhouse finds 'his cheerful manner always did me good'. He has no time for finessing; he says of Frank Churchill:

> 'There is one thing, Emma, which a man can always do, if he chooses, and that is, his duty; not by manoeuvring and finessing but by vigour and resolution.'

The vigour of his person, 'his tall, firm, upright figure', is paralleled by the vigour of his mind and conscience. 'He always moved with the alertness of mind which could neither be undecided nor dilatory.' He is kindly without ostentation and mixes easily with everyone of high or low estate. He does not like fancy manners and sees through everyone who makes a parade of them. He has a prejudice against French manners:

> 'No, Emma, your amiable young man can be amiable only in French, not in English. He may be very "aimable", have very good manners, and be very agreeable; but he can have no English delicacy towards the feelings of other people: nothing really amiable about him.'

It is true, however, that English delicacy towards the feelings of other people is remarkably absent in most of Jane Austen's fictional characters, but it is what she prizes above all the other qualities and it is the means by which she judges people. Mr Knightley is an ideal but he is flesh and blood as well and I, like many women, fell in love with him. His house, his estate, his management of his land and his tenants represent for Jane Austen the best values that England stands for. She allows herself no ironical comment in describing them. His house, Donwell Abbey, is symbolic, rare in Austen – Done-well and Abbey associate doing well with religious values. The house is modest, useful and used, unostentatious like its owner. As Emma surveys it:

She felt all the honest pride and complacency which her alliance with the present and future proprietor could fairly warrant, as she viewed the respectable size and style of the building, its suitable, becoming, characteristic situation, low and sheltered – its ample gardens stretching down to meadows washed by a stream, of which the Abbey, with all the old neglect of prospect, had scarcely a sight – and its abundance of timber in rows and avenues, which neither fashion nor extravagance had rooted up. – The house was larger than Hartfield, and totally unlike it, covering a good deal of ground, rambling and irregular, with many comfortable and one or two handsome rooms. – It was just what it ought to be, and it looked what it was – and Emma felt an increasing respect for it, as the residence of a family of such true gentility, untainted in blood and understanding.

Its Englishness is made unambiguous:

It was a sweet view – sweet to the eye and the mind. English verdure, English culture, English comfort, seen under a sun bright, without being oppressive'.

Mr Knightley is the only man fit to be the husband and moral mentor of that most witty and wilful, saucy and bewitching heroine, Emma Woodhouse. Under his guidance the good understanding which he claims that Emma has inherited by nature and the good principles instilled in her by Miss Taylor, her governess, will not too long be overrun by fancy and illusion. She is more like the Rosalind of *As You Like It* and the Beatrice of *Much Ado About Nothing* than anyone else in English literature. If she is 'faultless in spite of all her faults' it is because Austen disliked perfection; 'Pictures of perfection make me sick and wicked,' she declared in one of her letters.

The brilliance of character, wit, conversation and plot in *Emma* make it the best comic novel in English literature as Mr Knightley and Emma together display what Jane Austen considers the finest and most English of qualities. The wit, the conversation, the irony are all qualities which I, as an Irishwoman, loved, for these very qualities have always been practised and enjoyed in Ireland; but for Austen they are always severely at the service of morality.

E.M. FORSTER
AND THE LIFE OF THE FEELINGS

Mr Knightley's prejudice against the French was the only thing that ill became him in my eyes. I fell in love with him, I, an Irish girl, with a sane and sensible Englishman and scarce a giddy turn in him . . . I wondered at myself. I preferred him to Rochester or Heathcliff who would have swept me off my feet into a tempestuous emotional world. I puzzled over my preference. Mr Knightley loved the witty, vivacious Emma; he loved an independent-minded woman as long as her heart was in the right place; he loved to be teased and to tease in his turn. I liked to think myself more like Emma Woodhouse than Jane Eyre for Emma 'dearly loved a laugh' and with Mr Knightley for a lover and companion, I would have a laugh at least once a day.

Jane Austen had found the English gentleman wanting, often severely so, but she also found him redeemable like Mr Darcy, and once, all that he should be in Mr Knightley. By her last novel, *Persuasion*, she seems to have lost faith with the landed proprietor of the Big House which, for over two hundred years, had been the unit of political and cultural authority in England. Sir Walter Elliot of Kellynch Hall in *Persuasion* is utterly irredeemable. 'Vanity was the beginning and end of Sir Walter Elliot's character.' It was the new men of the Royal Navy, dependent not upon land but upon their own courage and initiative, who gave her hope. Was her hope justified in the years that followed her death?

Nearly a century after *Persuasion* (1818) was the time of my father's youth and naval career. Enormous changes had come over

England by then, such as an expansion of manufacturing and industry which was unthinkable to the rural Jane Austen. (I remembered Mrs Elton's remarks on one growing industrial city in *Emma*: 'Birmingham, one has not high hopes for Birmingham. I always say there is something direful in that sound.') Trade, the expanding empire, the huge growth of the cities, the transformation of the Yorkshire and Lancashire dales into 'dark Satanic mills', all came together to make England rich and confident. My father served in Royal Navy stations all over the world before the First World War, and the golden sovereign, he told me, spoke louder then than any other currency. When the sailors went ashore, gold coins in their pockets, the whole world welcomed them. Just at this time E.M. Forster published *Howards End* (1910), a novel which I read with immense interest for I was linked to the period he describes through my living father. What, I wondered, had become of the English gentleman since Jane Austen?

Like her, Forster surveys the English social scene and finds it (as I expected) confident, prosperous and sure of itself. Like her, he wants to know if the conditions then existing are conducive to the growth of satisfying personal relationships, for on this he will judge them, as she does. She had revealed through irony a very disturbing moral darkness at the heart of her society. Forster reveals as profound a darkness in his, 'a darkness in high places which comes with a commercial eye'. He takes as a representative Englishman not a landed proprietor or a naval officer, but a successful financier. Henry Wilcox lives in the commuter belt of London, his only connection with rural life being through his wife and her family home, Howards End. Imaginatively, he no longer has any connection with the soil or the seasons. Like Jane Austen, Forster takes a few families, has them cross each other's paths and sets up relationships between them so that he can reveal the inadequacies of the new men in the face of the demands of the personal life.

The Wilcoxes meet the Schlegel sisters, Margaret and Helen. Both girls are intelligent and imaginative, like Jane Austen's heroines, but unlike hers they are financially independent and living on their own. Though so like Elinor and Marianne in *Sense and Sensibility*, the hundred years that have since passed have given these sisters much greater freedom. Margaret is more practical than Helen who, like Marianne, is idealistic, impulsive and pretty. Mr Wilcox is a representative male of the class that Forster now finds distasteful: he is authoritative, confident, successful, sure of his own identity. It is natural for him to take charge of situations, especially where women are concerned. 'He was one of those men who knew the principal hotel by instinct.' 'When he took Margaret out to dinner, he told her what to eat.' He inhabits 'the world of motor-cars, telephones, estate agents' lists . . . of telegrams and anger'. He is not interested in the past: 'He lived for the five minutes that had passed and the five to come: he had the business mind.' Like Bounderby in *Hard Times*, he is proud of being a self-made man, proud of the way he has understood his world and gone about things. 'Hard facts were enough for him.' He is patronising to those less successful than himself.

'A word of advice. Don't take up that sentimental attitude over the poor. The poor are poor and one's sorry for them, but there it is.'

When Helen tells him of an intellectual discussion group she and Margaret had attended:

The man of business smiled. Since his wife's death, he had almost doubled his income. He was an important figure at last, a reassuring name on company prospectuses, and life had treated him very well. The world seemed in his grasp as he listened to the river Thames, which still flowed inland from the sea. So wonderful to the girls, it had no mysteries for him. He had helped to shorten its long tidal trough by taking shares in the lock at Teddington, and, if he and other capitalists thought good, some day it could be shortened again. With a good dinner inside him and an amiable but academic woman on each flank, he felt that his hands were on all the ropes of life, and that what he did not know could not be worth knowing.

He answers Helen:

'I often wished I had gone in for them [debates] when I was a youngster. It would have helped me no end.' . . . But Helen was nettled. The aim of *their* debates, she implied, was Truth.

'Oh, yes, it doesn't much matter what subject you take,' said he.

The irony is worthy of Jane Austen!

Forster kills off Mrs Wilcox so that Mr Wilcox can marry Margaret and 'the prose and the passion' can be united. Helen is outraged, warning her sister, 'I shall never speak to your husband.' Margaret is unafraid. 'There are heaps of things in me that he doesn't, and shall never, understand.' She accepts compromise. 'Yet he did alter her character – a little. There was an unforeseen surprise, a cessation of the winds and odours of life, a social pressure that would have her think conjugally.' I had often observed that conjugal thinking in married couples, one partner giving up, on the surface at least, a set of independent thoughts to sink them in the team. 'You go with your husband in religion and politics,' I had often heard said. I wondered at women who could so easily abandon their own ideals to often inferior husbands. I determined that, should I ever marry, I would be careful to avoid this conjugal trap.

It is Forster's purpose to bring Mr Wilcox to a situation where his protective male armour will be stripped from him, stripped as a result of his complacent entry into the lives of these two sisters, stripped by his inability to understand and respect the feelings, by lack of imagination, those useless qualities which he never valued. He had inherited the myth of maleness, just as my father had. Men, like women, are often victims of the roles prescribed for them. Thomas Hardy notices this in *Tess of the D'Urbervilles* when he says:

'Men have much more opportunity for expression rather than observation.'

Men were expected to have opinions rather than to listen which often makes them deaf to what they should hear. Mr Wilcox has a very unsubtle attitude to women.

Sensitive women he called 'nervous'. He liked his wife to be clever enough to shed radiance upon his enlightened choice but not so clever as to put him in the shade.

For all his business success, he is starved emotionally:

He simply did not notice things . . . he never noticed the lights and shades that exist in the greyest conversation, the finger posts the mile stones, the collisions and illimitable views.

When Margaret criticises him for this deficiency, he replies:

'I've no intention of frittering away my strength on that sort of thing.'

'It isn't frittering away the strength,' she protested. 'It's enlarging the space in which you may be strong.'

He answered: 'You're a very clever little woman, but my motto's concentrate.'

And again going in the roads of Mr Wilcox's soul. From boyhood, he had neglected them. 'I'm not a fellow who bothers about my own inside.'

The engaged Margaret longs for 'the mystery of love' to descend upon her. She believes that 'by quiet indications a bridge would be built and span their lives with beauty'. For him 'there was no mystery in love: it was a case of arrangements for property, money, rights. There was no radiance, no poetry in Mr Wilcox's vision of things.' Forster eventually brings Margaret to diagnose her husband's mind with deadly accuracy:

He had been spoilt, he had always been spoilt; he has always been obeyed . . . Duty was for him to consider, sometimes, other people's welfare but not their feelings.

Margaret is a fascinating study in the ability of the intelligent woman to accept a weaker partner and build him up in his own estimation without his being in the least aware of it. I have often wondered at that phenomenon.

In dealing with a Wilcox, how tempting it was to lapse from comradeship and to give him the kind of woman that he desired! Henry took the bait at once . . .

And:

Henry would resent so strong a grasp of the situation. She must not comment; comment is unfeminine.

Helen is incapable of creating a man in his own image in this way. So was I.

Helen runs off with a working-class clerk, who is interested in ideas, and has a child by him. For the Wilcoxes, the code of the gentleman in this situation is clear: one pursues and punishes a man who has seduced one of the women of one's clan. Mr Wilcox's son, worthy son of his father, means to thrash Leonard to within an inch of his life, but he goes further and kills him. There is a trial and Wilcox junior is sentenced to three years' imprisonment. Henry Wilcox's world collapses around him. Forster pushes him further. Margaret learns that he has had, in the past, an affair with Leonard's wife. His respectability is paper-thin. Caught out, he blusters, appealing to the male code which allows 'a bit on the side'.

> 'It is no good,' said Henry. 'Those things leak out; you cannot stop a story once it has started. I have known cases of other men – I despised them once, I thought that *I'm* different, *I* shall never be tempted. Oh, Margaret –.' He came and sat down near her, improvising emotion. She could not bear to listen to him.
>
> 'We fellows all come to grief once in our time. Will you believe that?' . . .
>
> 'I have' – he lowered his voice – 'have been through hell.'

And:

> Henry was anxious to be terrible, but had not got it in him. He was a good average Englishman, who had slipped.

It is Helen who sees clearly that

> '. . . he is just a wall of newspapers, motor-cars and golf-clubs . . . and behind it, nothing but panic and emptiness.'

She sees his collapsed state:

> 'Meg, is or isn't he ill? I can't make out.'
> 'Not ill. Eternally tired, has worked very hard all his life, and noticed nothing. Those are the people who collapse when they do notice a thing.'

His is the 'untutored heart', the subject of all Forster's novels; one of those whose feelings have never been educated nor their imagination nourished, and who have never even suspected the lack.

It is the starved imagination, not the well-nourished, that is afraid.

It is women who rescue him, as Sissy Jupe rescues the Gradgrinds in *Hard Times*, for it is the women who have a surer knowledge of the feelings. Margaret, Helen and the baby are found at the end of the novel living with Henry in Howards End, in precious harmony with the most enduring thing – the earth. But the house, Howards End, is a far more fragile representative of stability than the Big House in Jane Austen. It has less moral authority, less of a nourishing hold on the imagination of English men and women than in her novels. Everything has shrunk to the unsupported personal relationship.

> Margaret was silent. Marriage had not saved her from the sense of flux. London was but a foretaste of this nomadic civilisation which is altering human nature so profoundly, and throws upon personal relations a stress greater than any they have ever borne before. Under cosmopolitanism, if it comes (and it has) we shall receive no help from the earth, and the binding force that they once exercised on character must be entrusted to Love alone. May Love be equal to the task!

D.H. Lawrence, writing at the same time as Forster, faced the same task – how to make Love alone carry all the weight of human happiness. Nearly one hundred years after Forster, at the start of the twenty-first century, no novelist could call upon a house to represent common traditional values. Society in England had become more atomised and the spiritual starvation of Wilcox souls more pronounced than before. Where Jane Austen looked with hope to the future at the end of *Persuasion*, Forster is fearful:

> 'All the same, London's creeping.'
> She pointed over the meadow – over eight or nine meadows, but at the end of them was a red rust.
> 'You see that in Surrey and even in Hampshire now,' she continued. 'I can see it from the Purbeck downs. And London

is only part of something else, I'm afraid. Life's going to be melted down all over the world.' . . .

'Because a thing is going strong now, it need not go strong for ever,' she said. 'This craze for motion has only set in during the last hundred years. It may be followed by a civilisation that won't be a movement, because it will rest on the earth. All the signs are against it now, but I can't help hoping, and very early in the morning in the garden I feel that our house is the future as well as the past.'

Was his hope justified? I do not think so.

MY FATHER'S SPIRIT OF LIFE

[A poet] rejoices more than other men
in the spirit of life that is in him . . .
WORDSWORTH

Although my father's disappointments with many aspects of his life after he left the navy, together with his difficulty in expressing affection or inspiring it, issued frequently in contemptuous dismissal of the generous motives for action of other people, he had in fact another side to him. In spite of his nervous constitution, his worries, real and imagined, his irritability and moodiness, he had 'a spirit of life' in him and he did rejoice in it. When his mental horizons cleared and his mind and body were at peace, he rejoiced in the colours and shapes of the visible universe and his imagination was set on fire by the thought of the teeming life of nature. In this benign state, he noticed trees, flowers, birds, but above all else he noticed the sky. As we went on our walks he would lift his head to gaze at the vast expanse above him and remark, 'Look! See how that long cloud sits on the horizon like a stretched-out cat.' He would point to the skyscapes and cloudscapes and explain the clouds called cumulus and the herringbone clouds with their portents for the morrow. It was as if the patterns of the sky with its clouds, sun, moon and stars had entered into his very being in those twenty-four years when he had moved between ocean and sky, often for months on end. His light blue eyes had that faraway look of one whose natural focus was the distant horizon, a look I have noticed in the eyes of seafaring men.

It seemed fitting that when he died he should be buried at sea. We had discussed the options in those last weeks of his life. I had to allay

243

his fear that his lifelong agnosticism would be betrayed when, too weak and helpless to prevent it, a clergyman would be brought in to pray over him. We agreed that cremation was a clean end and that his ashes should be scattered on the sea. He seemed satisfied with this. During these last six years of his life when he lived with me, I had dreaded the moment when I should see him dead, he who for so long had dominated my life and made his presence felt in every moment of my day. To see death overcome him would be too awful to behold. When it came, it was as fearful as I had imagined. Although stricken to physical helplessness, wraith-like from the cancer which devoured him, he fought relentlessly on. 'Get me out of this bed and help me on with my clothes! I am going out!' I did as he bade me, buttoning on his underwear knowing that I would have to unbutton it again five minutes later. He stood up, resolute, only to fall back, helpless, into the chair. The next day and the next we repeated the performance. I did the office of nurse, an office which offended his dignity and shocked my feelings. Had we been easy with one another, how different those last weeks might have been. When at last the racking breathing which had afflicted him for a week ceased, I knew that the terrible moment had come. I had to screw my courage to the sticking point to look at him, conquered at last and frigid in death. I sat on the stairs afterwards and cried in a kind of long pent-up hysteria.

The cremation took place without any religious ceremony whatsoever. Only the strains of Handel's Largo, a favourite with him, gave solemnity to the occasion as, in front of a tasteless star-studded back wall, the coffin descended slowly out of our sight and our father out of our lives. When we collected his ashes from the crematorium we were all unnaturally subdued by the thought of such a powerful man having been reduced to a canister of ashes. We took them to Portaferry, the lovely unspoilt little town near the mouth of his favourite Strangford Lough, hired a boat and a fisherman to take us downstream towards the bar of the lough where the currents are strong and dangerous. It seemed fitting that Hugh should recite Tennyson's 'Crossing the Bar' as he scattered his ashes on the water and we all looked pensively on as what remained of our father joined the great continuum of waters which wash earth's shores.

Sunset and evening star,
And one clear call for me!
And may there be no moaning of the bar,
When I put out to sea.
But such a tide as moving seems asleep,
Too full for sound and foam,
When that which drew from out the boundless deep
Turns again home.

Such a rather unusual burial for a small place merited a report in a local newspaper. A sailor who had been a shipmate of my father's got in touch with me.

Your father had the keenest eye of anyone I ever knew. He could spot a mine a mile off in the water. I was his junior then, a mere youngster. When we were on watch together at night and the stars were sparkling in the great canopy of the heavens above us, he would point to the constellations, tell me their Greek names and explain how they had come by them. He would recount the thrilling stories of the Greek heroes and I listened, spellbound. 'Do you know why this ship is called the *Bellerophon*?' he asked. And he told me the story of the hero, Bellerophon, who had fought the Chimaera, that fire-breathing monster, lion in front, serpent behind and she-goat in the middle, and killed it. He had then taken on those fierce fighting women, the Amazons, and defeated them, and all with the help of the famous winged horse Pegasus. 'Look! You can see Pegasus right up above you in the sky now!' The stars seemed to be watching over us. 'We will come through this war (it was 1915), through mines and submarines and come home safe at the end.' I was strangely consoled, young fellow as I was. He was very well up was your father. He made me see that every ship in the Navy had a personality of its own.

(I later learned of the absurd proposition by the Admiralty during the Second World War to dispense with names on ships and have them called by numbers only. Fortunately, Churchill was there, humane and imaginative, to foil such a plan to rob ships of their personalities. There were Gradgrinds in the Admiralty then as there are Gradgrinds still in all the managements of human affairs.)

My father was often so penetrated by the beauty of the world that he felt surging within him the pressure to express this feeling. 'If I had had the chance I could have been an artist or a poet,' he said. Though he believed he was guided in all things by reason it was his senses, nourished by field and sea and sky in his childhood, which gave him this joy and delight. Though loss, fear and bewilderment were part of that childhood, awe and wonder were powerful counterbalances. I am glad that my father's 'spirit of life' has been passed on to me, for fear and anxiety needed to be counterbalanced in me, too. I am grateful that I am one of the 'noticers' of this world, that I am awake to shapes and colours, sounds and textures, both natural and human. (I often find myself looking at the way a man's ears grow out of his head when I should be listening to him.) The painter Turner tells how he overheard a spectator of one of his canvases saying, sceptically, 'Well, I have never seen a sunset like that!' Turner turned to her and said, 'No, you did not, but don't you wish you had!' The point is succinctly made: 'Don't you wish you had the eyes, the imagination, the spirit within you to enable you to see what I saw?' It was Turner who gave the sunset life, who lent us his eyes, for the world is fixed and dead unless we give it life, and it is our life that we give it. We do not all see the same show as we look out from behind our eyes, nor do we see the same show in the same way all of the time. It depends on our state, physical and mental. Sometimes the world is grey and lifeless while at other times it is bright and vivid.

Coleridge could express with exactness the feeling of depression; Wordsworth's genius was to express the opposite state, not the separation, but the union of mind with what lives outside itself and the peace and joy which that union creates in the soul. He sees likeness, union, relationship as the key to wisdom. In his Preface to the *Lyrical Ballads* (1802) he says of the poet:

> He is the rock of defence of human nature; an upholder and preserver, carrying every where with him *relationship and love*. In spite of difference of soil and climate, of language and manners, of laws and customs, in spite of things silently gone out of

mind and things violently destroyed, the poet binds together by passion and knowledge the vast empire of human society, as it is spread over the whole earth, and over all time [my italics].

I do not know any finer definition.

FRANCE

'Going abroad' – 'the honeymoon will be spent abroad' – what seduction in those words, what glamour, what romance! From our hard seats in the cheapest part of the cinema we raised our eyes to the screen and watched, absorbed, our romantic dreams being acted out by rich Americans gathered on the quays of New York harbour, preparing to 'go abroad' on luxurious transatlantic liners to exotic parts of the globe – to Paris, Rome, Vienna, even to India and China. Baggage piled high on porters' trolleys, cabin trunks bedecked with the labels of cruise lines (Cunard, North Pacific) and of five-star foreign hotels, fur coats, pug-dogs, they were on their way to adventure and romance where the beautiful would encounter the beautiful and all would end in joy and happiness. Then the lights went up and the tawdry surroundings of the cinema brought us back to reality . . . These were the fairy-tales that fed our innocent imaginations.

During the war years, my school years, not even the rich could 'go abroad'. Rich and poor alike were boxed into their own countries. Travel to England was very difficult, and to Europe impossible. Not even well-off schoolgirls could be sent abroad to learn a language. At school, we spoke French hardly at all so severely academic was the teaching. Trinity continued the pattern set at school but increased the difficulty of the weekly prose and translation. Students were far too self-conscious to break out of the mould, and to speak together in French was simply not done. Then Monsieur Jacques Viot arrived in Trinity. He was sent by the French government to converse with us in French and to pass on to us the riches of

French culture. Monsieur Viot was one of the triumphs of the French highly competitive intellectual system of education; he had jumped every hurdle of that difficult system and was now a postgraduate student at the prestigious École Normale Supérieure in Paris. We felt his intellectual fire scorching us.

A small, neat man, he presented himself before us once a week. He was *très correct* in dark academic suit, remote, serious, unsmiling. Without preliminaries, he opened his mouth and let flow a sequence of brilliant ideas on philosophical, political and literary topics in rapid, impeccable French. He paused and asked for questions... there were none. So overawed were we by this unusual performance in a language we but imperfectly understood, especially when delivered at such a rate, that we had not the courage to open our mouths. Monsieur Viot looked at us, looked at the inert, inarticulate mass before him and despaired. He was not used to this. His look was not encouraging for neither his temperament nor his training had prepared him for helping the timid and weak. In a short time he gave us up altogether and resigned himself to passing the prescribed hour in listening to his own sparkling soliloquies unimpeded by contradiction and debate. He was bored, very bored. Soon, our ears attuned, we were able to comprehend his rapid French and could register the scepticism, even cynicism, with which he treated most subjects. I never knew if he found other attractions in Dublin to make up for the hours he was obliged to spend with us.

I wanted to be a fluent French speaker more than I wanted to be an expert in the written language. How was I to do it? Penfriends were then very popular. (I had a keen penfriend on the Ivory Coast in Africa who sent me feathers as presents. His last letter to me was addressed 'the Prison' and although I replied to it, I heard no more from him.) Two of us decided to apply to the Sorbonne for penfriends. We wrote our names, addresses, ages and tastes on a piece of paper and addressed it to 'La Sorbonne, Paris, France'. Somehow that letter arrived at its destination, was pinned up on a noticeboard somewhere in that august institution, was noticed by a passing student of chemistry whose eye was caught by the word Ireland. 'Ireland! I have always wanted to visit that green and romantic country,' he said to himself. 'I'll write to one of them but which one shall I choose?' He closed his eyes, pointed his pen at the paper on the noticeboard and it came to rest on – my name. By such a quirk of fate began a firm and interesting friendship which has lasted to this day.

Letters with French stamps began to come through our letter box. Photographs were exchanged. I was sure my round, smiling face and curly hair would be too rustic for a Parisian used to elegance and refinement. Maurice's photo showed a pleasant, intelligent face and humorous eyes. Soon, he proposed an exchange of visits; it would be nice to get to know each other better and to see a little of each other's country. As for him, he could not wait to get to know Ireland. 'You must come to France, first,' he wrote, 'for I have so many wonderful things to show you in Paris now that the war is over. We still have rationing and everyone must furnish tickets for food but we shall manage very well; of that I am quite sure. You must spend a month with us here in Paris and a second month with the Ducos family; you are invited by this business friend of my father's to go on holiday *en famille* to Arcachon and teach his children English.' Two whole months in France! I could hardly believe my luck. If happiness is the possibility of satisfying the desires of the imagination, this possibility was now mine. My euphoria was soon dampened, however, by the hard facts of my position: I had no money to pay the fare to Paris and how could I then receive Maurice in our house with the unpredictability of my father's moods and the modesty of our accommodation? I was sure that Maurice lived in a luxurious apartment in Paris and the contrast with our house would be shocking. No, it was impossible . . . I was moody, irritable, unhappy. I could not easily let go of my dream.

Then something almost miraculous happened: I won £125 in a crossword puzzle competition. My mind was numbed by the amount. With such a sum not only could I pay my way to France and buy some new clothes but I would have something left over to provide little luxuries and excursions for Maurice when his time came to visit me. I could scarcely believe my good fortune. I was strangely reminded of a dream I frequently had: I was walking the streets of Dublin when, suddenly, on the pavement in front of me, I saw a bundle of five-pound notes. Riveted by the sight, I bent down and picked them up: there was at least £100 in that bundle, a small fortune. Flushed and triumphant, I hastily pushed the money into my pocket. Then, a terrible thought flashed through my mind – someone, somewhere, had lost this money, was at that very moment feverishly searching for it. I must take it right away to the police station and declare it. Declare it? Give it all up? I could not do it . . . and, pulled this way and that in an agony of conscience, I woke up. In my dream, I had avoided the moral decision. Once, not in a dream but in reality, I had come upon a ten-shilling note lying on the step of our stairs. My eyes fixed upon it, exulting; my father must have dropped it, he who was so careful; he would not know where he had lost it. I picked it up furtively and quickly hid it in my pocket. I then went through the same agony of conscience as in my dream but this time I did not wake up. I kept the money. For weeks afterwards I waited in real terror for the heavens to strike me down in retribution with some terrible disease. I learned from this experience that the pains of a bad and frightened conscience were not worth the pleasure of deceit.

My prize money, however, was no deceit. Nothing now stood in the way of my realising my dream; I *could* and *would* go to France. My euphoria was short-lived. Following closely on the heels of the letter announcing my success came another informing me that, as I was not yet twenty-one and so was, in law, a minor, I could not be awarded my prize money. I would be made a ward of court and the money would be put into secure gilts until I came of age. I could not take in this extraordinary turn of events: it was unjust, it was outrageous. All the importance of swearing affidavits, seeing solicitors, visiting the Four Courts did nothing to diminish my bitter disappointment. Although it was less than a year to my twenty-first birthday, the visit to France was to come months before it. I thought of applying to my father for a loan but I did not have the courage to do so. No transaction was easy with him for, if in a bad mood, any request might lead to a quarrel over something quite unconnected with the request. He was given to quoting as a maxim of life 'Neither a borrower nor a lender be', and I knew how sternly he put this precept into practice. Finally, I brought myself to ask him for a loan of £100 against the guaranteed security of gilts. After a few familiar warnings about never enjoying anything you could not pay for, he agreed to the loan. The wheel of fortune had turned upwards again for me! (When, at twenty-one, I applied to the courts for the £125, I was informed that gilts had gone down in value and what with a small fee here and a small fee there, the total coming to me would be no more than £90: my father was never repaid in full.)

At once I began to make plans for my visit to France. Maurice wrote that, as his mother was long since dead, it was not fitting that I should stay with himself, his father and his brother in a small apartment and that, accordingly, I would be lodged in a hotel but would, of course, have all my meals with them. This was reassuring. Frank, who always enjoyed being mischievous, saw his chance. 'Be warned, this fellow is certainly in the white slave traffic' (much talked about in our day) 'and he is making arrangements to cover his tracks. Hotel? Don't believe it! You will be welcomed, offered a drink which will be heavily laced with drugs and you will wake up in a tent in Algeria!' I was horrified by this scenario. No use turning to my father for advice: he would tell me to stand on my own two feet. The fact of my being young and female did not appear to concern him. Here was I, said I to myself, proposing to be alone with three men I did not know and who might well be in the white slave traffic in the wicked city of Paris! I was amazed at my own intrepidity. Next day, I talked myself out of these ridiculous and manufactured fears but when a letter arrived from Maurice telling me that he had been in a motorbike accident and that his face was heavily scarred, Frank renewed his attack: 'I told you!' he crowed. 'He got those scars in a fight with other gangsters in Algeria!'

After that, dark imaginings of disaster descended upon me. I pondered the problem of my security for many days until I came up with a solution. Two fellow students were travelling to Paris about the same time as myself. I asked if I might travel with them so that, at the Gare Saint-Lazare in Paris, I could emerge well concealed behind their backs. If I did not like the look of the man who was waiting for me at the ticket barrier I would slip through it unnoticed, stay in a hotel for the night and return to Dublin the next day. They agreed to help me. We travelled from Dublin by boat and train, the cheapest and most uncomfortable way. As the train hurried us along from Dieppe to Paris and ever nearer the fateful ticket barrier, I began to feel extremely nervous. I turned to Charlie and John for reassurance: Charlie was too absorbed in his own thoughts to provide it, and John was too preoccupied with note-book and dictionary taking down every French word and phrase he did not know from the hoardings on the stations that we passed (he was later to become a professor of French) to pay much atten-tion to my *cri de cœur*. Could I count on them? I began seriously to doubt it . . .

As the great steam engine jolted to a halt underneath the glass roof of the Gare Saint-Lazare I felt weak in all my limbs. Sheltering behind the two of them, head down, I moved forward in the thick of the crowd towards the barrier. But before I could take a quick, furtive look at the figure waiting there, a hand was held out to-wards me and a cultured voice said, 'Vous devez être Edith, je pense?' It was Maurice. I looked up at a tall, blond, blue-eyed, de-bonair young man and so unremarkable were his scars that I forgot to notice whether they were there or not (he had had plastic sur-gery). He was shaking my hand, taking care of my luggage, steer-ing me through the crowd. I turned to introduce Charlie and John – they had melted away. I was alone in a strange city with a strange young man. Tired now by the fatigue of the journey and by the toll on my emotions, I let myself be led forward down steep stairways and along crowded corridors and out onto an underground train platform. This was unexpected; I had imagined Maurice rich and car-owning. To find a foothold in the compartment, Maurice had to push me and my luggage into an already bursting crowd of people jammed inside it. I could scarcely keep my balance in the crush of bodies around me. I noticed how closed, almost hostile were the expressions on people's faces, unlike the friendly Dublin smile. The smell of garlic was new and offensive. I was shocked to see couples embracing intimately, oblivious of the people around them; I had never seen anything like that in Dublin. Maurice smiled at me encouragingly from his position near the door.

We got off at the Pré Saint-Gervais and made our way up into the blessed open air. Before my curious gaze stretched solid apart-ment blocks, shops and hurrying people. Maurice stopped before a tall iron gate through which we passed into a neat courtyard. A small, unpretentious house stood before us. We entered the hall, which was communal, with the flat above, said Maurice. He turned the handle of a door and we were at once in a small living room. A middle-aged man rose to greet me: he had greying hair, light blue eyes like Maurice's and fine features. 'Papa, c'est Edith; Edith, mon père.' Just then a young man, dark-skinned, brown-eyed, emerged from the kitchen: 'Edith, mon frère André; André, Edith.' The introductions were over. I wondered when Maurice would take me to the hotel as I was exhausted and longing to escape from the hard work of talking continually in French. Maurice turned to me: 'Edith, voulez-vous déposer vos bagages dans votre chambre?' Ma chambre? Ma chambre? And the hotel? I became greatly alarmed; had Frank been right in his terrible prophecy? Maurice escorted me across the hall into a room opposite: 'Voilà votre chambre. Nous sommes, tous les trois, dans la chambre à côté. Je viendrai vous chercher tout à l'heure pour diner', and he was gone.

I stood, very nervous now, and looked about me. A double bed, a wardrobe, a chest of drawers and a chair sombrely furnished the room. I took off my coat and sat down, anxiously pondering my situation. Soon, a voice called out, 'Vous venez prendre l'apéritif?' and my heart sank. Was this the heavily drugged drink that Frank had warned me of? I declined on grounds of not being accustomed to alcohol. I was shown my place at the table and from the kitchen the two boys brought course after course of food and put them before us but I could scarcely touch anything. Dinner over, they rose one by one, shook my hand and bid me 'bonne nuit' and I was once more in my room. I sat bolt upright on the bed listening intently to every sound. After a while I heard the creak of a bedspring and the murmur of a voice. I stared at the communicating door. Did I see it open or was I imagining it? Sick with worry and exhaustion and unimaginable terrors, I rose, eyes still fixed on the door, and got ready to defend myself. The door remained closed. I noticed a key, unturned, in the lock. I crept slowly forward and put my hand on it. Should I turn it? If they were good and decent people, they would know how unworthily suspicious I was, but if they were not...

I did not turn the key. I returned to my position on the bed, upright, alert. Soon I felt an urgent need to go to the lavatory but I could not remember how to get to it. It was somewhere between the kitchen and the men's room. I opened the door, crossed the hall and tried the handle of the living room door opposite. It was locked on the inside. I tried the handle of the door leading into the court-yard but it, too, was locked and the key removed, so the only way to reach the lavatory was through the men's room. I considered my situation afresh. There was only one solution: I must get through the window and drop into the courtyard below. Gingerly, I tried the unknown mechanism of the shutters but could not get it to work. Desperate, I turned and twisted until suddenly the mechanism gave way and I was staring out into the blackness of the French night. A new obstacle now confronted me in the form of an iron balustrade which came halfway up the window space. I climbed over it very awkwardly for fear of making a noise and dropped onto the ground below. I found the furthest corner of the small courtyard and blessed relief came at last. I prayed for rain before morning to wash away my sin.

Back inside my room I positioned myself once more, fully dressed, on the bed and determined to stay awake until morning, but by four o'clock, tired beyond endurance, I fell over and slept. I awoke the next morning to find myself still fully dressed and to hear the cheerful sound of Maurice's voice: 'Il est déjà dix heures! Vous étiez bien fatiguée, il me semble, car vous avez dormi douze heures de suite.' I looked around me, everything was as it had been and so was I. It had rained lightly before dawn! Relieved and re-freshed, I sat down at my place at table as Maurice put before me my first café au lait and a 'tartine' of bread and butter. He showed me how to dip the bread in the hot coffee until a delicious buttery foam rose to the surface. I dipped and dipped again.

Both father and brother had left for work at 6.20 a.m., André as a mechanic in one factory and Monsieur Chaslot as an engineer in an-other. Maurice's father had been obliged to work for the Germans in that factory all through the occupation but the personnel had made sure that production was held up and the enemy impeded. He was very reserved and never talked about his feelings but he had, said Maurice, seen and endured many awful things. He had witnessed the march of the triumphant German army into Paris on the Champs-Elysées as he had later watched it march out again. He had seen with his own eyes collaborators lynched and girls having their hair cut off for fraternising with German soldiers and he knew that the effects of the experience on returned prisoners of war were far from over. Had I noticed how thin his father was? He had been even thinner, like a blade, two years ago when the war ended for he had lost four stone in that last terrible year of starvation when no food at all got through to the people. 'Never mention Jerusalem artichokes to him!' André, as a soldier, had been a prisoner of war in Germany but had not been too badly treated. Decidedly, the war was becoming more real to me. Maurice, being younger, had been sent to his grandmother in Champtocé-sur-Loire. Food was still scarce in Paris, he said, but we would be invited to eat with friends where I would see what good French food was. Hélène, a hat-maker, bought food on the black market or exchanged hats for food and she would give us a meal to remember! Did I know that she got her best felt for her hats from County Tyrone in Ireland? We would call into her hat shop that very day!

Thus began an energetic round of visits to museums, châteaux, parks, galleries, cemeteries crowded with history and all under the burning sun of the summer of 1947. Maurice was never tired. The unaccustomed food and wine, the heat, the walking, the effort of speaking in French tired me out but I never gave in. We pushed our way into packed metros, we rode on buses, we fell into cafés when we were hot and tired, we talked and laughed and little by little, my French got better and better. Maurice's charm captivated the older ladies of his acquaintance and 'la petite Irlandaise' was in-vited along to aperitifs, to white wine and dry biscuits at five o'clock and to large dinners in the evening. 'How should I conduct myself at table?' I asked Maurice, conscious of the difference be-tween French table manners and our own. 'Watch Madame Lecoeur and do everything she does,' said Maurice. 'She is always "correct".' So I watched Madame Lecoeur and did everything she did: I kept both hands on my lap when not eating and only allowed one hand to lean gently on the table when the cheese course was put in front of us. I never allowed myself to lean against the back of my chair, contrary to my usual custom.

'And what does the little Irish girl do? What does her father do?' came enquiringly from many mouths. Maurice had warned me that a French person could tell your social status by the cut of your coat. A foreigner's coat did not offer the same clues. His father, seeing what was afoot, put a quick end to such embarrassing questions: 'Edith n'a pas de classe. Elle fait partie de l'élite intellectuelle', and there was silence. I met members of the family, a writer, a musician, an artist. I was dazzled by the conversation, by the brilliantly lucid sentences with which they could analyse an idea. I felt dull and stupid. They seemed to me able to articulate with beautiful finality the thoughts I had been confusedly thinking about for years. Even the French language sounded more brilliant than the English. (It was many years before I saw the danger of being beguiled by a beautiful phrase and of taking for the truth something that was only well expressed.)

Maurice spoke lovingly of the Loire Valley, of Champtocé, where his father and grandparents had been born and where his relations still lived. He would take me there. As we travelled south from Paris, I noticed through the windows of the train the dilapidated houses, the empty, deserted-looking villages. Maurice explained that rents had been frozen by law for many years so that the landlords had not been able to repair the exteriors, but the interiors were well kept by the tenants. We stayed in his father's house in Varades on the Loire twelve miles from Champtocé. His father had inherited the house from his uncle, the miller, and we could see the hoist over the door where the sacks of grains had been hauled up. It was sombre inside with those uncomfortable upright chairs you find everywhere in France. We shopped in the market, we walked along the banks of the Loire, we went to visit relations in the little village of Saint-Florent-le-Vieil on the opposite side of the river. This was a wonderful excursion. The bridge across the river had, in company with other bridges, been bombed during the war to hinder the retreating German army and only two arches still stood. To cross the river, we took a ferryboat from our side to a wide sandbank in the middle of the water and this we crossed on foot; then we took a second ferry from the other side of the sandbank to the far shore. We visited cousins and aunts, we walked through the pretty little towns on the banks of the river, we examined the grapes in the family vineyard, we tasted the new wine.

I loved the Loire; I loved the bluish atmosphere which hung dense and still over its bordering forests and fields; I loved its broad waters, broader than any I had ever seen; I loved the way it stretched its great arms around islands and sandbanks only to bring them together again in a unified, serene expanse; I loved the way it gave back to the sky above the subtle, ever-changing play of blues and greens and greys, the silvery Loire of poetry. I found myself continually saying, 'Isn't it beautiful, so beautiful...' 'Dangerous too,' said Maurice, 'for it regularly floods houses and fields. It flattened our big garden wall and came halfway up our wine cellar. And more than one unwary person has been sucked into its quicksands and disappeared.'

At the end of that summer I returned to my studies in Trinity College with a growing love for the country I had previously known only from books. I was no longer afraid to speak the language and I had a far keener interest in the literature which the college authorities had ordained for us to read.

My 'romantic' views, my moral philistinism, my naive ideals fostered by books and by the narrow judgements of the Ireland in which I lived were to receive salutary shocks from the books Trinity required me to read in English and French literature. If we want to get to know the soul of a people, we must read its literature, listen to its music, look at its art. It is literature, the written word, which is 'getting to know on all matters which most concern us, the best which has been thought and said in the world and through this knowledge, turning a fresh stream of thought upon our stock notions and habits' (Matthew Arnold). Literature is called *creative* because it can give us the very feel and flavour of experience rather than its 'meaning'. Ideas, too, when seized by the mind, can have a unique feeling and flavour and poetry of their own. I am very glad that I was obliged to study two languages and literatures instead of one at Trinity College, for French literature opened up new and exciting ways of thinking about ideas which I did not find in English literature.

The reverence for all life for which my nature craved was fully met, years later, not in a French novel but in a Russian one. It was *Anna Karenina* by Tolstoy, whose *War and Peace* I had so indiscriminately devoured when I was fourteen years old.

ANNA KARENINA
AND THE LIFE OF THE FEELINGS

I am a Frenchman by accident
but I am a human being by necessity.

MONTESQUIEU

My naive idea of 'the fallen woman' was to receive its death blow in a Russian novel. *Anna Karenina* tells the story of a married woman who commits adultery and leaves her husband and son to live with her lover. His passion gradually wanes and Tolstoy is moved to awe at what happens to Anna. He endows her with so much life, good-heartedness, openness and energy that even after she has thrown herself to her death, she lives on in our imagination, a free spirit, rich in other unrealised possibilities. Nothing ever seems final and fixed in her life. Tolstoy does not judge her: he brings her before us with such imaginative understanding that judgement does not even occur to us. The labels I had grown up with, 'the fallen woman', 'the adulteress', 'the fate worse than death', all fell before the generosity and vision of this book.

'Happy families are all alike; every unhappy family is unhappy in its own way' – thus the book opens. The unhappy family is the Oblonsky family.

> Everything was in confusion in the Oblonskys' house. The wife had discovered that the husband was carrying on with a French girl, who had been a governess in the family, and she had announced to her husband that she could not go on living in the same house with him. This position of affairs had now lasted three days, and not only the husband and wife

themselves, but all the members of the family and household, were painfully conscious of it. Every person in the house felt that there was no sense in their living together, and that the stray people brought together by chance in any inn had more in common with one another than they, the members of the family and household of the Oblonskys. The wife did not leave her own room, the husband had not been at home for three days. The children ran wild all over the house; the English governess quarrelled with the housekeeper, and wrote to a friend asking her to look out for a new situation for her; the main cook had walked off the day before just at dinnertime; the kitchen-maid and the coachman had given warning.

The rollicking pace of the narrative belies the sensitivity with which Dolly (Darya Alexandrovna) and Stiva (Stepan Arkadyevitch), her husband, are to be treated. We expect Stiva, the cause of all this misery, to be seen as superficial and immoral but Tolstoy sees him in quite a different way; he sees him as he sees himself – innocent. This surprises readers of English novels. He comes before us, as everyone comes before us in the novel, immensely 'there' and alive. (Even a character who only looks into the novel for one sentence is alive in this way: 'A young deacon, whose long back showed in two distinct halves through his thin undercassock.') Stiva is radiant with health and energy, open, generous-hearted, loved by everyone with whom he comes into contact, and 'deceit and lying were opposed to his nature'. He is very distressed to have caused his wife pain:

Stepan Arkadyevitch was a truthful man in his relations with himself. He was incapable of deceiving himself and persuading himself that he repented of his conduct. He could not at this date repent of the fact that he, a handsome, susceptible man of thirty-four, was not in love with his wife, the mother of five living and two dead children, and only a year younger than himself. All he repented of was that he had not succeeded better in hiding it from his wife.

He feels no sense of sin, nor does Tolstoy ironically suggest that he should.

He had never clearly thought out the subject, but he had vaguely conceived that his wife must long ago have suspected him of being unfaithful to her, and shut her eyes to the fact. He had even supposed that she, a worn-out woman no longer young or good-looking, and in no way remarkable or interesting, merely a good mother, ought from a sense of fairness to take an indulgent view. It had turned out quite the other way.

And the worn-out woman is one of the most tenderly presented characters in the book. We see her, as Tolstoy sees her, faded,

> her now scant, once luxurious and beautiful hair fastened up with hairpins at the nape of her neck, with a sunken thin face and large, startled eyes . . .

> She still continued to tell herself that she should leave him, but she was conscious that this was impossible; it was impossible because she could not get out of the habit of regarding him as her husband and loving him. Besides this, she realised that if even here in her own house she could hardly manage to look after her five children properly, they would be still worse off where she was going with them all. As it was, even in the course of these three days, the youngest was unwell from being given unwholesome soup, and the others had almost gone without their dinner the day before. She was conscious that it was impossible to go away; but cheating herself, she went on all the same sorting out her things and pretending she was going.

She is always carrying a child or looking after half a dozen of them but never so happy as when surrounded by her children and in her own home. She loves to bathe with her children in the river:

> To go over all those fat little legs, pulling on their stockings, to take in her arms and dip those little naked bodies, and to hear their screams of delight and alarm, to see the breathless faces with wide-open, scared, and happy eyes of all her splashing cherubs, was a great pleasure to her.

Only someone who loved children could have written that. There is no shade of contempt, no condescension in Tolstoy's portrayal.

We are taken into Dolly's heart, into her lack of self-confidence before Anna, into her dreams and hopes and disappointments. On a visit to Anna and her lover, she is at first overwhelmed by Anna's beauty and by the sophistication of her home and manners and loses her confidence in herself. She retires to bed and suddenly her feelings change:

> Left alone, Darya Alexandrovna said her prayers and went to bed. She had felt for Anna with all her heart while she was speaking to her, but now she could not force herself to think of her. The memories of home and of her children rose up in her imagination with a peculiar charm quite new to her, with a sort of new brilliance. The world of her own seemed to her now so sweet and precious that she would not on any account spend an extra day outside it, and she made up her mind that she would certainly go back next day.

Tolstoy honours the inner feelings of this 'mere mother' as much as he honours the feelings of the brilliant and sexually attractive Anna. He follows as the characters make new and startling discoveries about their own hearts.

Levin, Stiva's friend, occupies a large part of the book. He is the opposite to Stiva, idealistic, romantic and puritan, in search of the ideal wife, intolerant, suspicious of social beings and social talk.

> 'I understand myself less well when I talk than when I am silent.'

He, too, though a philosopher, listens to his heart to find out the truth of himself:

> He did not, as he had done at other times, recall the whole train of thought – that he did not need. He fell back at once into the feeling which had guided him, which was connected with those thoughts, and he found that feeling in his soul even stronger and more definite than before ... thought could not keep pace with feeling.

He is earnestly and intelligently seeking for the meaning of life and cannot rest until he finds it. He loves the country and his soul never ceases to hear the music of the earth, whose poetry accompanies us all through the book. Stiva and Levin discuss 'fallen women'. To Levin they are 'vermin'. Stiva's answer is arresting:

> 'You're very much of a piece. That's your strong point and your failing. You have a character that's all of a piece and you want the whole of life to be all of a piece, too – but that's not how it is. You despise public official work because you want the reality to be invariably corresponding all the while with the aim – and that's not how it is. You want a man's work, too, always to have a defined aim, and love and family life always to be undivided – and that's not how it is. All the variety, all the charm, all the beauty of life is made up of light and shadow.'

I needed to be told that, too. I was an intolerant and romantic idealist like Levin. Tolstoy changed all that.

Anna now steps into the book and into our lives. She has come to heal the breach between her brother, Stiva, and Dolly. We are not told that she is full of life, we *feel* the life that is in her: 'her nature is brimming over', 'her light, resolute step', 'the energetic squeeze with which she freely and vigorously shook his hand', ' the rapid step which bore her rather fully-developed figure with such lightness', 'the elasticity of her movements', 'the freshness and unflagging eagerness which persisted in her face and broke out in a smile'. Her gaiety and charm infect everyone; 'her charm was such that she always stood out against her attire . . . her dress could never be noticed on her'. Anna had been married young, a made marriage and a loveless one to an important government minister. She has one son whom she adores. And so it might have contentedly continued had not chance (the author) made her encounter a handsome army officer full of personal authority, Alexey Vronsky. A powerful passion overwhelms them both such as neither had known before and which Anna never even suspected in herself.

> She gave him no encouragement but every time she met him there surged up in her heart a feeling of quickened life . . .

We feel the extraordinary power of her beauty and personality over Vronsky; for the first time in a life well acquainted with the opposite sex, he falls in humble worship and adoration before a woman. In an English novel of the period, Anna would have fought hard against this terrible temptation but Tolstoy shows her as knowing at once that it is useless to resist it. 'There was no other way.' Their passion grows over a year of intense and contradictory emotions: joy in each other, shame before the life of concealment they have to live and the hurt done to others, until, inexorably, the consummation comes:

> She felt that at that moment, she could not put into words the sense of shame, of rapture, and of horror at this stepping into a new life, and she did not want to speak of it, to vulgarise this feeling by inappropriate words. But later too, and the next day and the third day, she still found no words in which she could express the complexity of her feelings; indeed, she could not even find thoughts in which she could clearly think out all that was in her soul.

All the complexity of emotion that pours into her soul, Tolstoy honours – rapture, shame, shame before her beloved son but not before her husband:

> 'For eight years he has squeezed the life out of me. Now I love, I live!'

She moves through the book, as do all the characters, with an exhilarating openness to emotion and to changes of emotion which make them amazed at themselves, make them discover new feelings in themselves – revenge, hatred, generosity, forgiveness... Even Karenin, Anna's husband, 'whose soul has been brutalised by social convention' and who longs to punish Anna, knows moments of blissful forgiveness when 'what had seemed insoluble when he was judging, blaming, and hating, had become clear and simple when he forgave and loved... he had not known his own heart'. Tolstoy knows the soul, the deepest part of us and the best, which can suddenly make us feel our being in a new way, if we will but let it. This knowledge, which is Tolstoy's genius to understand and convey, gives to his novel a unique spiritual quality rarely found elsewhere.

Tolstoy follows the vibrations of Anna's soul, the restlessness, the ecstasy, the shame, the embarrassment, with total respect. As a woman of her time, she had to give up everything – reputation, family, friends – for Vronsky, and he, a man of sensitivity and honour, has sacrificed his career for her, but it is the women who bear the greater weight of social censure. (I thought of all those women in similar situations at home, in Ireland.) Little by little the burden thrown upon the exclusive personal relationship becomes too much. Without the wider support of family and friends and all the little occupations and distractions of social living which uphold a marriage (for they have been ostracised) the relationship grows tense and strained. Vronsky begins, secretly, to be bored with his life. Anna's great fear is to lose the only thing she has now got – his love. The unbearable thing we have to watch is Anna's loss of her once proud, free self and her slow and awful descent into obsessive and morbid jealousy. 'Some evil spirit of strife had grown up between them.' Her soul, that best and most beautiful part of her, grows sick – even unto death. She does violence to her deepest and innermost feelings. The last act of her sick soul is to punish Vronsky by killing herself and we watch it happening with awe and compassion. Vronsky is not made out to be a shallow man: his sufferings before and after Anna's death are terrible, much more terrible than Stephen Guest's for Maggie Tulliver.

This novel arouses in us pity and sorrow, but at the same time a vivid sense of the sacredness of all life, and this is literature's highest gift to posterity. Literature is here doing its job of making us feel to the full a sense of our common and best humanity.

POSTSCRIPT

Life at Trinity continued full of purpose and possibility, the frantic, intellectual life always intertwined with thoughts of the opposite sex even for those highly ambitious northerners who were working non-stop for a first. Some of the latter, intellectually so advanced, were much less so emotionally. They sought advice on how best to conduct themselves with girls. One ex-serviceman in particular made himself available for this purpose, having seen the world and having had experience of women. Sometimes a small queue formed in the evening outside his rooms. Advice, given freely, was mostly bad as I had occasion to learn on the receiving end. Some nervous persons were advised to try strong-arm tactics but they were poor actors and sometimes made themselves ridiculous. Tales of girls who had broken college rules and dared to stay overnight in a boy's room kept our imagination on the stretch. Who was interested in whom? Who was suffering a romantically hopeless passion? Who, I asked myself, could possibly be interested in me?

Busy with conjecture, nothing escaped our eye as we crossed Front Square or sat motionless in front of our book in the Reading Room. One girl confided that one of the most unlikely candidates for romance, a senior lecturer, was madly in love with her and was showering her with presents. Was he mad or was she mad herself? I was never to find out. Others reported that some of the lecturers were not as academic as they looked. I marvelled at this news. I remembered it when I was asked to tea by our English professor, a bachelor living alone in rooms in the college. No romantic heart could possibly beat under that innocently benign exterior. I had nothing to fear despite the rumours I heard about him. Nevertheless, as I mounted the two flights of stairs to his rooms, my heart beat a little faster than usual. I knocked, the door opened, and there he was in a dressing gown in the middle of the afternoon! He welcomed me before disappearing into his bedroom and staying there for at least three minutes. Was he (and here my heart jumped) getting the bed ready? He re-emerged, still in his dressing gown, and proposed something to drink – a danger sign surely. 'What will you have, my dear, Keemun? Lapsang Souchong? Orange Pekoe?' Never having heard that there was any more than one variety of tea, I concluded, more nervous than ever, that he was offering me alcohol, that he was going to make me drunk. 'Nothing too strong,' I stammered out, rigid now on my chair and eyeing the passageway to the door. When he reappeared from his tiny kitchen carrying a cup of tea in his hand, I nearly laughed aloud with relief. We talked for an hour about this and that and he encouraged me to think of a Ph.D. – I was in my last year – but he did not omit to say how lonely he often felt in those bachelor rooms . . .

Literature, both English and French, was such a huge subject and the teaching in Trinity, often so ineffective, seemed to offer no plan for understanding it. I read everything and hoped for inspiration. It was only in my final year that one thing began to connect with another and footholds that we call knowledge were slowly gained. All this reading meant much more to me than mere fodder for examinations but I kept my enthusiasm moderated in front of others for fear of seeming affected. I was longing for someone with whom I could share my passion without fear of being misunderstood. Was there anyone who felt like me?

We went about in groups. For those studying the different modern languages, the Modern Languages Society offered informal and social occasions to meet. There were academic talks given by students themselves and a French play was put on once a year for a whole week in the Peacock Theatre. Excursions into the nearby Wicklow and Dublin Mountains were especially popular. We took the bus to Bray and started our walk, drifting into twos as if by accident. Conversation peppered with laughter spiced the day. Afterwards we fell into a cheap café in Bray and broached more solemn subjects, as if the still evening light and the pleasant fatigue of our limbs called for a little more seriousness. Someone asked if we believed in platonic love. Was the noblest kind of love not the platonic variety (this from someone who had something else in mind)? Yes, we said, we did believe in it: a noble and true ideal, surely. But secretly it was not platonic love but romance we longed for. Every novel I had read was about romance. I was sure that it would exalt and give meaning to my life as it did in novels. I determined, however, that should it happen to me, I would continue to earn my own living as did Charlotte Brontë's heroines. But no matter how hard I tried, I could not feel romantically inclined towards any of these new friends. Was I incapable of feeling love?

In my third year at Trinity, I was auditioned for a part in the annual French play, one which I had little hope of getting as the producer, a German student, was very demanding and there was much competition for parts. When I was offered one of the main parts in *Asmodée* by François Mauriac, I was delighted, especially as I felt I could understand the role – that of an ingénue. Cast as my younger brother was a young student from Belfast. He was a year behind me at Trinity as he had served three years as a volunteer in the Royal Navy. Both the North and the navy rang alarm bells, after the experience of my father! After rehearsals, the group would adjourn to a nearby cinema café in O'Connell Street and linger deliciously over a cup of coffee. Sometimes he was with us, sometimes he was not. I could not help admiring his sensitive face and his lean figure which was always clad in the same tan sports coat. Like many of the northern students, he was witty and funny, but unlike most of them, he was deeply private about his feelings. I sensed that at once and liked him for it. Sometimes we met casually in Trinity but it was always with others. I felt myself more and more drawn to this independent, sensitive and enigmatic person.

One day in the severe winter of 1947, when there was no heat anywhere in Trinity as there was no coal and only wet turf available, I came into college for a lecture although I was suffering from a sore throat and a hacking cough and expected to get pneumonia too in the below-zero lecture room. I was well aware of the deficiencies of my hair, of my red nose and of my coat which was a hand-me-down of my sister's which I had lengthened with a large piece of astrakhan. After the lecture I made my way to Front Gate, determined to keep my head down and to escape to home where I could nurse both my throat and my humiliation in private. Suddenly there was a face in front of me atop a well-known tan sports coat. It was Peter Devlin. I was forced to stop and pass the time of day with him, far as I was from wishing such an encounter.

'Have you been to a lecture?'

'Yes, I have. It was on Pascal. I particularly like Pascal.'

'So do I,' he muttered and I could see the depth of feeling in his eyes.

I made to move off when, quite unexpectedly, he said: 'What about a cup of coffee in Roberts? It will help your cough.' As in a dream, I found myself walking alongside him, we two alone for the first time. We took our seats at a small table for two in the upstairs café where the cigarette smoke rose thickly to the low ceiling and made me take such a wicked fit of coughing that I became more mortified than ever. I saw his brother throw a curious glance at the two of us from a nearby table – Peter was not usually to be seen tête-à-tête with a girl. What did we talk about? 'Just what we ought, of course.' We talked about the books we loved in a very natural and unaffected way. It was delightful. That was how literature served me best of all. It led me into romance and a lifelong companionship. It also led me to revise my ideas on northeners and sailors! 'Reader, I married him!'